W9-AJO-522

PRO/CON VOLUME 24

WORK AND THE WORKPLACE

Published 2005 by Grolier,
an imprint of Scholastic Library Publishing
Old Sherman Turnpike
Danbury, Connecticut 06816

Library of Congress Cataloging-in-Publication Data

Pro/con

p. cm

Includes bibliographical references and index.

Contents: v. 19. World Politics - v. 20 Religion and Morality - v. 21. U.S. Judiciary - v. 22. International Law - v. 23. Poverty and Wealth - v. 24. Work and the Workplace.

ISBN 0-7172-5950-1 (set : alk. paper) - ISBN 0-7172-5951-X (vol. 19 : alk. paper) - ISBN 0-7172-5952-8 (vol. 20 : alk. paper) - ISBN 0-7172-5953-6 (vol. 21 : alk. paper) - ISBN 0-7172-5954-4 (vol. 22 : alk. paper) - ISBN 0-7172-5955-2 (vol. 23 : alk. paper) - ISBN 0-7172-5956-0 (vol. 24 : alk. paper)

1. Social problems. I. Scholastic Publishing Ltd Grolier (Firm)

HN17.5 P756 2002
361.1–dc22

2001053234

Printed and bound in Singapore

SET ISBN 0-7172-5950-1
VOLUME ISBN 0-7172-5956-0

For The Brown Reference Group plc
Project Editors: Claire Chandler, Aruna Vasudevan
Editors: Fiona Plowman, Chris Marshall, Jonathan Dore, Mark Fletcher
Consultant Editor: David Grusky, Professor of Sociology, Cornell University, Ithaca, NY
Designer: Sarah Williams
Picture Research and Permissions: Clare Newman, Susy Forbes
Set Index: Kay Ollerenshaw

Senior Managing Editor: Tim Cooke
Art Director: Dave Goodman
Production Director: Alastair Gourlay

GENERAL PREFACE

"All that is necessary for evil to triumph is for good men to do nothing."
—Edmund Burke, 18th-century English political philosopher

Decisions

Life is full of choices and decisions. Some are more important than others. Some affect only your daily life—the route you take to school, for example, or what you prefer to eat for supper—while others are more abstract and concern questions of right and wrong rather than practicality. That does not mean that your choice of presidential candidate or your views on abortion are necessarily more important than your answers to purely personal questions. But it is likely that those wider questions are more complex and subtle and that you therefore will need to know more information about the subject before you can try to answer them. They are also likely to be questions about which you might have to justify your views to other people. In order to do that, you need to be able to make informed decisions, be able to analyze every fact at your disposal, and evaluate them in an unbiased manner.

What Is *Pro/Con*?

Pro/Con is a collection of debates that presents conflicting views on some of the more complex and general issues facing Americans today. By bringing together extracts from a wide range of sources—mainstream newspapers and magazines, books, famous speeches, legal judgments, religious tracts, government surveys—the set reflects current informed attitudes toward dilemmas that range from the best way to feed the world's growing population to gay rights, from the connection between political freedom and capitalism to the fate of Napster.

The people whose arguments make up the set are for the most part acknowledged experts in their fields, making the vast differences in their points of view even more remarkable. The arguments are presented in the form of debates for and against various propositions, such as "Do extradition treaties violate human rights?" or "Should companies be allowed to relocate abroad?" This question format reflects the way in which ideas often occur in daily life: in the classroom, on TV shows, in business meetings, or even in state or federal politics.

The contents

The subjects of the six volumes of *Pro/Con 4—World Politics, Religion and Morality, U.S. Judiciary, International Law, Poverty and Wealth,* and *Work and the Workplace*—are issues on which it is preferable that people's opinions be based on information rather than personal bias.

Special boxes throughout *Pro/Con* comment on the debates as you are reading them, pointing out facts, explaining terms, or analyzing arguments to help you think about what is being said.

Introductions and summaries also provide background information that might help you reach your own conclusions. There are also tips about how to structure an argument that you can apply on an everyday basis to any debate or conversation, learning how to present your point of view as effectively and persuasively as possible.

VOLUME PREFACE
Work and the Workplace

Sociologists and other experts have become increasingly interested in work and the culture of the workplace. As more and more people work longer days, the boundaries between office and home have become blurred. An increasingly litigious society has meant that both employers and employees have to be more responsible—the former in the measures they take to protect workers' rights during office hours, the latter in the way they behave toward their colleagues and their bosses.

Protection

Longer office hours and accusations of a culture of overwork in the United States in particular have complicated any discussion about rights and exploitation. Although unions have been incredibly important in fighting for leglislation to protect their members, their power and influence declined during the 20th century, partly due to extreme opposition from government. Organizations also now exist to break up unions. Supporters argue that this has weakened protection for workers in the office. They also believe that unions can help fight the trend by large businesses of relocating their production facilities abroad and employing cheap native labor in the jobs previously filled by U.S. workers, for example. Many people in western nations have lost work in this way. Another criticism of reallocating jobs abroad is that companies often choose to set up business in states with poor human and civil rights. It is therefore easy for them to abuse laborers, employ child labor, or make people work in hazardous conditions that would simply be unacceptable in developed countries.

New problems

Changes in patterns of how people choose to work also raise new issues. Some younger people in particular are deciding to give up highly pressured careers and relocate out of cities to quieter, less stressful places. Many employers also encourage workers to jobshare or to work at least part of the week at home. This, observers say, is extremely beneficial to parents with young children who can rejig their work day to spend more time with their families. Despite this, many parents complain that employers are still not giving them enough rights, especially fathers. In the past 30 years or so most developed countries have introduced legislation to grant parents leave to spend with their children.

The work environment has also changed in such a way as to make sexual conduct in the office a matter of concern. Reports of sexual harassment not just by women but same-sex and female harassment of men as well have increased, leading some to question if legislation is adequate. Many employers also dissuade employees from having intimate relationships with each other; but as people spend long hours in the office, this has become more common.

Critical thinking

Work and the Workplace will help its readers think critically about significant and topical issues.

HOW TO USE THIS BOOK

Each volume of *Pro/Con* is divided into sections, each of which has an introduction that examines its theme. Within each section are a series of debates that present arguments for and against a proposition, such as whether or not the death penalty should be abolished. An introduction to each debate puts it into its wider context, and a summary and key map (see below) highlight the main points of the debate clearly and concisely. Each debate has marginal boxes that focus on particular points, give tips on how to present an argument, or help question the writer's case. The summary page to the debates contains supplementary material to help you do further research.

Boxes and other materials provide additional background information. There are also special spreads on how to improve your debating and writing skills. At the end of each book is a glossary and an index. The glossary provides explanations of key words in the volume. The index covers all 24 books; it will help you find topics throughout this set and previous ones.

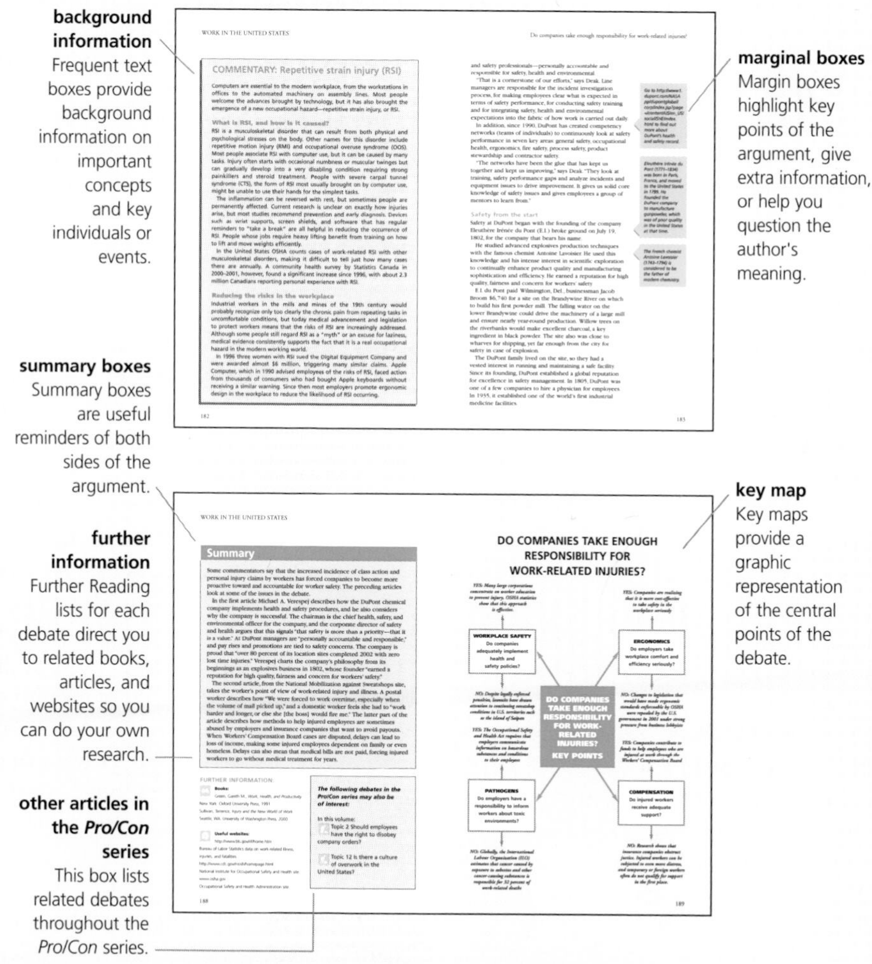

background information
Frequent text boxes provide background information on important concepts and key individuals or events.
marginal boxes
Margin boxes highlight key points of the argument, give extra information, or help you question the author's meaning.
summary boxes
Summary boxes are useful reminders of both sides of the argument.
key map
Key maps provide a graphic representation of the central points of the debate.
further information
Further Reading lists for each debate direct you to related books, articles, and websites so you can do your own research.
other articles in the *Pro/Con* series
This box lists related debates throughout the *Pro/Con* series.
COMMENTARY: Repetitive strain injury (RSI)
Summary
DO COMPANIES TAKE ENOUGH RESPONSIBILITY FOR WORK-RELATED INJURIES?

CONTENTS

PART 1
WORKER RIGHTS

INTRODUCTION

Present-day labor legislation and associated rights, both national and international, are the culmination of the political, social, and legal struggle of working people around the globe to achieve fairer and more humane treatment by their employers.

Governments, human and civil rights organizations, and labor unions, among others, have worked hard to ensure that employees are protected in the workplace, not just from exploitation but also from injury and harassment. However, as rights protection has improved and employees have increasingly taken legal action against wrongful practice, companies have also taken steps to reduce the likelihood of malpractice suits by their workers or members of the public. In doing so, some of the protections previously afforded to workers, such as the right to privacy in the office, have been challenged, with mixed results.

Globalization and trade liberalization have also created changes in the workplace. Many enterprises have taken advantage of the opening up of new markets to relocate their business operations abroad, often at the expense of domestic labor. The use of cheap workers in developing nations with far weaker employment protection laws has led some experts to call for international labor legislation affording the same protection to laborers, wherever they live.

More equality for some

Historically most people have objected to exploitation, and laborers quickly discovered that there was strength in numbers. Winning better wages, shorter hours, and improved working conditions was far more achievable if employees joined together to state their grievances. Increasingly workers began to organize into guilds, professional associations, and unions.

For many years labor unions were illegal in most countries. Penalties for attempting to organize a union included execution in some places. Despite this, workers around the world formed labor unions, and they began to acquire power. The eventual result was a body of labor law regarding the recruitment and treatment of people in work and legalizing the organization of labor unions in most industrialized nations.

International labor standards

In addition to national laws there also emerged a large body of international labor standards put in place as part of broader moves toward social justice and internationally recognized human rights on the part of the international community in the aftermath of World War II. Many such standards were formulated by the International Labor Organization (ILO), a UN specialized agency originally founded in 1919. ILO conventions and recommendations set minimum standards of basic labor rights on issues such as the right to organize, freedom of association, collective bargaining, abolition of forced labor, and equality of opportunity and treatment.

Modern times

Despite, or perhaps because of, the successes of labor movements in industrialized nations, unions in the United States and elsewhere have suffered falling membership in recent decades, particularly in the private sector. Many large corporations are also opposed to their workers unionizing, and there have been accusations of TNCs colluding with local gangs to threaten or bully union representatives in poor nations. Others argue that worker protection has advanced so far, covering everything from the maximum hours worked to the minimum wage, that unions are simply not needed anymore. Yet at the same time, many social and political commentators believe that many worker rights are under threat, and that some issues are not being properly addressed by employers or lawyers. They argue that there is a pressing need to reexamine many hard-won rights and protections for employees. Others believe that the problem is not with the amount of cover workers get under the law but the way in which existing legislation is applied when cases come to court.

Long working hours mean that many workers use e-mail and the Internet for private use. Many employers now have strict codes of practice that allow them to monitor their employees in the workplace and even to carry out searches and drug tests to prove they are fit to work. Although viewed by some as an infringement on worker privacy, many companies argue that they are just protecting themselves from potential law suits. Workers are also sometimes penalized for bringing certain wrongdoings to light or for disobeying orders if they think they are wrong. Critics argue that employers have a right to expect loyalty from their employees. The first three topics examine some of these these issues.

The last three topics in this section examine discriminatory behavior; they focus on sexual harassment, parental rights, and age. Although discrimination is viewed unfavorably, in practice workers are often ridiculed if they complain about inappropriate sexual behavior, for example. Men as well as women are victims of harassment, but some argue that their claims are often dismissed. Some feel that this extends to other areas including parental rights, although critics counter that employers are still not giving working parents enough rights in the workplace.

Topic 6 tackles the issue of having a mandatory retirement age. An increasing number of elderly people either want or have to work; they view such forced retirement as wrong.

"Let the workers organize ... for the future of labor is the future of America."

—JOHN L. LEWIS (1880–1969), UNION ORGANIZER

Topic 1
SHOULD WORKERS HAVE A RIGHT TO PRIVACY IN THE WORKPLACE?

YES
"WHERE TO DRAW THE LINE"
PERSONNEL TODAY, JUNE 1, 2004
LIZ HALL

NO
FROM "WORKPLACE SURVEILLANCE REDUCES LIABILITY, RAISES ETHICAL CONCERNS"
HTTP://WWW.VA-INTERACTIVE.COM/INBUSINESS/EDITORIAL/LEGAL/ARTICLES/WORKPLACE.HTML
JENNIFER LECLAIRE

INTRODUCTION

In 1928 Supreme Court Justice Louis Brandeis wrote that the "right to be left alone" was the right most valued by Americans. There is, however, much discussion about how far the right to privacy extends in the workplace: Increasingly, employers are using surveillance cameras, telephone recording devices, and Internet programs to monitor what their workers do and say during office hours.

Civil rights organizations such as the American Civil Liberties Union (ACLU) claim that this is an unconstitutional invasion of privacy. They fear the emergence of a "Big Brother" society in which employers will be able to monitor everything their workers do or say (see page 13). Others argue that such surveillance is a necessary evil in 21st-century society. They claim that companies are losing billions of dollars each year through employees misusing work facilities and selling trade secrets and through hostile-environment lawsuits in which employees claim that their companies have failed to protect them from harassment, bullying, or racism. Others counter that minor abuses of company time for personal use have always occurred, and that it is only because it is now technologically possible to monitor such activity that this is seen as a major problem. They contend that obsessive monitoring in the workplace shows there has been a collapse of trust, indicating a failure of management that surveillance only makes worse.

In any discussion of privacy in the workplace the Constitution, especially the Fourth Amendment, is always raised: It provides "[t]he right of people to be secure in their persons, houses, papers and effects, against unreasonable searches and seizures." While the Fourth Amendment has been used in many privacy defense cases, some commentators argue that only the federal government is subject to its restrictions, so it is not effective against private entities. Others argue that the Framers of the Bill of Rights could not have foreseen such developments as the enormous increase in the power of private corporations and the ways in which workers would consequently need to be protected.

> *"The Constitution itself … stands in the way of Big Brother.… [L]iberty, and the safeguards inherent in due process, remain strong."*
>
> —ADAM L. PENENBERG, AUTHOR OF *SPOOKED: ESPIONAGE IN CORPORATE AMERICA*

Research conducted in 2002 found that the average U.S. employee spends about six hours a week surfing the Net for personal reasons; 62 percent of companies also reported that some employees used the Net to find sexually explicit material. The cost to companies due to loss of productivity through personal Internet use has been estimated at about $5.3 billion a year. Opponents argue, however, that this figure should be seen in the context of the much greater productivity gains that the Internet has brought by increasing the speed, quality, and quantity of communication. They also contend that some of this "personal" Internet time replaces previously unrecorded "unproductive" time such as unofficial smoking breaks or chats at the coffee machine.

Advocates of workplace surveillance, however, claim that while the Internet has made global communication much easier and faster, it has also created greater opportunities for employees to sell company secrets. Monitoring e-mails is one method to prevent this.

Among the other major reasons cited for taking such action is the increasing number of hostile-environment lawsuits brought against companies. Some workers are suing their bosses after being sexually harassed or bullied in the workplace, claiming that they must or should have known about the abuse. Many companies believe that by monitoring such things as Internet use and e-mail, they can protect both their workers against discriminatory behavior and also themselves from such lawsuits.

Workers are also being penalized if their employers discover that they have sent e-mails containing offensive material. In *Bourke v. Nissan Motor Corporation* (1993) Bonita Bourke sued the company for wrongful discharge and invasion of privacy after an e-mail she had sent, containing sexual and personal information, was randomly selected as an example during a training session. Since the company had already disclosed that it was monitoring employees' e-mails, the judge ruled in Nissan's favor. Some people believe that such decisions are unfair: Employees spend so much time at work and exist in a culture of "overwork," commentators argue, it is inevitable that they have to send personal messages during work hours.

The following two articles examine this issue in greater depth.

WHERE TO DRAW THE LINE
Liz Hall

Liz Hall is a journalist at Personnel Today *magazine and author of books on employee screening and monitoring.*

In the 1997 case Western Provident Association v. Norwich Union *WPA alleged that NU's staff had been circulating e-mails claiming that WPA was insolvent. NU paid out £450,000 ($820,866 at mid-2004 rates), plus costs. The case was important since it showed that "publication" occurred as soon as someone other than the author of the e-mail read it, and also that a company has limited protection against incurring defamation liability. This led some experts to state that companies should develop a clear policy regarding employee use of Internet and e-mail, and that monitoring could act as a safeguard.*

YES

✓ Employers are increasingly adding employee monitoring to their ammunition box in their bid to combat problems such as legal liability, reduced productivity, and the threat of the exposure of trade secrets and intellectual property. But are employers going too far in their attempts to stop employees misusing and abusing technology at work?

Employer liability

Employers can be held vicariously liable for their employees' activities when using the internet and are responsible if staff send e-mail messages that breach confidentiality or are defamatory. In the case of *Western Provident [Association] v Norwich Union,* Norwich Union was forced to shell out £450,000 in damages and costs for slander and libel after Western Provident discovered damaging and untrue rumours circulating on Norwich Union's internal e-mail system. They were about Western Provident being in financial difficulties, and being investigated by the Department of Trade and Industry (DTI).

If an employee commits an act of harassment or discrimination via e-mail or by downloading and distributing inappropriate material, the employer is also vicariously liable—even if the act was unauthorised. Staff can sue employers for failing to provide a workplace free of harassment, which can extend to the electronic distribution of offensive material. Nearly a quarter of organisations have had complaints about staff accessing internet chat rooms and 17 percent have had complaints relating to games on the web, according to a survey by *Personnel Today* and law firm K-Legal in 2002.

Redressing problems caused by the misuse of technology is a costly business. The 2002 Annual Security Survey by the DTI revealed that some 44 per cent of businesses reported suffering an e-mail breach, with clear-up costs averaging £33,000.

Then there is the cost of lost productivity. One of the problems with employees browsing the internet is that it can become highly time-consuming and unfocused, even if done

COMMENTARY: Orwell's vision

The phrase "Big Brother" has become part of everyday language as a way of describing today's increasingly surveillance-oriented society. It comes from the novel *Nineteen Eighty-Four* by the English writer George Orwell (1903–1950). Although Orwell's book warns of a future in which every thought and idea is monitored or controlled by government, some people argue that Orwell's vision has come true. Many people are concerned that more and more aspects of our lives are under scrutiny at home, during leisure time, and especially in the workplace—in this modern version corporations as well as governments monitor our lives.

Life and times

Eric Arthur Blair was born in 1903 in Bengal, India (he adopted the pen name George Orwell in 1933). When he was one year old, Orwell moved with his mother and sister to England, where he remained until 1922. When he failed to win a scholarship to college, he went to Burma and worked in the administration of the Indian Imperial Police (1922–1927). Appalled by British colonialism, Orwell resigned and returned to Europe, where he took any jobs he could find in France and England. He later used his experiences to write his first novel, *Down and Out in Paris and London* (1933).

During the 1930s Orwell became increasingly influenced by socialism. He traveled to Spain and reported on the civil war. He eventually joined and fought on the side of the United Workers Marxist Party militia. He grew to dislike communism, preferring British socialism instead.

During World War II (1939–1945) Orwell also served as a sergeant in the Home Guard and worked as a journalist for the BBC and *The Observer* newspaper. Toward the end of the war he began to write his most well-known books, *Animal Farm* (1945) and *Nineteen Eighty-Four* (1949). He claimed that the latter was written "to alter other people's idea of the kind of society they should strive after." Orwell did not live to enjoy his success, however. He died in 1950, but his ideas remain topical today.

Premonition?

In *Nineteen Eighty-Four* Big Brother is the head of INGSOC, the party that rules Oceania. Winston Smith, the book's protagonist, works in the Records Department of the Ministry of Truth. His job is to alter records and newspaper articles. Winston becomes increasingly dissatisfied with the society in which he lives, but Big Brother monitors every action of his citizens through telescreens, which are used to show propaganda and to preach hate, but which also contain microphones and cameras to monitor citizens' actions. The Thought Police monitor Thought Crimes—thoughts against the party. Critics argue that Orwell foretold the world in which we live today—societies in which every thought and action are monitored.

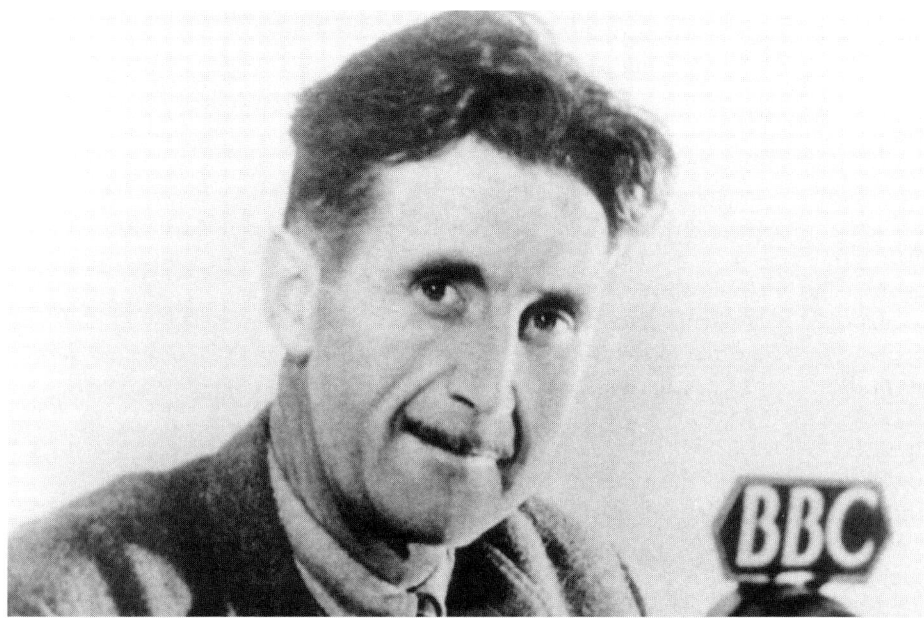

George Orwell wrote of a culture of conformity ruthlessly enforced by universal surveillance in his novel Nineteen Eighty-Four *(1949).*

Could this problem be solved simply by using filtering software to block access to certain types of websites, as is done in many schools and libraries?

for genuine business reasons. Some 70 per cent of pornographic traffic occurs during regular business hours, according to Sex Tracker, a service that monitors pornography site usage.

Companies are becoming increasingly heavy-handed when dealing with internet and e-mail abuse, backing up their monitoring policies with firm action. In 2002, Hewlett Packard Compaq disciplined 150 workers in the UK, firing some staff for "viewing and sharing unauthorised and inappropriate material." *Personnel Today*'s research found that UK employers spent more time disciplining staff over internet and e-mail abuse than any other workplace issue.

Striking a balance

Is it better to ban all nonwork use of the phone and the Internet, or should the pressures of increased work hours be recognized by allowing employees to use facilities during their breaks for personal use?

In an environment where staff monitoring is becoming commonplace, employers should strike a balance between being able to detect misconduct, criminal behaviour, abuse of company equipment, and poor work performance on the one hand, and making sure they protect employees' rights to privacy and maintain staff morale on the other.

In seeking to get the balance right, employers should bear in mind that working days have lengthened in many cases, forcing people to carry out many errands at work. So while people are being increasingly forced to take care of personal business at work—such as online shopping—they are then being criticised for slacking off.

The problem with a Big Brother society

As long as 10 years ago, a report on workplace privacy by the International Labour Organization (ILO)—a UN agency that seeks to promote social justice and internationally recognised employment rights—looked at evidence from 19 countries. It concluded that "Big Brother" looms large in the workplace, and that workers' health and welfare is being damaged as they are scrutinised by computers, cameras and assorted bugs.

See http://www.fecl.org/circular/2807.htm for a summary of the findings of this ILO report.

The ILO report examined research from US government agencies the Office of Technological Assessment and the National Institute for Occupational Safety and Health, and concluded that electronic monitoring causes stress and can create adverse working conditions, such as:

How would you feel if you knew you were being filmed while you were in the classroom? Would it have an effect on your behavior? Would you consider it an invasion of privacy and an infringement on your right to free speech as guaranteed by the Constitution?

- lack of involvement
- lack of control over tasks
- reduced task variety and clarity
- reduced supervisory support
- fear of job loss
- routinised work activities
- reduced social support from peers.

The Trades Union Congress (www.tuc.org.uk) is the British federation of 70 affiliated unions. It has around 7 million members. The TUC is similar to the AFL–CIO in the United States.

The TUC is among those bodies claiming that employee monitoring initiatives have led to an invasion of employee privacy, a drop in productivity and an increase in stress levels, saying that such initiatives are actually counter-productive. The use of monitoring with CCTV is one of the TUC's main concerns. Excessive monitoring undermines staff, leading to greater job-related depression and poorer well-being. Stress levels among frontline call handlers in UK call centres were found to be significantly higher than among benchmark groups in other occupations, according to a study from the Health and Safety Laboratory, *Psychosocial Risk Factors in Call Centres*, 2004. The report reveals that eavesdropping—electronic performance monitoring by supervisors listening in on calls—is a major cause of work-related stress.

See http://www.hse.gov.uk/research/rrpdf/rr169.pdf for the full text of this report.

Using technology to monitor staff should not replace good people management skills. It should only ever be used as support, setting clear boundaries and making sure good management skills are in place at all times. It should ensure that the work environment balances the equation of rights.

Is monitoring calls in a call center the same as monitoring calls in another, less customer-oriented organization?

WORKPLACE SURVEILLANCE REDUCES LIABILITY, RAISES ETHICAL CONCERNS
Jennifer LeClaire

Jennifer LeClaire is a Florida-based freelance journalist specializing in business and health issues.

NO

Workplace surveillance is replacing workplace privacy as businesses of all sizes begin to consider monitoring employee communications. Monitoring services are an increasingly popular method of reducing employee liability, as well as screening performance and productivity. However, many workers are challenging such security measures as an invasion of their personal rights. A recent poll conducted by the Center for Democracy and Technology (CDT) suggests 83 percent of Americans are "very concerned about their privacy."

The privacy, levels of trust, and viability of public life in a community all contribute to its "social capital." See http://www.cfsv.org /communitysurvey/ index.html for results of a large-scale survey of social capital in U.S. communities.

Big Brother reality

We live in a society that is increasingly lacking in personal privacy, individual trust and a viable public life that supports and maintains democratic values and practices, says William Staples, a University of Kansas professor of sociology and author of *The Culture of Surveillance—Discipline and Social Control in the United States*. [He says:]

> *The monitoring and invasion of our privacy by others is becoming increasingly taken for granted. In fact, people exhibit a strange, almost voyeuristic intrigue about the technology, right down to their own video cameras.*

See http:// www.uri.edu/ personal2/sammyjo/ ECPAwebpage.htm for an outline of the provisions of the act, as well as the full text of the act itself and the changes brought about by its revision in 2000.

Electronic Communication Privacy Act

Experts warn that businesses should still take precautions before monitoring an employee's communications in the workplace.

According to the Electronic Communication Privacy Act (ECPA), employees who have had communications wrongfully intercepted are afforded the right to challenge the system's operator for invading their right to privacy.

Michael R. Overly is an Internet law specialist with the firm Foley & Lardner.

"To protect themselves from liability and to ensure their computer resources are used only for authorized purposes, employers must have the right to monitor employee files and e-mail," insists attorney Michael R. Overly....

Workers often use their office phone, sometimes on company time, to carry out personal business such as buying goods with a credit card. Some people believe such activities are inevitable given the long hours that most people spend at work.

U.S. businesses surveillance

TYPE OF SURVEILLANCE	% companies using it
Monitoring Internet connections	62.8
Storage & review of e-mail messages	46.5
Storage & review of computer files	36.1
Video recording of employee job performance	11.9
Recording & review of telephone conversations	7.8
Storage & review of voice mail messages	7.8
Total, active monitoring of communications	77.7
Telephone use (time spent, numbers called)	43.3
Video surveillance for security purposes	37.7
Computer use (time logged on, keystroke counts, etc.)	18.9
Total, all forms of electronic monitoring	82.2

Based on AMA study of 1,627 U.S. businesses, 2001.

Rules of monitoring

"In order to avoid potential invasion of privacy claims, monitoring must be done properly," says Patricia Butler, an attorney with Ford & Harrison LLP.

"Courts have also held that when employees are warned that their e-mail and other electronic communications are subject to monitoring and have signed a statement agreeing to restrict their use of company-owned hardware and software to company business, an employee has no legitimate expectation of privacy and consequently cannot make a claim for invasion of privacy under state law," she explains.

Under Michael Tamer, Teknekron invented the first quality-monitoring software program. Tamer has long championed the importance of call centers delivering superior customer service, and he is a popular industry speaker. He has testified before Congress in hearings on call-monitoring legislation.

Success

Monitoring has been successful for many years in customer service call centers, says Michael Tamer, president and CEO of Teknekron Infoswitch Corp., a leading provider of monitoring technology. Tamer has been active in Congress concerning employee monitoring since the technology emerged in the early '90s.

"I have seen monitoring programs change the way companies do business by strengthening relationships in the call center. It brings management closer to customers because they hear what the customer experiences," he says.

See http://www.uwua.org/callcenter.htm for a 2002 study on the effect of monitoring in U.S. call centers.

WebSENSE

Phil Trubey, founder and president of the San Diego-based NetPartners Internet Solutions, has created WebSENSE, an advanced Internet-filtering software used by the majority of schools and libraries across the nation. By giving employers the ability to track and log which Web sites their employees visit, WebSENSE allows management to block sites that distract employees from work, and protect their company from sexual harassment claims directly related to inappropriate Internet use.

See www.internetfilterreview.com for an evaluation of various Internet filtering products and a glossary of terms explaining how they work. Do you think this is censorship?

Summary

The preceding two articles examine issues in the hotly debated topic of whether employees have a right to privacy in the workplace.

Liz Hall, in the first article, focuses on the situation in Britain. She claims that although employers are monitoring their staff to help reduce inefficiency and inappropriate behavior, there is a danger of them going too far. She states that it is important to get the right balance between protecting business from potential legal cases arising from employees misusing the Internet and having a proper regard for workers' rights, including the right to privacy. Hall asserts that employees are now suffering from stress, poor morale, and depression as a result of heavy-handed policies that some employers take in monitoring staff. "Using technology to monitor staff should not replace good people management skills.... It should ensure that the work environment balances the equation of rights," Hall concludes.

Jennifer LeClaire, writing in the second article on the situation in the United States, claims that surveillance is here to stay; and although she acknowledges that it can contribute to a loss of trust between people in the workplace, she quotes commentators who regard it as a valid and justifiable exercise, and even one that has a positive contribution to make. Lawyer Michael R. Overly states that "employers must have the right to monitor employee files and e-mail." Similarly lawyer Patricia Butler contends that employees have no basis for complaint if a policy of surveillance is openly stated at the outset, while CEO Michael Tamer argues that monitoring in call centers helps managers "hear what the customer experiences."

FURTHER INFORMATION:

Books:

Lane, Frederick S., *The Naked Employee: How Technology Is Compromising Workplace Privacy.* New York: American Management Association, 2003.

Staples, William, *The Culture of Surveillance: Discipline and Social Control in the United States.* New York: St. Martin's Press, 1997.

Weckert, John (ed.), *Electronic Monitoring in the Workplace: Controversies and Solutions.* Hershey, PA: Idea Group, 2004.

Useful websites:

www.aclu.org

American Civil Liberties Union site. Includes reports on worker privacy and links to court cases on the issue.

www.privacy.org

Useful site about surveillance/privacy issues.

The following debates in the Pro/Con series may also be of interest:

In this volume:

Part 1: Worker rights, pages 8–9

In *The Constitution:*

Topic 15 Is Internet surveillance constitutional?

In *Human Rights*:

Topic 6 Do threats to national security ever justify restrictions on human rights?

SHOULD WORKERS HAVE A RIGHT TO PRIVACY IN THE WORKPLACE?

SHOULD WORKERS HAVE A RIGHT TO PRIVACY IN THE WORKPLACE? KEY POINTS

CONSTITUTION
Does the Constitution protect workers' rights to privacy?

YES: The Constitution protects the right to privacy. Employers are in breach of this if they monitor phone calls and e-mails, for example.

NO: A worker's right to privacy is not specifically protected, and it is not clear in any case if the Fourth Amendment applies to private corporations

SURVEILLANCE
Is there too much surveillance in the workplace?

YES: Some employers even install cameras in the washroom to monitor workers. This is unjustifiable and shows that trust has collapsed.

NO: Statistics show that drug and other forms of substance abuse are on the increase; employers have a duty to make sure that this is not happening

INDIVIDUAL VS. GROUP RIGHTS
Are individual rights more important that group rights?

YES: By giving up individual rights to privacy for the collective good, employees are paving the way for the erosion of other rights

NO: Individuals have to give up certain rights if it is better for group rights. Employers are protecting workers' rights by making sure they are not sexually harassed or bullied—by monitoring e-mails, for example.

CHANGING CULTURE
Do long office hours mean that workers will have to use the Internet for personal use during work hours?

YES: Americans live in a culture of "overwork" and spend long hours in the office, often with no breaks. This makes it inevitable that workers will have to do personal chores during office hours. They should not be penalized for doing this.

NO: Worker legislation guarantees employees breaks and limits the number of man-hours in most nations. There is therefore no excuse to abuse the Internet or e-mail for personal use.

Topic 2

SHOULD EMPLOYEES HAVE THE RIGHT TO DISOBEY COMPANY ORDERS?

YES

"FACING ANTHRAX THREAT, EMPLOYEES HAVE LIMITED RIGHT NOT TO WORK "
WWW.GOVEXEC.COM, OCTOBER 30, 2001
BRIAN FRIEL

NO

"CAUGHT ON THE NET"
THE GUARDIAN, DECEMBER 3, 1999
HELEN HAGUE

INTRODUCTION

In the developed world there are established employment laws that govern what an employer can legally ask of an employee in the workplace. In most circumstances employees are expected to fulfill the requirements of their job. Occasionally situations can arise in which workers feel justified in refusing to obey an order. This can be prompted by the belief that the order could have dangerous consequences, or employees may simply disagree with the ethics of doing a certain job. Some experts argue that this is inherently wrong; workers, they claim, have a duty to carry out company orders.

When an employee starts working for a company, he or she agrees to abide by the terms of a contract that can contain certain requirements or "clauses." Some companies ask employees to sign a "nondisclosure agreement" (NDA) to prevent them from divulging information to the media or to other companies—for example, a software company might want to prevent leaked information on a new computer game. Although some experts claim that NDA clauses are essential in the cut-throat world of big business, others counter that employers often abuse this contractual feature to silence or "gag" employees who are aware of company malpractice.

In America the Occupational Safety and Health Administration (OSHA) provides regulations regarding hazards and dangers at work. The law says employees can refuse to work only if they are in imminent danger and are unable to follow normal reporting procedures. Such workers can include health workers exposed to highly infectious diseases or public service staff, such as postal workers, exposed to biochemical terrorism in the course of their jobs. For example, in 1999 three people died and thousands more were tested following exposure to anthrax spores during a terrorist campaign.

Some critics argue that people are justified in refusing to work in conditions that put their personal safety at risk. They claim that such employees disobey orders only if other official mechanisms have broken down, and they are either not receiving adequate protection, or they have few or no means of complaint. Since they are left with no other option, workers have the right to refuse orders that could harm themselves, colleagues, or the public.

> *"Reasonable orders are easy enough to obey; it is capricious, bureaucratic or plain idiotic demands that form the habit of discipline."*
>
> —BARBARA TUCHMAN (1912–1989), HISTORIAN

However, some people are employed in high-risk jobs such as national security, and they should not have the option of refusing an order, some observers assert. In the United States disobeying military orders can result in severe punishment and even death in extreme situations such as in time of war. Military personnel swear an oath of enlistment that includes their agreement to obey all orders regardless of their personal feelings. Once enlisted, they are bound by the Uniform Code of Military Justice (UCMJ), which supersedes most U.S. employment legislation. Many believe that this kind of obedience is essential in combat since individual questioning of orders could result in loss of life for many more hundreds of people. Although personnel can refuse to perform an illegal order, in practice this is often frowned on, critics say. Some experts argue that even soldiers should not blindly follow orders if they consider them to be morally wrong. They refer to the example of Lieutenant William Calley, who ordered his unit to open fire on the Vietnamese village of My Lai in 1968, resulting in the deaths of 500 unarmed civilians, mostly women and children. Calley claimed that he had acted under orders from a superior officer. He was court-martialed in 1971.

Unlike Calley, many people choose to stand up to their employers when they disagree with a work-related order or policy. If this fails, some decide to go public and tell society at large about alleged abuses. However, these people, called "whistleblowers," often suffer both professionally and personally as a result of their actions. Some observers believe that they should be applauded and encouraged since in most cases they highlight a company abuse or a health and safety problem. It is unfair, they claim, that whistleblowers should incur the wrath not only of the companies they take on but also that of the largely disapproving media.

In the last 30 years or so there have been several notable cases involving whistleblowers. In 1994, for example, Jeffrey Wigand, a vice president of the Brown & Williamson Tobacco company, breached his NDA by revealing on the TV show *60 Minutes* that nicotine in cigarettes was being chemically strengthened. B&W sued Wigand, allegedly conducted a smear campaign against him, and put his personal life under investigation.

This issue causes much debate. The articles that follow examine it further.

FACING ANTHRAX THREAT, EMPLOYEES HAVE LIMITED RIGHT NOT TO WORK Brian Friel

Brian Friel published this article on www.govexec.com, the government business news daily.

Anthrax is an acute infectious disease caused by the spore-forming bacteria Bacillus anthracis. *In October 2001 U.S. authorities became concerned when three people died and thousands more had to be tested following several bioterrorist attacks involving anthrax. See http://www.holistic-online.com/Remedies/Biot/biot_introduction.htm for more information.*

Go to http://laws.findlaw.com/us/445/1.html for more information on this case, which resulted from two employees being suspended after they refused to do their duties: They claimed that their safety equipment was unsafe.

YES

With deadly anthrax bacteria turning up in more and more federal workplaces, a little-known right has gained sudden importance: In extreme circumstances, federal employees have a limited right to refuse a manager's order if the order would place employees in imminent danger, under a federal regulation and case law.

With two Postal Service workers dead and anthrax spores discovered at Postal Service facilities, the State Department, Justice Department, White House, Supreme Court and the Senate, the threat of catching a deadly disease at work has alarmed many federal workers. Postal workers at several facilities have walked off the job to protect themselves from possible infection by the bacteria.

While the right of federal workers to refuse to work because of such an emergency has never been tested, a review of Occupational Safety and Health Administration regulations, Merit Systems Protection Board rulings and Federal Labor Relations Authority decisions shows that employees have a basic right to disobey orders that would place them in imminent danger. But that right is severely circumscribed, so workers who refuse to work because of concerns for their health and safety can still be fired for insubordination.

OSHA's regulations say that, in the federal government, there is "the right of an employee to decline to perform his or her assigned task because of a reasonable belief that, under the circumstances the task poses an imminent risk of death or serious bodily harm coupled with a reasonable belief that there is insufficient time to seek effective redress through normal hazard reporting and abatement procedures" (29 CFR 1960.46(a)).

The OSHA regulation mirrors a 1980 Supreme Court decision (*Whirlpool Corp. v. Marshall,* 445 U.S. 1) in which the court found that private sector employees can refuse to do work that would place them in imminent danger.

In general, however, federal employees must follow their supervisors' orders, according to Merit Systems Protection

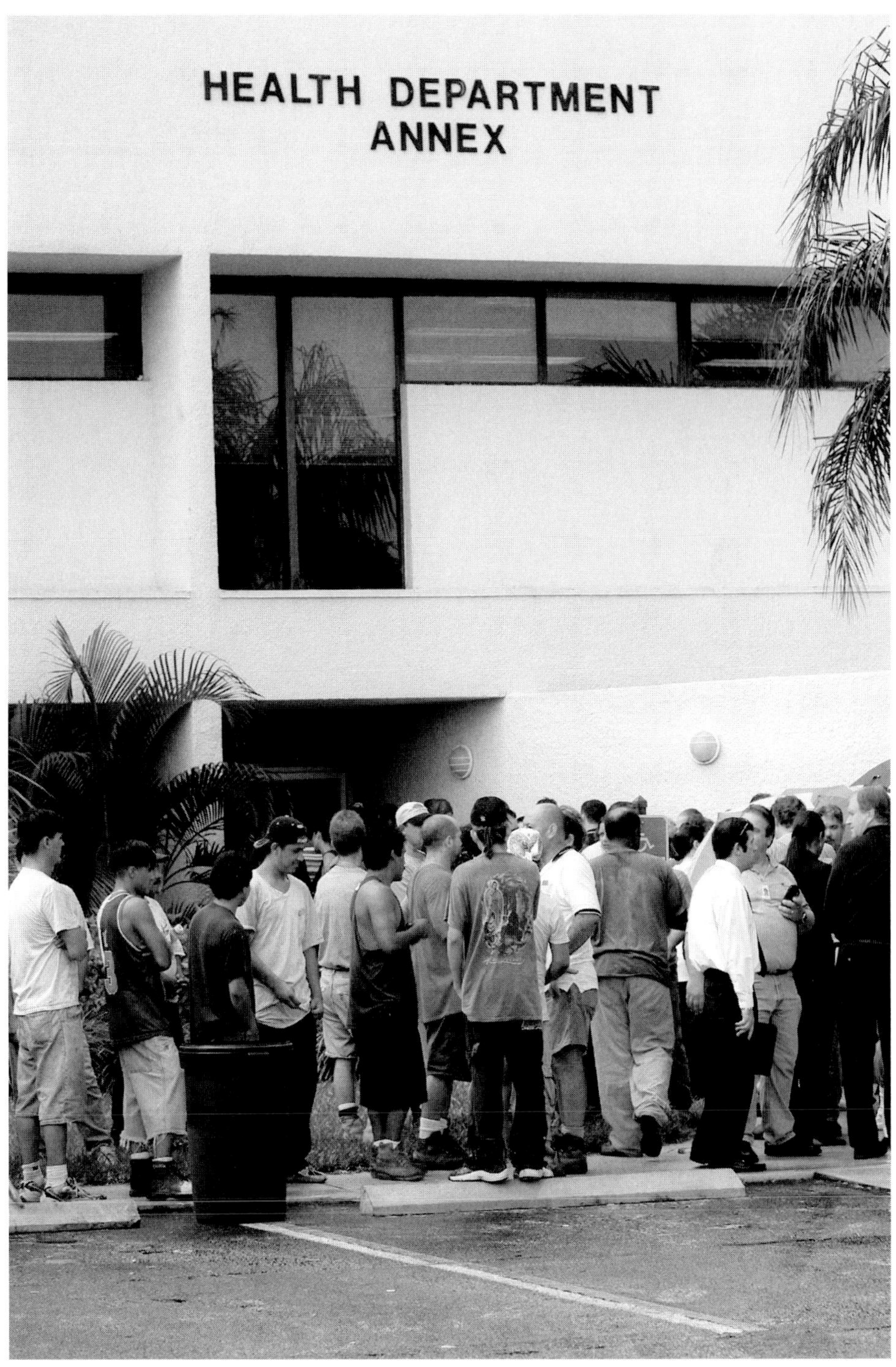

Employees wait their turn to be tested for anthrax poisoning at a Palm Springs health clinic. Many refused to work in conditions endangering their health or safety.

In a democratic society do workers have the right to make decisions concerning their own safety and health without fear of being penalized later? Is this a human rights issue? Go to Volume 15, Human Rights to explore this further.

Board rulings. "An employee does not have the unfettered right to disregard an order merely because there is substantial reason to believe that the order is not proper," the board said in *Gomez v. Department of Agriculture* (63 MSPR 36, 37–39, 1994). "He must first comply with the order and then register his complaint or grievance, except in certain limited circumstances where obedience would place the employee in a clearly dangerous situation."

The so-called "obey then grieve" rule is frequently cited in cases in which employees say they refused to work because of concerns about their health and safety. In other words, employees should generally follow orders and then complain through the appropriate channels afterwards.

When confronted with unsafe working conditions, an employee should let his or her supervisor know about the problem and discuss solutions before refusing to work, MSPB case law suggests. Employees can request safety inspections as well. Failing to take those steps can hurt employees' chances of showing that refusing to work was their only option.

Quoting from law cases helps give your argument credence. Does it work here?

"The employee who refuses to perform work for a health-related reason must show the reasonableness of his concerns," the board said in *Parker v. Department of Interior* (4 MSPR 97, 1980). "The defense will ... likely fail if the employee fails to make known to a supervisor his fear of harm," the board said in *Taylor v. USPS* (41 MSPR 374, 1989).

The Federal Labor Relations Authority has found in several cases over the last 20 years that the OSHA regulation does not prevent managers from issuing orders or from disciplining employees who refuse to obey orders. Employees can disobey orders only if the danger imposed by them meets three criteria:

Can you think of any jobs in which these criteria could not be applied?

- The threat is imminent.
- It poses a risk of death or serious bodily injury.
- It cannot be abated through normal procedures.

In *American Federation of Government Employees v. Army and Air Force Exchange Service* (30 FLRA No. 102), the labor relations authority ruled that the following provision should be included in a labor relations agreement between the union and the agency:

> *The employee has the right to decline to perform assigned tasks because of a reasonable belief that, under the circumstances, the tasks pose an imminent*

risk of death or serious bodily harm coupled with a reasonable belief that there is insufficient time to effectively seek corrective action through normal hazard reporting and abatement procedures.

The authority noted that the provision would interfere with a supervisor's ability to assign work, but that interference would come up in very few cases. Furthermore, employees would have an obligation to explain their concerns to a supervisor. The provision "does not protect employees who feel themselves to be in danger where there is no clear evidence to support that conviction," the authority decision said.

Does this seem adequate?

The authority added that employees would still risk disciplinary action because a manager may not agree with their danger assessment. An employee who refused to work and was then disciplined could file a grievance protesting the discipline. Ultimately, an arbitrator could decide whether the employee or the manager was right.

Employees in bargaining units should check their labor relations agreements to see if similar provisions cover them.

In the post-September 11, 2001, world could any work situation be argued to be hazardous?

William Bransford, a Washington attorney who specializes in federal employment law, said safety and health cases are so fact-specific that it would be difficult to guess how an employee's refusal to work in an area exposed to anthrax would play out in the grievance process or at MSPB. Bransford added that federal managers should do everything they can to create safe working environments for their employees.

"Managers should recognize their responsibility and get expert advice to make sure their employees are safe in carrying out their work," Bransford said. "A manager who fails to do that is setting himself up for trouble. A manager could be disciplined, marked down or investigated by the inspector general because he placed employees in unsafe conditions."

CAUGHT ON THE NET
Helen Hague

Helen Hague is a writer. She published this article in the British newspaper The Guardian *on December 3, 1999.*

If a company has a clear policy on Internet and e-mail use, do you think it is it right to fire people who abuse it in such circumstances?

There have been several cases of workers being fired for sending inappropriate e-mails at work; but if the average working week is far longer than 30 years ago, and people are spending more time in the office, is it inevitable that employees will use work Internet and e-mail for personal purposes?

NO

✗ There have probably been a good few angst-fuelled emails whizzing around the world over the past 24 hours as news of mass sackings for cyberspace abuse have seeped through the system. Twenty-three office staff at *The New York Times* were fired this week after company managers discovered they'd been emailing smutty notes, jokes about bosses and pornographic pictures while tapping away on screen.

The New York Times has a policy specifying that "communications must be consistent with conventional standards of ethical and proper conduct, behaviour and manners". Staff are banned from using their computers to "create, forward or display any offensive or disruptive messages", so it looks like a fair cop. But in Britain, most companies are still on the nursery slopes when it comes to keeping abreast of employees' internet habits. And employees, it seems, are getting a taste for personal emailing and leisure surfing in company time.

Tara, a 27-year-old receptionist in a local authority, reckons she sends around 50 emails a day. Earlier this week she delved into her family tree on the net and was soon emailing potential second cousins twice removed across the pond who share her distinctive surname. "I suppose it's a bit tragic really, but I get on the net whenever I can at work," she says. "Everyone's at it here. I'm not linked up at home and the job is pretty boring. Nobody's ever told me not to."

Breach of contract

But if your workstation routine regularly includes email banter, downloading smut or spending hours online trading Jpegs, be warned. The new growth area for employment lawyers is drafting email and internet policies, which become part of your employment contract. Oh yes, and the IT department can read and log all those risqué references to the head of personnel you thought were such a hoot.

Many employers are not yet aware that defamation by email can cost the company dear. Two years ago, Norwich Union paid £450,000 in an out-of-court settlement and had to make a public apology when an email on the intranet disparaging a competitor got out. Workers in the City have been sacked for downloading and distributing porn. One female company director, who has just drafted an email and internet policy, admitted she had sent a rather ripe "visual joke" to a friend in the City, only to be emailed back with a terse "Don't do that again—I could be sacked". Working with a sexually explicit screensaver could constitute harassment if it offended other staff.

The author is referring to the financial district in London, England.

Many companies are cracking down on what they deem is inappropriate use of the Internet or e-mails in an effort to prevent "hostile work environment" lawsuits against them, particularly to do with sexual harassment.
Go to Topic 4 Is workplace sexual harassment legislation adequate?

Simon Halberstam, head of internet and e-commerce law at city firm Sprecher, Grier, Halberstam, has drafted a standard email and internet use policy for clients—and demand is surging. He is frequently asked to lecture on the legal implications of the internet and email. "So many companies are unaware that they are liable for everything that employers do. They are most commonly exposed to defamation, downloading material that may be infected with viruses, sexual harassment, and entering into unauthorised contracts online. It's a minefield."

Under the draft contract, employees who abuse the internet and email can be summarily dismissed for accessing inappropriate websites, sending inappropriate email, using it to defame third parties, and excessive use for personal purposes inside working hours.

But some companies balk at such draconian policies. The Industrial Society, for instance, has found that company phone bills have dropped as people have begun to send emails to fix personal appointments rather than spend time on the telephone. In the time-poor, cash-rich economy, employees who can do a bit of shopping online aren't slipping out to Bond Street in the lunch hour, and companies can reward the loyalty of valued employees by allowing them access to the net and email for personal use.

Reasonable solutions?

There is also a debate going on as to whether employees should be given private email addresses so that the messages they send do not leave the screen with the company footer, which makes it look as if they've been sanctioned by the firm. Questionable emails can not only tarnish the company's image but also open up exposure in the growing area of cyber-liability for defamation, harassment or breach of copyright.

Sue Nickson, head of the national employment unit at Hammond Suddards, advises the Institute of Personnel and Development on email and net issues. "Employers should

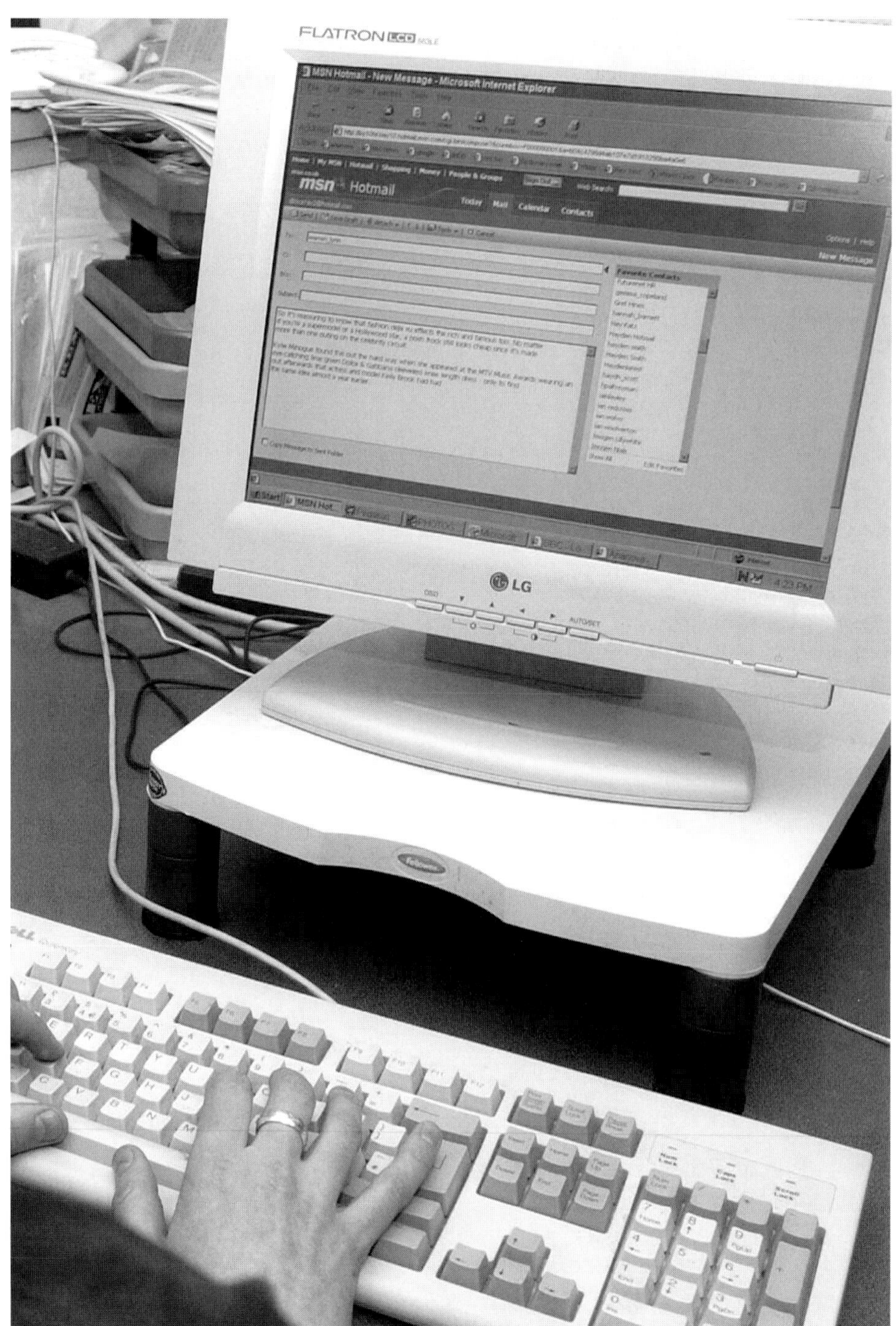

Many workers use e-mail during work hours. Some employers monitor usage, and there have been cases of employees being dismissed for improper use of e-mail at such workplaces as The New York Times.

spell out what is and isn't acceptable. They should get the policy in place, make it clear what the parameters are and what the penalties will be if employees breach them. Abuse of email will be treated as a disciplinary offence and will trigger company disciplinary procedures.

> *For instance, a few personal emails to a boyfriend in Hong Kong could result in an oral warning, while 60 emails a day may well mean immediate dismissal. It's a question of degree, and companies need to build flexibility into their policies while making it clear that the principal use is for business and that harassment or exchange of abusive or pornographic materials will not be tolerated.*

Does the Constitution protect privacy in the workplace? If not, how can employees protect themselves from employer abuse? Go to Volume 7, The Constitution, Topic 15 Is Internet surveillance constitutional?

It should, she says, be spelled out to employees that they are being monitored.

> *At the end of the day, if you are abusing email in company time, the company has the right to look into it and it's not a privacy issue when you sign up to the contract. It is beginning to dawn on employees that their companies are monitoring them and they are starting to realise it's all capable of being tracked back to them.*

Robert Pullen, editor of law cases at Incomes Data Services, says UK companies are waking up to the need to protect themselves from cyber-liabilities by getting proper internet and email policies in place. "Those who don't will find themselves increasingly exposed. However, it will be very difficult to sack people summarily in the first instance of abuse."

The days of cyber-slacking are not necessarily numbered, but once they sign the company's internet policy, email-happy employees who are regulars in online shopping malls should think about changing their workstation habits.

Does this seem fair? Do you think that offenses such as shopping online for a present for a friend, surfing the Net for porn, or e-mailing work secrets to another company should be given different penalties?

Summary

The issue of whether employees always have to follow orders causes heated discussion, especially following several high-profile whistleblowing cases involving abuses by big businesses. The articles by Brian Friel and Helen Hague look at this issue. Brian Friel, in the first extract, examines whether federal employees have the right to refuse to work in situations that place them in danger, such as the 2001 deadly anthrax contamination. Friel asserts that legislation does grant this right in such extreme cases, although such action "has never been tested." Drawing on OSHA regulations for private companies, he explains employees should "follow orders and then complain." He refers to several test cases and to the Federal Labor Relations Authority's conclusion that employees should face disciplinary measures if a supervisor disagrees that a work situation is imminently dangerous. Washington-based attorney William Bransford says it is difficult to generalize when every case is "so fact-specific," and he suggests that managers ensure safe work conditions so that such situations do not arise.

Helen Hague examines employee "abuse" of Internet access at work. She warns employees that companies' IT departments can read the e-mails that "you thought were such a hoot." Employees might see Internet use at work as a harmless "perk," but Hague cites a $700,000 settlement paid by a British company after disparaging e-mails about a competitor became public. Some companies draft Internet policies that make employees subject to dismissal if they do not comply. Others balk at such "draconian policies," saying the Internet costs them less than personal phone calls. Employment expert Sue Nickson claims that employers need to spell out what is and is not acceptable practice in the workplace.

FURTHER INFORMATION:

Books:

Dempsey, James X., and David Cole, *Terrorism and the Constitution: Sacrificing Civil Liberties in the Name of National Security* (2nd edition). Washington, D.C.: First Amendment Foundation, 2002.

Useful websites:

http://www.nolo.com/lawcenter/ency/article.cfm/ObjectID/1710112D-A8C2-4DBC-97A3E271E3C8A169/catID/0A323459-4B09-4D32-BB8CD8E6058BE1CF#9307F654-ECD3-4332-80626F50D96EC85E
Health and safety question and answer site that details when employees can refuse to perform jobs for safety reasons.

The following debates in the Pro/Con series may also be of interest:

In this volume:

Part 1: Worker rights, pages 8–9

Whistleblowing: Inez Austin and the Hanford Nuclear Reservation, pages 34–35

Part 2: Work culture, pages 86–87

SHOULD EMPLOYEES HAVE THE RIGHT TO DISOBEY COMPANY ORDERS?

SHOULD EMPLOYEES HAVE THE RIGHT TO DISOBEY COMPANY ORDERS? KEY POINTS

SAFETY
Do employees have the right to refuse to work?

YES: If employees think that hazards in the workplace put their health and safety at risk, they can refuse to work

NO: The Office of Safety and Health Administration states that employees have a very limited right to refuse to work. They should carry out their duties and complain afterward.

WHISTLEBLOWING
Is whistleblowing ethical?

YES: If employees have evidence that a company is conducting illegal or improper business, they have a duty to inform the public

NO: Employers, especially those working in politically sensitive areas, must be able to trust their workers. Sometimes people have to suspend their moral or ethical beliefs in order to do their jobs.

NONDISCLOSURE
Is it ever acceptable for employees to breach their contracts?

YES: An employee who has signed an NDA should still breach its terms if an employer has asked him or her to keep quiet about illegal practices or falsifications

NO: Many NDA clauses are designed to ensure that trade secrets are not leaked to competitors by employees. They are needed to protect employers.

ETHICS
If employees disagree with an order on moral grounds, should they be able to refuse to carry it out?

YES: Even in such occupations as the military, if a superior officer orders someone to do something that is morally wrong, such as kill unarmed civilians, he or she must have the right to refuse

NO: In jobs involving national security employers have to be certain that their employees will carry out their orders, even seemingly unpalatable ones

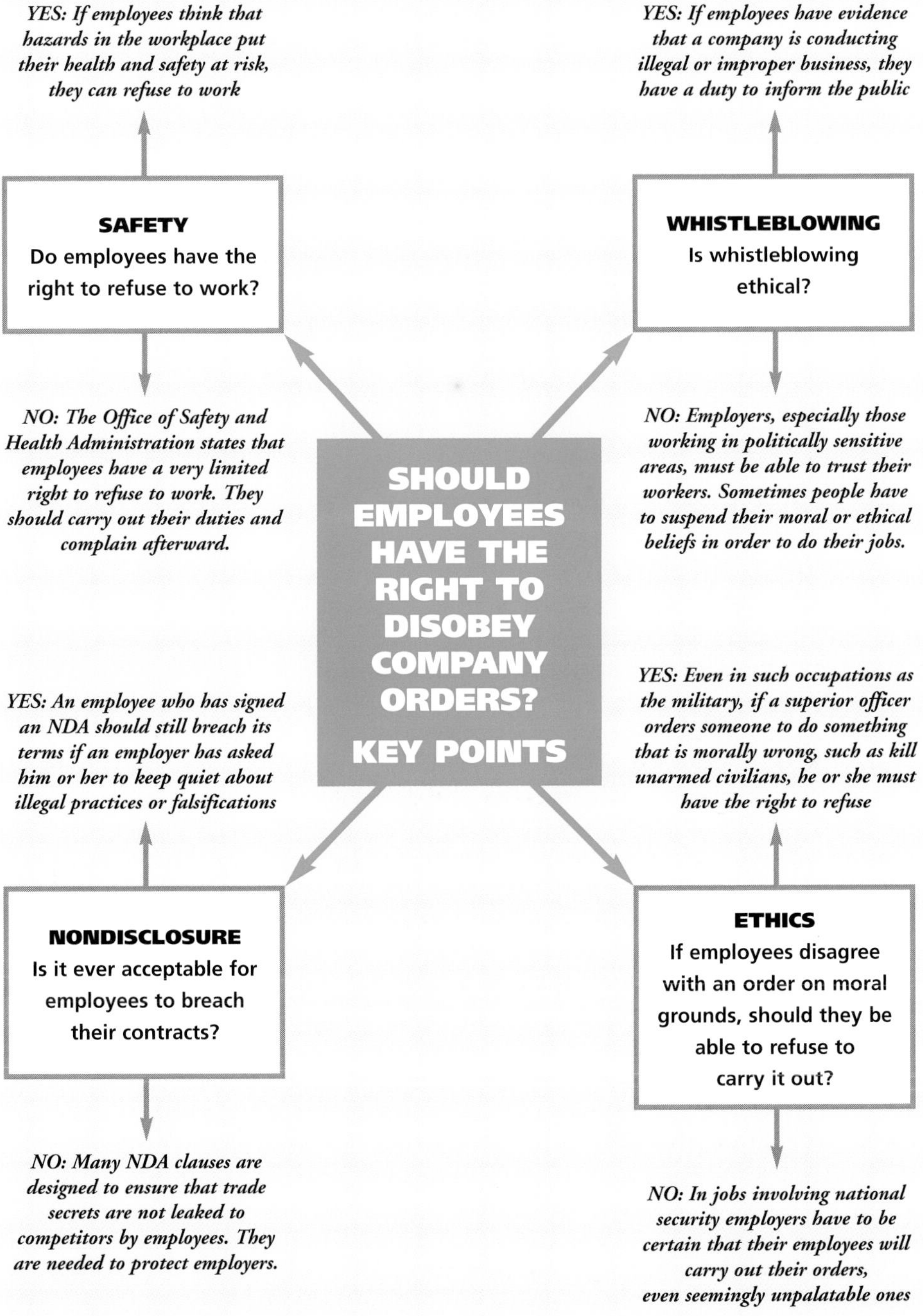

WHISTLEBLOWING: INEZ AUSTIN AND THE HANFORD NUCLEAR RESERVATION

"Ms. Austin's stand in the face of harassment and intimidation reflects the paramount professional duty of engineers—to protect the public's health and safety—and has served as an inspiration to her coworkers."

—AMERICAN ASSOCIATION FOR THE ADVANCEMENT OF SCIENCE (1992)

In 1990 Inez Austin, a senior engineer at Hanford Nuclear Reservation in Washington state, made a decision that would change her life and lead her to be both vilified and praised. Austin refused to approve a plan to pump radioactive waste from one underground tank to another, since she believed the process was far too dangerous. Despite pressure to sign the plan off as safe, Austin refused to do so. Over the next few years she was subjected to physical and mental abuse by her employers, she was threatened, and her professional reputation was attacked. Austin received validation for her actions, however, when she received the 1992 Scientific Freedom and Responsibility Award from the American Association for the Advancement of Science for her efforts to prevent "potential safety hazards involving nuclear waste contamination."

The events of 1990

Inez Austin was one of the few women engineers in the Westinghouse company. Extremely pleased with her work, the company transferred Austin to a new position as senior process engineer. A major part of her new role was to approve safety procedures involving the pumping of radioactive wastes such as ferrocyanide—a substance that the U.S. Senate had concluded could be highly explosive under certain conditions. In June 1990 Austin was asked to look at the safety of pumping hazardous liquid wastes out of five single-shell tanks in order to stabilize the tanks. The pumping formed part of a 30-year cleanup program certified by the Energy Department and the Environmental Protection Agency, and had to occur by July 1, 1990. Austin, however, became concerned that two of the tanks contained extremely volatile and unstable amounts of ferrocyanide. She believed that there was about a 10 percent chance of an accident occurring, so she recommended that the two tanks in question not be certified until certain studies into ferrocyanide were concluded. This, however, could have meant up to a three-year delay, which could have resulted in a lawsuit by the state against the federal government for failure to meet the July pumping deadline.

Austin thought the risks involved justified the delay, and she put her findings in writing to her boss, Richard Kimura. When her report was returned to her for signing on June 25, 1990, however, Austin discovered that Kimura had removed any reference to her safety concerns. She refused to sign the document despite threats of disciplinary action from Kimura. After further threats Austin resigned from the review board rather than put her signature on something she disagreed with.

Consequences

What Austin could not foresee was that her actions would have such long-lasting consequences for her career. For the 10 years prior to the Hanford incident Austin had received consistently excellent ratings for her work, but afterward, for the first time in her career, she was given a poor rating. She was also harassed, her mail was not delivered, and her office and home were broken into. Remarks were made in the workplace about her mental health and her need to see a psychiatrist. Finally, Austin filed an action with the Energy Department on October 11, 1990, alleging harassment by her employers following her whistleblowing. She dropped the charges two months later in exchange for a new job, a month off with pay, removal of a letter of reprimand from her work file, and compensation for her legal fees. She was allowed to choose a new position and moved to West Tank Farms Operations (WTFO). Once there, however, she found that her new boss had been told not to give her any work. Over the next three years any work Austin did was on a volunteer basis only, and she found that it was duplicated by another employee. She was effectively being paid to do nothing. She was finally demoted in October 1993. On October 7 Austin went public, calling a news conference and informing the press that in the nearly three years since her settlement with the Energy Department, she had received no work. Her actions led her to be assigned jobs, but she continued to be harassed in the workplace.

Unlawful practices

Many experts believe that Hanford was in breach of several safety requirements. It is alleged to have allowed untrained workers into restricted areas and covered up an asbestos spill, among other things. But while many people worked under these conditions without complaining, Austin could not, and in February 1996 she was fired. She decided to report her concerns regarding safety issues and her own treatment following the whistleblowing episode directly to the Federal Energy Secretary, Hazel O'Leary, in April 1996. Although O'Leary promised Austin that her termination would be put on hold and that she would still be paid, this did not happen. This prompted Austin to take her complaints to the Labor Department. Although she won her case and was awarded damages, they did not come even close to covering either Austin's loss of earnings or the damage to her professional reputation. Austin sued Westinghouse for unfair dismissal; a jury decided in 2000 that she had not been fired but had effectively resigned. They also rejected her contention that the company had constructed a paper trail of documents after the event to put themselves in the clear. "It's a company town," Austin said of Richland, Washington. "People are paid a lot to keep quiet." She stands by her actions.

Topic 3

IS MANDATORY DRUG TESTING IN THE WORKPLACE WRONG?

YES

FROM "PRIVACY IN AMERICA: WORKPLACE DRUG TESTING"
HTTP://ARCHIVE.ACLU.ORG/LIBRARY/PBR5.HTML
AMERICAN CIVIL LIBERTIES UNION

NO

FROM "DRUG TESTING"
HEALTH AND HUMAN SERVICES DEPARTMENT AND SAMHSA'S
NATIONAL CLEARING HOUSE FOR ALCHOHOL AND DRUG INFORMATION
EMPLOYER TIP SHEET NO. 9

INTRODUCTION

At the heart of any discussion about whether there should be compulsory drug testing of employees in the workplace are the issues of how much control employers ought to have over their workers' lives, and whether such testing is an invasion of worker privacy.

Drug testing has been widely accepted in jobs such as air-traffic control and fire fighting because of the danger that drug impairment could represent to the public and also out of fear of lawsuits against companies. More controversial has been testing in the private commercial sector, such as in manufacturing, where some 78.5 percent of U.S. firms practice it, and in retail, where 63 percent of firms use testing on employees.

Advocates of testing claim that U.S. studies show there is a real problem that needs addressing: Substance abusers (including alcoholics) are 33 percent less productive and four times as likely to hurt others at work or themselves. They also claim statistics show that testing is effective: Figures from Ohio show that when random testing was introduced in the state, absenteeism dropped 91 percent and job injuries 97 percent. Other countries also have work-drug problems. A study in Canada revealed that up to 10 percent of workers were drinking excessively. In Poland, 5.7 percent of workers were found to be drinking at work, and in Germany the figure was more than 10 percent. But many observers believe that drug testing in the workplace is wrong since it neither is accurate nor deals with the real problem. Some argue that counseling and medical help would be more effective options, for example.

Until 1975 U.S. testing was largely confined to the military, and legal opinion was that the Fourth

Amendment to the Constitution restricted it by guaranteeing "the right of the people to be secure in their persons … against unreasonable searches." Critics argued that this prevented testing that could not be justified for a specific reason. However, in the 1975 case of *Committee for GI Rights v. Callaway* the court ruled that drug testing did not violate the Fourth Amendment.

"An era of chemical McCarthyism is at hand, and 'guilty until proven innocent' is the new slogan."

—GEORGE LUNDBERG, EDITOR OF THE *AMERICAN MEDICAL ASSOCIATION JOURNAL* (1986)

In 1982 President Ronald Reagan (1981–1989) launched the "War on Drugs," which advocated "zero tolerance" of drug use and stiff penalties for offenders. In 1986 Reagan banned federal employees from using illegal substances. In 1988 the Drug Free Workplace Act further required contractors and grantees of federal agencies to provide drug-free workplaces as a precondition of receiving a contract or grant. Soon afterward insurance companies began to offer discounts to businesses that tested their employees.

Drug testing involves the collection of a sample (urine, a hair, or less frequently blood or saliva), which is analyzed to search for metabolites from a particular substance. This means the tests do not detect the substance itself but a byproduct that the body has produced by ingesting the substance. Since the same metabolite can sometimes be produced by both legal and illegal substances, critics have questioned the tests' validity. They also claim that employees may be unfairly penalized for positive results from drugs taken outside of the workplace. Supporters claim that most drugs are illegal, and where they are consumed is largely irrelevant; they also claim that false results can be overruled through retesting.

Among other criticisms leveled at drug testing is that companies can use testing to look for medical conditions that employees are not under obligation to tell them about. Whereas early testing only targeted illegal narcotics, over the years the list of drugs tested has increased to include prescription drugs such as tranquilizers. Opponents, including civil rights groups such as the American Civil Liberties Union, claim that in today's Big Brother society other industries such as insurance companies or federal agencies may be able to get hold of test results. They are concerned that mandatory testing is yet another sign that U.S. workers' rights—already weaker, they argue, than in western Europe, for example—are being further undermined.

Another point raised against testing is that employees are obliged to prove their innocence. This reverses the basic legal principles that a person is innocent until proven guilty, and that the burden of proof lies with the accuser. Advocates insist, however, that mandatory testing ensures that minority groups are not unfairly targeted.

The following articles take a more detailed look into the issue.

PRIVACY IN AMERICA: WORKPLACE DRUG TESTING
American Civil Liberties Union

The American Civil Liberties Union was founded in 1920. It aims "to conserve America's original civic values —the Constitution and the Bill of Rights." See www.aclu.org for further details.

YES

✓ In fact, workplace drug testing is up 277 percent from 1987—despite the fact that random drug testing is unfair, often inaccurate and unproven as a means of stopping drug use. But because there are few laws protecting our privacy in the workplace, millions of American workers are tested yearly—even though they aren't suspected of drug use.

Employers have the right to expect workers not to be high or drunk on the job. But they shouldn't have the right to require employees to prove their innocence by taking a drug test. That's not how America should work.

Methods of tampering with urine specimens have ranged from adding salt or soap to the sample to make it unusable, to substituting another person's urine, brought to the test in a hidden container.

Invasion and error

However routine drug tests have become, they're still intrusive. Often, another person is there to observe the employee to ensure there is no specimen tampering. Even indirect observation can be degrading; typically, workers must remove their outer garments and urinate in a bathroom in which the water supply has been turned off.

The lab procedure is a second invasion of privacy. Urinalysis reveals not only the presence of illegal drugs, but also the existence of many other physical and medical conditions, including genetic predisposition to disease—or pregnancy. In 1988, the Washington, D.C. Police Department admitted it used urine samples collected for drug tests to screen female employees for pregnancy—without their knowledge or consent. Furthermore, human error in the lab, or the test's failure to distinguish between legal and illegal substances, can make even a small margin of error add up to a huge potential for false positive results. In 1992, an estimated 22 million tests were administered. If five percent yielded false positive results (a conservative estimate of false positive rates) that means 1.1 million people who could have been fired, or denied jobs—because of a mistake.

A "false positive" is a result that seems to indicate the presence of a particular substance but in fact has been caused by a different substance.

I waited for the attendant to turn her back before pulling down my pants, but she told me she had to

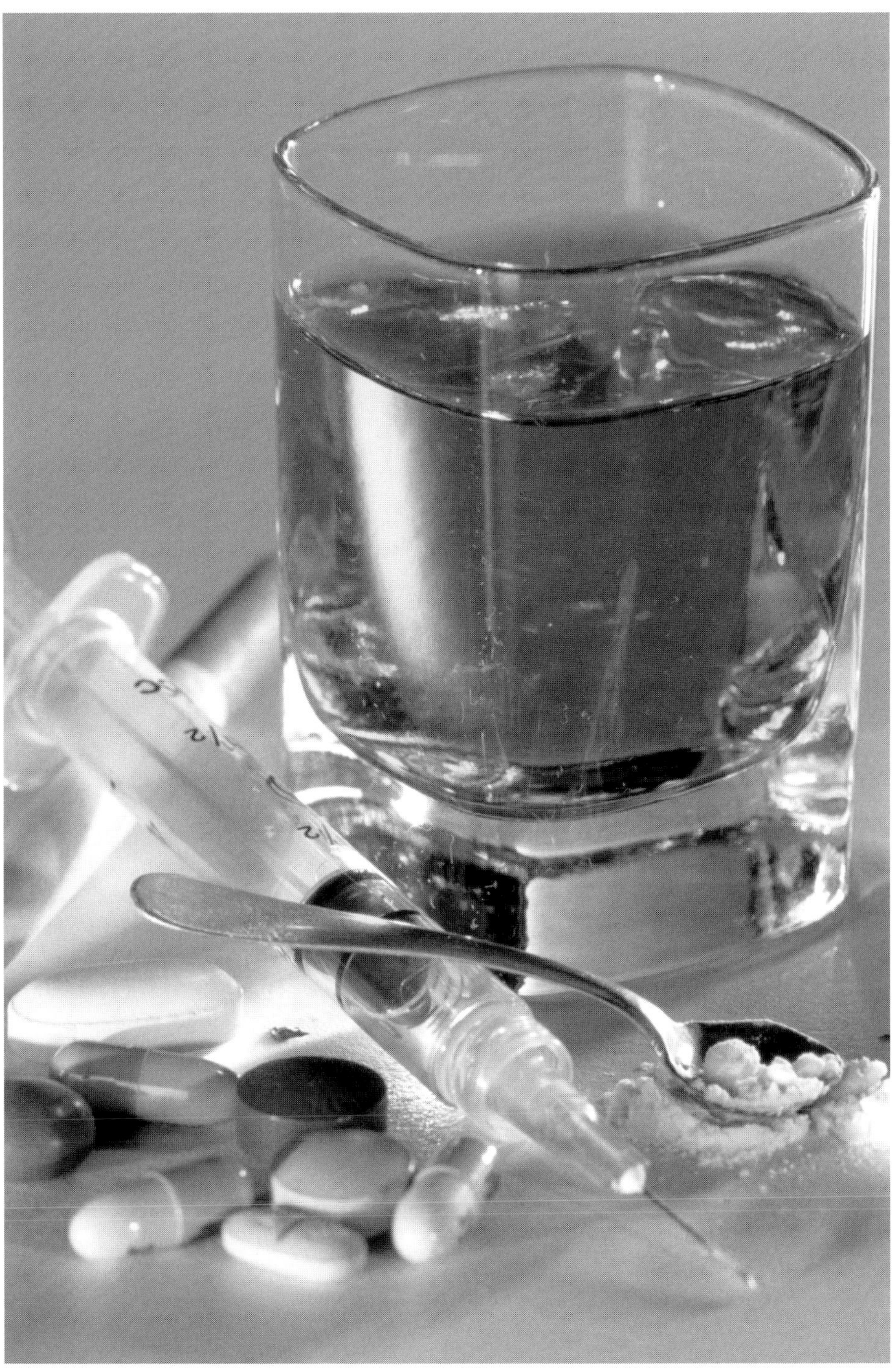

According to estimates, hundreds of thousands of workers have alcohol or drug addictions. But would mandatory drug testing help stop this?

watch everything I did. I am a 40-year-old mother of three: nothing I have ever done in my life equals or deserves the humiliation, degradation and mortification I felt.
—From a letter to the ACLU describing a workplace drug test.

Tests that fail

See http://www.nap.edu/catalog/2118.html for the National Academy's 1994 report, "Under the Influence? Drugs and the American Work Force."

Claims of billions of dollars lost in employee productivity are based on guesswork, not real evidence. Drug abuse in the workplace affects a relatively small percentage of workers. A 1994 National Academy of Sciences report found workplace drug use "ranges from a modest to a moderate extent," and noted that much of reported drug use "may be single incident, perhaps even at events like office parties." Furthermore, drug tests are not work-related because they do not measure on-the-job impairment. A positive drug test only reveals that a drug was ingested at some time in the past. Nor do they distinguish between occasional and habitual use.

Do you agree that employers have no business knowing what their employees do at home? Or do employers have a legitimate interest in anything that might affect a worker's ability to do their job?

Drug testing is designed to detect and punish conduct that is usually engaged in off-duty and off the employer's premises—that is, in private. Employers who conduct random drug tests on workers who are not suspected of using drugs are policing private behavior that has no impact on job performance.

Far from foolproof

Poppy seeds are commonly found sprinkled on various bread products. Heroin is derived from opium gum, which is produced by the opium poppy.

Sometimes drug tests fail to distinguish between legal and illegal substances. Depronil, a prescription drug used to treat Parkinson's disease, has shown up as an amphetamine on standard drug tests. Over-the-counter antiinflammatory drugs like Ibuprofen have shown up positive on the marijuana test. Even the poppy seeds found in baked goods can produce a positive result for heroin.

About safety-sensitive occupations

Alertness and sobriety are, of course, imperative for certain occupations, such as train engineers, airline pilots, truck drivers and others. Yet even in these jobs, random drug testing does not guarantee safety. Firstly, drug-related employee impairment in safety-sensitive jobs is rare. There has never been a commercial airline accident linked to pilot drug use. And even after a 1994 Amtrak accident in which several lives were lost, investigators discovered the train engineer had a well known history of alcohol, not drug, abuse.

Computer-assisted performance tests, which measure hand-eye coordination and response time, are a better way of detecting whether employees are up to the job. NASA, for example, has long used task-performance tests to determine whether astronauts and pilots are unfit for work—whether the cause is substance abuse, fatigue, or physical illness.

Could performance tests be used more widely instead of drug tests? Are there any drawbacks compared to drug tests? See http://www.nontesterslist.com/nontesters/tlccomer1.html for an overview of performance testing and the issues it raises.

Drug tests don't prevent accidents because they don't address the root problems that lead to substance abuse. But good management and counseling can. Employee assistance programs (EAPs) help people facing emotional, health, financial or substance abuse problems that can affect job performance. EAP counselors decide what type of help is needed: staff support, inpatient treatment, AA meetings, and the like. In this context, the goal is rehabilitation and wellness—not punishment.

Employers need to kick the drug test habit.

What we are doing

Privacy—the right to be left alone—is one of our most cherished rights. Yet because so few laws protect our privacy, the ACLU's campaign for privacy in the workplace is very important—particularly in the private sector.

There is no specific clause concerning privacy in the Constitution, but the First, Third, Fourth, Fifth, and Ninth Amendments do include protections that draw on the idea of a right to privacy. See http://www.law.cornell.edu/constitution/constitution.billofrights.htm for the text of these amendments.

The ACLU is working in the states to help enact legislation to protect workplace privacy rights. We have created a model statute regulating workplace drug testing. In 1996 the ACLU launched a public education campaign to help individuals across the nation become aware of the need for increased workplace privacy rights. Our educational videotape *Through the Keyhole: Privacy in the Workplace—An Endangered Right* was featured on national television and at union meetings and other gatherings nationwide.

Much more work remains to be done. As of mid 1997, only a handful of states ban testing that is not based on individual suspicion: Montana, Iowa, Vermont, and Rhode Island. Minnesota, Maine and Connecticut permit not-for-cause testing, but only of employees in safety-sensitive positions. These laws also require confirmation testing, lab certification and test result confidentiality.

"Not-for-cause testing" is a test carried out on a random or universal basis, rather than because there is evidence that a particular individual might be alcohol or drug impaired.

Hawaii, Louisiana, Maryland, Nebraska, Oregon and Utah regulate drug testing in some fashion; Florida and Kansas protect government employee rights, but not those of private sector workers. Only in California, Massachusetts and New Jersey have the highest courts ruled out some forms of drug testing on state constitutional or statutory grounds. The ACLU is now continuing our efforts to protect workplace privacy rights. You can help....

DRUG TESTING
Employer Tip Sheet No. 9

This employer tip sheet was published by the Health and Human Services Department and SAMSHA's Clearinghouse for Alcohol and Drug Information. Go to www.health.org for more information and to see other publications.

NO

What is drug testing?

Drug testing is one way you can protect your workplace from the negative effects of alcohol and other drug abuse. A drug testing program can deter people from coming to work unfit for duty and also discourage alcohol and other drug abusers from joining your organization in the first place....

Some employers believe that a drug-free workplace program and drug testing are one and the same; however, drug testing is only one element of a program. Drug testing may be appropriate for some organizations and not others. In some cases drug testing is required; in others, it is optional.... When drug testing is optional, the decision about whether or not to test will depend on a variety of factors such as the cost, appropriateness, and feasibility....

In some cases drug testing is compulsory under state or federal law, for instance, the Drug Free Workplace Act of 1988 (see the Introduction to this topic, page 37).

When should you drug test?

Below are examples of situations in which drug testing might be appropriate or necessary:

Pre-employment tests. Offering employment only after a negative drug test result.
Goal: To decrease the chance of hiring someone who is currently using or abusing drugs.

Pre-promotion tests. Testing employees prior to promotion within the organization.
Goal: To decrease the chance of promoting someone who is currently using or abusing drugs.

Annual physical tests. Testing employees for alcohol and other drug use as part of their annual physical.
Goal: To identify current users and abusers so they can be referred for assistance and/or disciplinary action.

Critics say that, apart from those in safety-sensitive jobs, "reasonable suspicion" should be the only grounds for carrying out a drug test. Do you agree?

Reasonable suspicion and for cause tests. Testing employees who show obvious signs of being unfit for duty (For Cause) or have documented patterns of unsafe work behavior (Reasonable Suspicion).

Goal: To protect the safety and well-being of the employee and other coworkers and to provide the opportunity for rehabilitation if the employee tests positive.

Random tests. Testing a selected group of employees at random and unpredictable times. Most commonly used in safety- and security-sensitive positions.
Goal: To discourage use and abuse by making testing unpredictable, and to identify current users and abusers so they can be referred for assistance and/or disciplinary action if needed.

This wording suggests that only the timing of the tests is random, not the selection of people to take them. Is there a danger that testing will be used to focus unfairly on particular groups of workers, such as ethnic minorities?

Post-accident tests. Testing employees who are involved in an accident or unsafe practice incident to help determine whether alcohol or other drug use was a factor.
Goal: To protect the safety of the employees, and to identify and refer to treatment those persons whose alcohol or other drug use threatens the safety of the workplace....

An effective drug testing program needs a drug testing policy....

What should a drug testing policy include?

- The drugs you are testing for

Laboratories can test for a wide variety of drugs. Generally, employers test only for those that are most commonly used and abused: cocaine, phencyclidine (PCP), opiates, amphetamines, and cannabinoids (marijuana). Some employers also test for alcohol.

Unless a worker shows obvious signs of drunkenness or is unable to carry out his or her job, should alcohol be included among the substances tested for, since it is not illegal?

- Who will be tested and under what conditions

While the overall drug-free workplace policy should apply to everyone in an organization, the drug testing policy may apply only to some employees. Therefore, the testing policy should clearly identify the employee positions included in the testing program. The policy should also indicate under what circumstances employees in each position will be tested.

Why do you think drug testing would "apply only to some employees"? Do you think it would help workforces accept it more willingly if everyone in an organization was tested on the same basis?

Employers who are required to drug test by one or more Federal agencies should refer to the specific regulations to determine the types of testing that are required (e.g. random, post-accident, etc.). Employers whose employees are members of a union or collective bargaining unit should know that unless drug testing is required by law or regulation, it will likely be a mandatory subject of bargaining.

- Consequences of testing positive or refusing a test ...

Before beginning a drug testing program, carefully consider how you will handle a positive drug test result. The actions that will be taken in response to a positive drug test should be clearly detailed in the written policy. Although there are many options, common responses include referring the employee for treatment, disciplinary measures, or discharge....

Are urine tests justified if they do not give an indication of whether a person is impaired at work?

SAMHSA is the Substance Abuse and Mental Health Services Administration, an arm of the Health and Human Services Department. See www.samhsa.gov for further details.

If a person has shown no sign of being impaired at work, is it fair that they should be fired for refusing to take a drug test?

Drug testing methods

- **Urine test:** The most common form of drug testing is to analyze a sample of urine for traces of drugs. A positive test result only indicates that a drug was used sometime in the recent past; it does not tell whether or not the person was under the influence when giving the sample....
- **Blood test:** A blood test measures the actual amount of alcohol or other drugs in the blood at the time of the test. Unlike the urine test, the results tell whether or not the person was under the influence at the time the test was done.
- **Alternative specimen test:** Alternative specimens and technologies for the detection of the use of selected drugs of abuse, include hair, oral fluids, sweat, and point of collection initial test devices (for urine and oral fluids at this time). They have been under formal, ongoing evaluation by the SAMHSA-chartered Drug Testing Advisory Board (DTAB) since April 1997....

An employee who tests positive may be given paid or unpaid leave and referred to the employee assistance program (EAP) or other substance abuse assessment service, if available. Some employers automatically discharge anyone who tests positive. Usually, refusing to provide a sample for testing or attempting to tamper with, contaminate, or switch a sample is considered grounds for discipline or discharge.

It is important to have guidelines in place that explain the organization's procedures for appeal should an employee test positive. The appeal process will vary depending on the nature of the work done, State laws, contractual requirements, etc....

Drug testing procedures

A clear written description of the procedures that will be used for drug testing should be included either in the drug testing policy or in a separate document.... Below are examples of the type of information to include:

- Where employees will give their samples (name and phone number of the collection site)

- Where the samples will be tested (name and phone number of the testing laboratory)
- How results will be reported (will the laboratory contact the individual, or will a designated person in the company tell the employee?)

Employers will also want to know these terms:

- **Chain of custody.** A chain of custody form is used to document the handling and storage of a urine [or other] specimen from the time it is collected until the time of disposal. This form links the individual to the urine sample. It is written proof of everything that happens to the specimen while at the collection site and the laboratory.
- **Confirmation tests.** The first test of a urine sample is called an initial test. This test is fairly accurate and reliable but can also detect over-the-counter medications. Therefore, if the initial test is positive, a second test (by gas chromatography/mass spectrometry, or GC/MS) should be done on the sample immediately. This confirmatory test is highly accurate and will rule out any false positives (mistakes made) on the first test.
- **DHHS cut-off levels.** A cut-off level is a value that is used to determine whether a drug test is positive or negative. Many employers use the cut-off levels established by the Department of Health and Human Services....
- **Medical review officer (MRO).** Although not always required, an MRO is an important part of an effective drug testing program. An MRO is a licensed medical doctor who has special training in substance abuse. Using an MRO helps to protect both the employer and the employees....

See http://www.mshp.dps.missouri.gov/MSHPWeb/PatrolDivisions/CLD/Toxicology/Toxicology.html for more details about the processes involved in confirmatory tests.

Do you think cut-off levels should be set high to catch those who have definitely taken a drug, or low to catch all those who might have taken it?

What about legal challenges?

Many States have drug testing laws that determine what an employer can and cannot do. Resources are available to help you find out if there are any State drug testing laws you must comply with. An attorney with experience in labor and employment issues, or a professional consultant specializing in workplace drug testing can help ensure that the testing rules and procedures as outlined in your policy are in compliance with State regulations.

Avoid legal problems by using procedures that are clear, fair, consistent, and documented in a written policy. Because employment decisions based on a test result can be contested, it will be to your advantage to have a detailed policy and to understand the protections that are available to you....

These notes were written by a branch of the federal government, but many of them will not apply in some states since most law to do with drug testing is enacted at the state level. Would it be better if regulations on drug testing could be set by federal government so that they are the same for Americans everywhere?

Summary

In the first article the American Civil Liberties Union (ACLU) claims that drug testing is a violation of privacy and is fundamentally unfair because it humiliates employees by treating them as guilty until they can prove their innocence. Urine tests—the most common kind of test—also fail in their stated aim of testing fitness for work since they can only show that a substance has been ingested in the past, not that it is still having an effect. Testing, therefore, amounts to an attempt by employers to police private behavior. Urine tests are also unreliable, returning an unacceptable number of false positives, which potentially endanger careers for no reason. The ACLU claims that employers who really want to test fitness for work should use computerized performance tests instead. If they want to help employees with substance-abuse problems, they should invest in an employee assistance program.

The second extract, an employer's tip sheet by the Clearinghouse for Alcohol and Drug Information, defends mandatory drug testing in the workplace. It asserts that testing is a valid way of protecting employees who abuse illicit substances or alcohol from themselves and also protects their coworkers. The piece explores the conditions and situations in which a drug test might appropriately be implemented, such as after accidents, in the cases of odd or suspicious behavior, or just as part of an annual or ongoing assessment of the workforce. The tip sheet emphasizes that it is crucial for employers to have a clearly stated drug policy that is fairly and consistently applied, and includes procedures for appeals and legal challenges.

FURTHER INFORMATION:

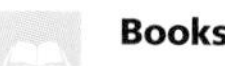

Books:

Bennett, Joel B., and Wayne E.K. Lehman, *Preventing Workplace Substance Abuse: Beyond Drug Testing to Wellness*. Washington, D.C.: American Psychological Association, 2002.

Holtorf, Kent, *Ur-Ine Trouble*. Palos Verdes Estates, CA: Vandalay Press, 1998.

Newton, David E., *Drug Testing: An Issue for School, Sports, and Work*. Springfield, NJ: Enslow, 1999.

Useful websites:

www.drugfreeworkplace.gov
SAMHSA's resource page for employers.

http://www.norml.org/index.cfm?Group_ID=4935
Background to the legal history of drug testing.

http://www.unodc.org/unodc/en/bulletin/
UN site with an overview of drug testing in the workplace.

The following debates in the Pro/Con series may also be of interest:

In this volume:
Part 1: Worker rights, pages 8–9

In *The Constitution*:
Topic 14 Are random drug tests of athletes constitutional?

In *Criminal Law and the Penal System*:
Topic 11 Should soft drugs be decriminalized?

IS MANDATORY DRUG TESTING IN THE WORKPLACE WRONG?

IS MANDATORY DRUG TESTING IN THE WORKPLACE WRONG? KEY POINTS

ASSUMPTION OF INNOCENCE
Do drug tests reverse the assumption of innocence at the base of our law?

YES: Tests treat everyone as a suspect who has to prove his or her innocence, and refusal to take a test is considered an admission of guilt

NO: Treating everyone the same way is the only way of ensuring that no assumptions are made either way, and everyone is treated fairly

COST
Are drug tests a waste of money?

YES: Tests are a costly use of laboratory resources that only tell employers about substances their workers might have ingested in the past. They reveal nothing about fitness for work, which can be tested much more cheaply.

NO: The Labor Department estimates that, particularly when associated with employee assistance programs, companies save between $5 and $16 for each dollar invested

PRODUCTIVITY
Is it a myth that drug tests help increase worker productivity?

YES: Recent studies in the High-Tech industry show that in fact it decreased productivity by creating a climate of suspicion, lowering morale, and increasing resentment

NO: U.S. studies demonstrate that substance abusers (including alcohol) are 33 percent less productive and 3 times more likely to be late for work

ABUSE OF RIGHTS
Is drug testing unconstitutional?

YES: Except where public safety is involved, any advantages gained from testing are not great enough to offset the damage to an individual's right to privacy

NO: The Constitution has no explicit "right to privacy." Courts have ruled that testing does not breach the Fourth Amendment.

Topic 4

IS WORKPLACE SEXUAL HARASSMENT LEGISLATION ADEQUATE?

YES

"AMERICA'S OVERPROTECTIVE SEXUAL HARASSMENT LAW"
CATO INSTITUTE, APRIL 10, 2000
JOAN KENNEDY TAYLOR

NO

"SAME-SEX SEXUAL HARASSMENT CASES TYPICALLY HELD TO DIFFERENT STANDARDS"
LAMBDA LEGAL, *LEGAL DIRECTOR'S UPDATE*: FALL 1997
BEATRICE DOHRN

INTRODUCTION

Sexual harassment is unwanted and one-sided behavior of a sexual nature that makes the recipient feel uncomfortable. It is a form of sexual discrimination and is particularly found in the workplace, where attention is focused on an individual's gender rather than on his or her professional qualifications or ability to do the job. Originally sexual harassment applied primarily to the harassment of women by men; today, however, it includes unwanted sexual behavior toward men by women or by people of the same gender as well.

Although some commentators perceive sexual harassment as purely sexual in character, others believe that it is connected with power. Most cases in the workplace involve inappropriate sexual conduct toward one worker by another holding a position of greater authority.

Since the 1960s legislation has been introduced to help protect workers from sexual harassment, which today is an offense under both federal and state law. Although many cases have been successfully brought against perpetrators and also employers who fail to protect their staff from sexual misconduct, critics argue that current legislation is inadequate, and that the compensation granted in some cases is insufficient given the emotional and psychological trauma caused.

In the United States sexual harassment is illegal under Title VII of the 1964 Civil Rights Act, which prohibits discrimination on the grounds of race, color, national origin, sex, and religion. The act also established the Equal Employment Opportunity Commission (EEOC), which ensures that the law is properly applied. The EEOC requires all organizations with more than 15 employees to develop a sexual harassment policy, to advertise that policy, and to educate employees about sexual harassment issues.

Sexual harassment cases usually fall under two headings in law. *Quid pro quo* (literally "this for that") harassment occurs when either someone is offered employment or career advancement based on his or her submission to the sexual advances of the employer or is told that he or she will be fired unless he or she complies. The second type of harassment is based on a "hostile work environment." This can include sexual jokes, suggestive remarks, sexually derogatory comments, and offensive cartoons and photos relating to gender, which are seen to demean or offend a particular sex. Critics, however, claim that there is no clear definition of what this type of harassment—which forms the basis of most sexual harassment cases—constitutes.

> *"Do we really want to live in a society where normal flirtations, courtships, and matings are routinely banned from the office and factory?"*
>
> —JUSTICE ALEX KOZINSKI, "GENDER BIAS," *SAN FRANCISCO RECORDER* (MAY 27, 1992)

According to research, men and women view sexual harassment very differently. Women are more likely to interpret a sexual situation at work as harassment. In one study women and men were given a series of hypothetical situations and were asked whether or not they would label the behaviors as sexual harassment. In one example a male supervisor invited a new female employee to lunch to discuss her work. The conversation focused on her personal life. Later, over drinks, he tried to fondle her. Most of the women questioned said that the harassment began with the lunch, while most of the men thought it began when the man attempted to fondle the woman.

Another issue is how much responsibility companies bear in sexual harassment cases. Some people claim that offenses are more likely to happen if a worker perceives that management does not take victims seriously, punishes women who complain about misconduct, or inadequately enforces sexual harassment policies. Factors such as the status of women in the organization, the perception of women as an outside group, and the general acceptance of sexual behavior can make sexual harassment more or less likely to occur in certain firms. Some observers argue that making it clear to employees what constitutes sexual harassment and taking a firm stance on the side of alleged victims could prevent many cases arising.

Others, such as Gwendolyn Mink, author of *Hostile Environment: The Political Betrayal of Sexually Harassed Women* (2000), argue that despite advances in sexual harassment law, only the most determined victims bring cases against their abusers. Mink claims that we live in a culture of disbelief that makes it difficult for the law to operate properly, as cases such as Paula Jones's allegations against former President Bill Clinton and Anita Hill's case against then Supreme Court nominee Clarence Thomas testify.

The following two articles look at this debate in greater detail.

AMERICA'S OVERPROTECTIVE SEXUAL HARASSMENT LAW
Joan Kennedy Taylor

Joan Kennedy Taylor is the author of What to Do When You Don't Want to Call the Cops: A Non-Adversarial Approach to Sexual Harassment, *a Cato Institute book published by New York University Press (1999).*

YES

We are letting something destructive happen to American business in the name of helping women. Current sexual harassment law—that is, the extension of anti-discrimination law to stifle and punish sexual speech in the workplace—is creating the very hostility between the sexes that it purports to correct.

Not natural enemies

Men and women are not natural enemies but are being told that they are. Men are warned that if they offend female co-workers they might be disciplined or even terminated. Women are being instructed that offensive speech, if heard from men in the workplace, is probably illegal. And to top it off, the Supreme Court is requiring businesses to give these warnings.

There is certainly a free speech issue involved, but from a management perspective the matter is worse than that: it's divisive. The workplace and society are changing. The American work force is becoming more diverse, while our work is less dependent on physical strength. Women are now needed in jobs for which, just a few decades ago, they had to struggle to be considered.

The author claims harassment in the workplace is not sexism, yet she later goes on to admit that some men bitterly resent the success of women at work. How does this affect her argument?

Misinformation

The problem is not one of sexism. It is a problem of expectation and communication and of misinformation given to workers of both genders. There are undoubtedly a few men who bitterly resent the success of women. But their problem and problems of sexual predation and male aggression are not the subjects discussed in the ubiquitous programs that management feels compelled to set up today. Rather, it's clear that those programs deal with faulty expectation and miscommunication: the joke couched in raw language, the playful misunderstood insult, the complimentary remark, the hazing of a newcomer—in other words, the staples of male culture.

"Hazing" means to harass by banter, ridicule, or criticism. It is also a practice used as initiation in college fraternities. See Volume 16, Education, Hazing in fraternities and sororities, pages 188–189.

The movie Disclosure *(1995), starring Demi Moore and Michael Douglas, featured a situation in which a male employee accused his female boss of sexual harassment.*

COMMENTARY: Employer responsibility

On June 26, 1998, the Supreme Court made employers more liable for incidents of sexual harassment. In two sexual harassment cases, *Faragher v. City of Boca Raton* and *Burlington Industries, Inc. v. Ellerth*, the Supreme Court ruled that the employer is responsible for the actions of the supervisor, even when the employer is unaware of the supervisor's behavior. This means that employers can no longer claim ignorance in sexual harassment cases: They cannot say that the employee did not inform them about alleged offenses, nor can they claim that they were unaware of the supervisor's behavior. Under the new ruling even an employee who refuses the unwelcome sexual advances of a superior, and who does not suffer any adverse job consequences, can still bring a lawsuit against his or her employer if the employee can prove that the harassment was sexual.

Critics argue that sexual harassment protection is now too extensive. Employers can still be held liable regardless of whether they have a sexual harassment policy in place or sexual harassment training is provided to their supervisors. Some commentators claim that this is unfair.

The test

The Supreme Court created a two-part test to be used by employers in defending themselves against a sexual harassment lawsuit. First, employers need to show that they have taken care to prevent and correct any sexual harassment behavior within their workplace; and second, they need to show that the employee failed to take advantage of any preventive or corrective opportunities provided by the employer. Preventative measures include having a strict policy that is made known to every employee, providing training to managers, and conducting surveys among staff to see if sexual harassment is occurring.

Critics say that although sexual harassment legislation has progressed greatly over the last few decades, society still has a long way to go before sexual harassment is eradicated from the workplace: Around 40 percent of women claim to have been sexually harassed at some point in their career, and around 11 percent of complaints of sexual harassment filed with the Equal Employment Opportunity Commission are made by men.

Women can't know the way men behave when women are not around. And men, used to all-male workplaces, are not sure how to treat female co-workers. They may treat them as sex objects rather than colleagues or be overly paternalistic. But such faulty expectations and miscommunications do not prove sexual harassment.

If the problem is not one of sexism, the solution is not one of legal remedy. Instead, the solution is to increase all workers' knowledge and to foster communication. We need a different attitude and a different kind of employee training.

Do you think the author's argument would be more effective if she proposed the kind of attitude and employee training she thinks is needed? Providing alternatives to the systems you are critiquing can add power to your argument.

Overly protective legislation?

This country tried once before to protect women from the effects of workplace transition. The protective labor legislation in effect from 1908 until the 1970s mandated special conditions for women: minimum wages, maximum hours, laws against night work and heavy lifting, and requirements for special rest breaks. Certain occupations, such as mining and wrestling, were banned for women altogether. Feminists realized in the 1970s that such regulations were "protecting" women out of good jobs and promotions.

Once more, an attempt to protect women at work is doing them harm. Like the labor legislation, sexual harassment protection spreads the assumption that women are too delicate to flourish in the workplace without government aid. Sexual harassment regulation has failed women in a changing world. It harms everyone. It violates free speech, creates rather than lessens workplace hostility and fosters a Victorian view of women. If some women find it difficult to speak up for themselves, we should help them empower themselves, not rely on the government to mandate worker relations.

Sexual harassment legislation also aims to protect men in the workplace. Do you think the author overly focuses on women as the victims of harassment in the workplace?

Being realistic

Not only should government not be relied on in social situations, it cannot be relied on. Women can learn what to expect in the workplace and how to handle problems that arise with their male co-workers. In so doing women will not only better protect themselves, they will also feel the satisfaction that comes from being effective personally as well as professionally.

Do you agree with the author's contention that sexual harassment legislation prevents women from taking personal responsibility in the workplace? What do you think this says about her attitude to women?

SAME-SEX SEXUAL HARASSMENT CASES TYPICALLY HELD TO DIFFERENT STANDARDS
Beatrice Dohrn

Beatrice Dohrn is the director of the Lambda Legal Defense and Education Fund, an organization that works to realize the civil rights of lesbians, gay men, bisexuals, the transgendered, and people with HIV and AIDS. Go to http://www.lambdalegal.org/cgi-bin/iowa/documents/record?record+1143 for an update on this case.

NO

Recently, I completed an amicus brief to the United States Supreme Court on the issue of same-sex sexual harassment. Ten women's and other civil rights groups joined Lambda Legal on the brief, which has now been submitted in the case, *Oncale v. Sundowner*.

Educating about sexual identity

The brief, and our efforts on this issue highlight a fascinating aspect of the work that we do here at Lambda Legal: presenting complex and sophisticated legal arguments at the same time as conveying very basic but critical education about sexual orientation and sexual identity. For example, there are decades of precedent for claims by women of sexual harassment from men (or in some cases, vice versa). Those cases did not involve discussion or speculation about the sexual orientation of the harassers—and that is how it should be. After all, does it matter whether a supervisor harasses an employee because he is attracted to her as a heterosexual or because he is trying to hide that he is gay?

The author sums up her argument in a nutshell: The sexual orientation of parties involved in sexual harassment cases is irrelevant. It can be helpful to reduce your argument to one brief statement early in the debate.

The point is, federal law provides a remedy for an employee who is consistently exposed to conduct that is so egregious and pervasive as to make unwelcome sex a term or condition of employment. The focus has been, and should remain, on the conduct. If a supervisor's behavior is actionable, it is actionable regardless of sex or sexual orientation.

Different standards for different sexes

Do you think the legal criteria for sexual harassment cases should be the same for same-sex cases as for cases involving different sexes? If not, why not?

Unfortunately, many circuit courts considering claims of harassment from a person whose harasser is of the same sex have held these claims to a different standard than that applied to different-sex cases. Several circuits focus extensively on the personal motivation of the harasser. For example, in addressing cases where a man is the victim of relentless sexual harassment from another man, these courts

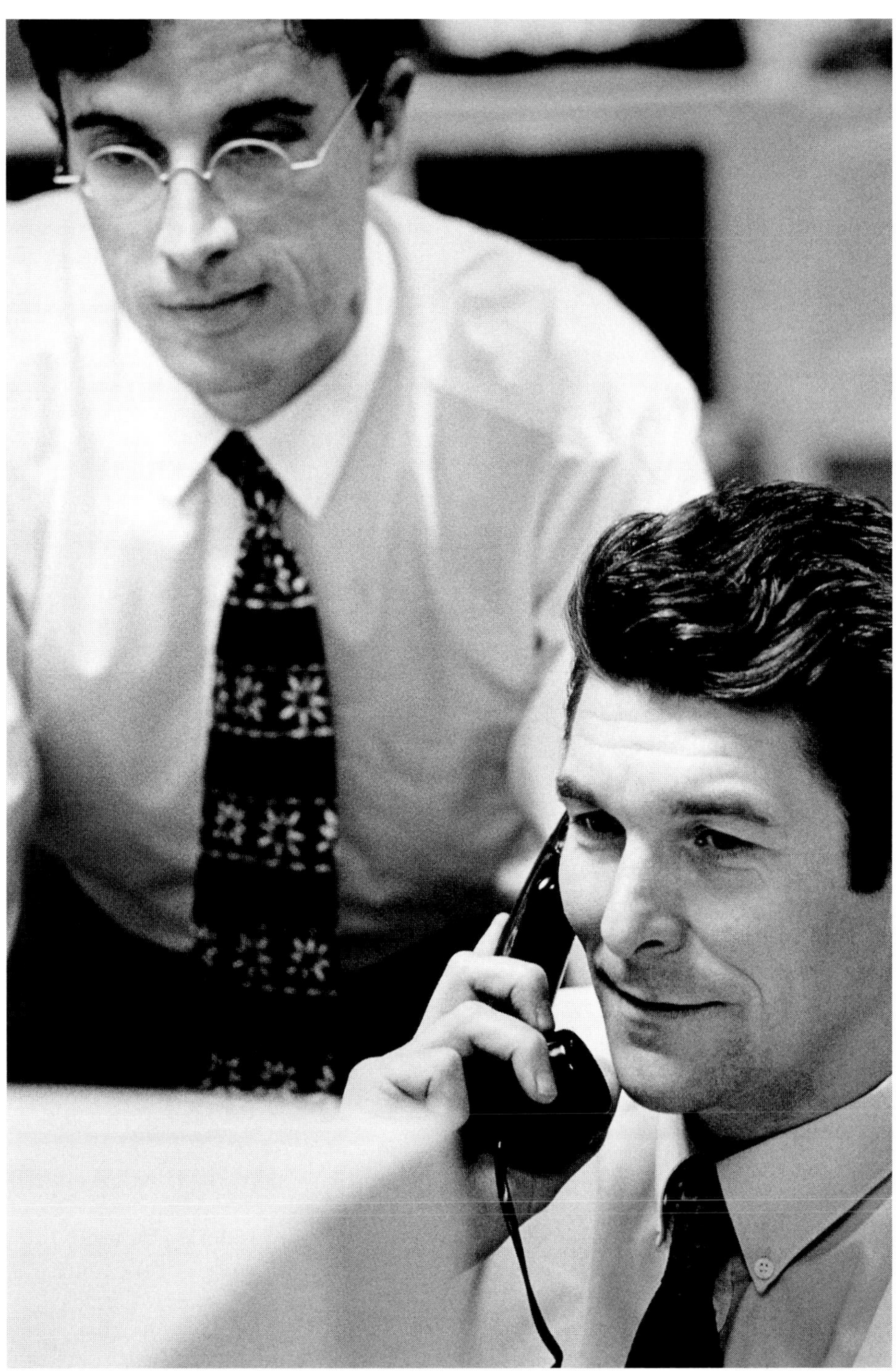

The number of allegations of sexual harassment involving people of the same sex is growing. Some legal commentators believe that this has led to more sexual discrimination.

actually have found that a lawsuit can be brought only if the harasser is gay. In other words, behavior is unlawful as employment discrimination if the harasser is gay, but the very same lawsuit will be dismissed if the harasser is heterosexual (or if the employee can't prove otherwise!)

Do you think that the law should be changed to recognize sexual orientation discrimination? See Topic 11 Does sexual orientation matter in the workplace?

Further, and equally outrageous, some courts go on to suggest that if the victim is gay, regardless of the harasser's gender, that victim is not protected because federal law does not cover sexual orientation discrimination. These courts seem not to comprehend that as lesbians and gay men, we are still subject to sex discrimination. In these courts' views, it's as if the introduction of a gay issue taints everything, and renders us outside the protections that the law affords all others.

No "special rules" for same-sex cases

Critical to presenting our case for why no "special rules" are needed in same-sex cases is a reminder to the Court that it should not suspend common sense or existing law when it must consider cases that involve sexual conduct among people of the same gender. So, just as the relationship between a person's libido and her or his misconduct is not at issue in different-sex cases, there is no reason to make it an issue in same-sex cases. Further, just as a heterosexual person who is sexually harassed by a supervisor deserves the law's protections, so too does a lesbian or gay man who is exposed to the same harassment.

"Libido" refers to a person's sexual drive.

First, we need the court to understand that sexual harassment isn't exclusively an expression of sexual feelings or desire. While sexual harassment sometimes occurs when a person admires an employee or finds her or him attractive, harassment is an equally inappropriate response to negative feelings. In either case, people of any sexual orientation are just as capable of feeling attracted to people of any sex as they are of disliking people of any sex. The important point is that it doesn't matter why a person engages in sexual harassment it simply matters whether he or she did so.

Do you think this point is valid? Could discovering the reasons why someone engages in sexual harassment help prevent other such offenses?

But, the court also needs to understand the fallacy in the assumption that sexual orientation dictates absolutely the possibility of sexual feelings for a person of one sex or another. Our brief discusses the complexity of determining who is and is not gay, and the inadvisability of requiring courts to make that determination to decide whether a case can or cannot proceed. The law must also be fair to us when we are accused of harassment. For example, at Lambda Legal we hear of cases where lesbians and gay men are accused of bringing sex into the workplace, based on behavior that is properly understood as unrelated to sex when straight people "share" (such as discussing one's weekend plans, family composition, dating, or relationships). Behavior that is appropriate for heterosexuals in the workplace is no more "sexual" when the workers involved are lesbian or gay.

Sexual harassment illustrates how our civil rights litigation always goes hand in hand with our education work. For example, our military cases often turn on how well a court understands that heterosexuals already share public bathrooms and bunkhouses with gay people, and our parenting cases often require us to make courts truly understand that displays of affection are just as important and appropriate in lesbian and gay households as in others....

For a debate on homosexuals and the military see Volume 7, Constitution, Topic 8 Should homosexuals be allowed to serve in the military?

Summary

In the first article Joan Kennedy Taylor argues that sexual harassment law causes the very hostility between the sexes that it is intended to prevent. She claims that men and women are being told that they are "natural enemies" when they are not. Taylor asserts that sexual harassment is a problem of communication and misinformation in the workplace rather than one of sexism. She is critical of the antisexual harassment programs provided by companies, which she says do not address the real issues. She suggests that since women today work in workplaces that were once all-male, some men do not know how to treat female coworkers. Taylor concludes by suggesting that women have to learn how to handle problems with male coworkers rather than relying on the law.

In the second article Beatrice Dohrn argues that a different standard is applied in cases of same-sex sexual harassment than in different-sex cases. She claims that there is a tendency to focus on the personal motivation of the harasser; and in cases in which a man is the victim of harassment by another man, courts have only allowed a case to proceed if the harasser is gay. Dohrn says that federal law fails to protect gay male victims regardless of the gender of the harasser. She holds that there is a legal inability to recognize that gays and lesbians are also subject to sexual discrimination. Dohrn says that there should be no "special rules" in same-sex cases of sexual harassment but asks that courts show common sense and attention to existing law.

FURTHER INFORMATION:

Books:

Kennedy Taylor, Joan, *What to Do When You Don't Want to Call the Cops: A Non-Adversarial Approach to Sexual Harassment*. New York: New York University Press, 1999.

Useful websites:

http://216.239.39.104/search?q=cache:697HYMOtxCsJ:www.time.com/time/classroom/archive/980323.pdf+Paglia+sexual+harassment+fast+making+us+an+infantile+nation&hl=en&start=1&ie=UTF-8
Looks at the evolution of sexual harassment law.

http://www.employer-employee.com/sexhar4.html
Examines same-sex harassment.

http://www.nolo.com/lawcenter/ency/article.cfm/ObjectID/0E020B2A-F7D9-0C2AB52398DFAAFDC6F/catID/57153B2E-F39E-48DA-830ADA31F5A23325
Information about sexual harassment legislation and definitions.

The following debates in the Pro/Con series may also be of interest:

In this volume:

Part 1: Worker rights, pages 8–9

Anita Hill: The legacy, pages 60–61

Topic 10 Should sexual relationships in the workplace be allowed?

Topic 11 Does sexual orientation matter in the workplace?

IS WORKPLACE SEXUAL HARASSMENT LEGISLATION ADEQUATE?

IS WORKPLACE SEXUAL HARASSMENT LEGISLATION ADEQUATE? KEY POINTS

CULTURE
Does the law have more influence than the "culture of disbelief" about harassment?

YES: The high incidence of successful lawsuits against perpetrators shows that sexual harassment is being addressed properly under law

NO: The Anita Hill case highlighted the fact that most people prefer to disbelieve victims of sexual harassment. This makes it difficult to apply laws.

GENDER BIAS
Are men adequately protected against sexual harassment?

YES: Recent cases and the media have illustrated the problem of men being sexually harassed by both their own sex and by women. Organizations such as Lambda Legal have helped address this issue.

NO: Most research and media attention are directed toward women and their treatment under law. Federal law does not adequately protect gay men.

STATE LAW
Is sexual harassment adequately protected under state law?

YES: Most states have their own sexual harassment legislation, and they work hard to enforce it properly

NO: The high estimates of unreported offenses and cases that never reach court prove that state legislation still has a long way to go

POWER VS. SEX
Is sexual harassment more about power than sex?

YES: Feminist scholars argue that power is a defining motive in harassment. Harassers are often in a position of authority over victims. Many high-profile cases show that people in power are more likely to commit offenses.

NO: It is hard to separate one from the other. While power can play a part, the physical/verbal offenses committed are of a sexual nature.

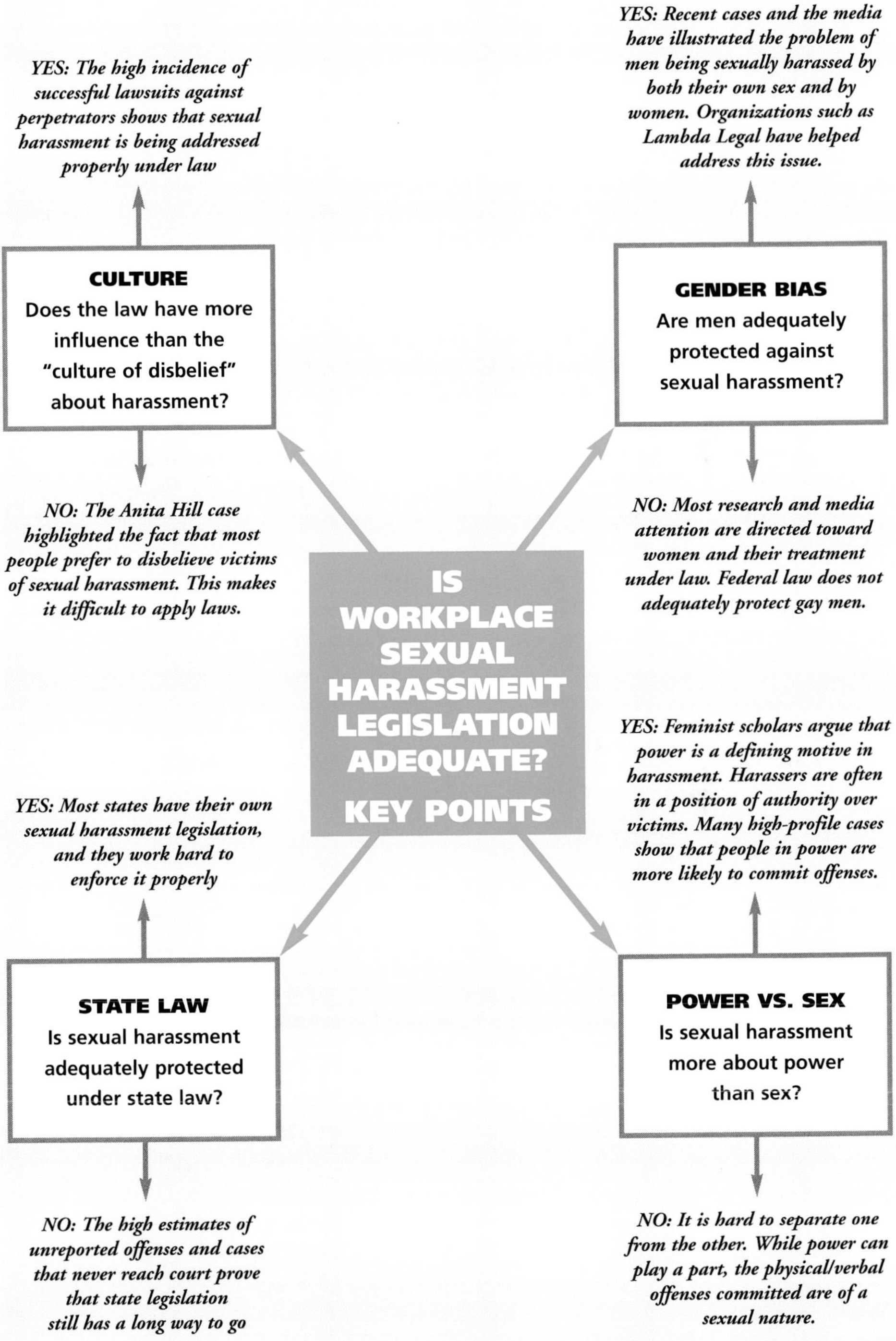

ANITA HILL: THE LEGACY

"It was, for me, about integrity."

—ANITA HILL, ON THE CONGRESSIONAL HEARINGS INTO HER ALLEGATIONS OF SEXUAL HARASSMENT AGAINST CLARENCE THOMAS

In 1991 Anita Hill, a University of Oklahoma law professor, alleged that Supreme Court nominee Clarence Thomas had sexually harassed her when they were coworkers from 1981 to 1983. The Hill–Thomas affair attracted huge media attention, not only because it involved a federal judicial nominee but also because both protagonists were highly intelligent, professional African Americans. It focused public attention on several gender- and race-based issues, but most importantly it highlighted the problem of sexual harassment in the workplace, despite the existence of legislation making such behavior illegal.

Allegations and hearings

The United States Senate Judiciary Committee conducted hearings to investigate Anita Hill's allegations of sexual harassment by Clarence Thomas. From October 11 to 13, 1991, Americans were allowed to watch the televised hearings, and viewer ratings broke previous records.

During the three days of hearings Hill spoke of Thomas's behavior toward her when she worked as his assistant at the Education Department and later at the Equal Employment Opportunities Commission. The alleged harassment included references to pornography, inappropriate discussion of sexual acts, frequent requests for dates, and comments on Hill's dress sense and sexual attractiveness. Thomas heatedly denied the claims. He called the hearings "a high-tech lynching for uppity blacks who in any way deign to think for themselves, to do for themselves." Opinion polls indicated that although minority groups were undecided about the truth of Hill's allegations, most people supported Thomas.

Although the hearings themselves had little legal significance, many observers thought them extremely important in focusing public attention on gender inequalities in U.S. society, sexual harassment in the workplace, and the issue of acceptable sexual conduct by public officials. Others believed that the hearings were little more than a witch hunt to discredit Thomas, President George Bush's nominee to replace Thurgood Marshall on the Supreme Court. Marshall had been the first African American to be appointed to the Supreme Court and was a leading advocate of civil rights. Thomas, on the other hand, was a well-known conservative, and his nomination drew opposition from groups as diverse as the National Association for the Advancement of Colored People (NAACP), the Bar Association, and various women's rights groups.

Although Thomas had already sat through confirmation hearings in September 1991, the Senate Judiciary Committee had been unable to make a recommendation to the full Senate. Hill's claims of sexual harassment by Thomas therefore placed his appointment to the bench in jeopardy. The allegations, made during interviews with the FBI, were leaked to the media in the days before the Senate's final vote on Thomas's appointment. The Senate delayed the vote so that it could hear more about Hill's accusations, but after the hearings it narrowly confirmed Thomas's nomination by 52 votes to 48.

Political bias?

Some observers found it strange that although both Hill and Thomas were at the center of media attention, and several news networks did their best to try to find women with similar allegations against Thomas, very little focus was given to Hill's political leanings. In his book *The Real Anita Hill: The Untold Story* (1993) journalist David Brock wrote that Joseph Biden, the chairman of the Judiciary Committee, had ruled the question of Hill's politics out of order. Brock alleged that Hill had been forced to testify through the manipulation of various interest groups and liberal Senate staffers, and was far from being a courageous woman who had decided to come forward to tell the truth about Thomas, as her supporters insisted. He further claimed that Hill was a liberal activist and committed feminist. Thomas, on the other hand, was extremely conservative: Today he is seen as one of the most right-wing members of the Supreme Court. In 2001, however, Brock published another book, *Blinded by the Right: The Conscience of an Ex-Conservative*, in which he admitted that he wrote things about Hill that he knew not to be true and also that he deliberately embellished Thomas's reputation.

The legacy

The hearings highlighted for many observers the extreme gender discrimination prevalent in U.S. society, even in the Senate. Americans watched Hill, an articulate African American law professor, having her professional and personal credibility tested by a group of predominantly unsympathetic and disbelieving white men. Many women felt dismay and anger when they saw that Hill's painful experiences were not taken seriously by male politicians, and some people believe this led to a record number of women choosing to run for public office—1992 was labeled the "Year of the Woman."

Commentators also believe that Hill's allegations were important in helping other women suffering from sexual harassment come forward and break their silence. In the five years following the hearings sexual harassment cases more than doubled, and awards more than quadrupled.

In addition, the hearings showed the influence that the media—television in particular—have in focusing public attention on matters of social, racial, or cultural significance. The often sensationalized supermarket-tabloid-style coverage of the case set the precedent for reporting on later events such as the O.J. Simpson murder trial in 1995 and the sex scandal involving President Bill Clinton and White House intern Monica Lewinsky, which hit the headlines in 1998.

Topic 5
DO PARENTS HAVE ENOUGH RIGHTS IN THE WORKPLACE?

YES
"COURTS BOLSTER RIGHTS OF WORKING MOTHERS"
THE PHILADELPHIA INQUIRER, JULY 24, 2004
DAVID CRARY

NO
FROM "BREASTFEEDING MOTHERS NEED WORKPLACE SUPPORT"
HTTP://WWW.MOMSVOICE.COM/PAGES/ARTICLES/BREASTFEEDING_SUPPORT.HTML
TAMARA W. WILSON

INTRODUCTION

Increasing numbers of men and women are juggling work and family commitments. Single-parent families comprise one-third of all American families with children, and according to a 2002 study by the Families and Work Institute in New York, both parents work in 78 percent of two-parent families. With more women working today than ever before, changes in the labor force are leading commentators to debate whether parents have enough rights in the workplace.

Historically childcare was usually the woman's domain: Mothers cared for their children, while fathers worked to support their families. In the 19th century, however, the Industrial Revolution and the growth of manufacturing industry resulted in people moving from rural, agrarian areas to live and work in industrial, urban centers, and many more women entered the workforce. This trend grew in the 20th century, first through the suffrage movement, which fought for equal rights for women, and later during both world wars, when women took over the jobs of men who had gone abroad to fight. As a result, increasing numbers of women chose to marry later, if they married at all, and the number of children born out of wedlock also rose. The number of divorces likewise increased, leading to more single-parent families dependent on the income earned by the mother or father. Employers gradually came under pressure to create work conditions conducive to their workers who had the day-to-day responsibilities for their children's wellbeing. Today many companies try to accommodate parents by offering work arrangements such as job sharing, flextime, and teleworking.

Some experts claim that legislation has also made it easier for parents in the United States to fulfill their work and family duties. The 1993 Family and Medical Leave Act (FMLA) requires employers with 50 or more staff to grant employees of both sexes up to a total of 12 weeks' unpaid, job-protected leave for the birth or adoption of a child or to care for a sick family member. Although this law has helped millions of families, critics point out that only about half of all U.S. workers are covered by FMLA, and even among those that are, many simply cannot afford to take unpaid time off work.

"Can we afford to do more for American working families and still compete in the global economy?"

—DR. JODY HEYMANN, PROJECT ON GLOBAL WORKING FAMILIES (2004)

FMLA prompted some employers to offer better benefits to their workers, and more companies began providing paid maternity leave in an attempt to retain talented female staff. Today, according to the Families and Work Institute, about 13 percent of firms with more than 100 employees also offer paid paternity leave. Companies that have instituted paid leave for new fathers include IBM, financial services firms Merrill Lynch and J.P. Morgan Chase & Co., and accountants KPMG.

Advocates of parental rights have also praised California, which in 2004 became the first state to create a paid family leave program, guaranteeing workers up to six weeks' leave on partial pay. Similar legislation has been drafted in other states.

These measures have been broadly welcomed, but observers claim that the United States still lags far behind most nations in offering protections to working families. "The Work, Family, and Equity Index," a study of 168 countries published in 2004 by the Project on Global Working Families at Harvard University, found that 163 countries offered paid leave to women for the birth or adoption of a child; 45 countries offered fathers paid paternity leave; and at least 37 had policies guaranteeing parents some kind of paid leave when their children are ill—the United States guarantees none of these protections. In fact, it ranks among the bottom five countries in terms of family benefits. In a bid to improve this situation, the Healthy Families Act was introduced to Congress in June 2004. The bill proposes providing seven days of paid sick leave each year that workers can use either for themselves or to care for a family member.

Critics contend, however, that laws cannot eradicate prejudices that are entrenched in working culture. Many fathers remain reluctant to take paternity leave because they think it might damage their careers. They fear that their employers and coworkers will regard childcare as a female activity that is incompatible with the macho impulses of go-getters who want to do well at work. Mothers often feel they are discriminated against by employers, who assume they will not be fully committed to their jobs. On the other hand, some people criticize the growth of workplace benefits for mothers and fathers, claiming that policies such as flextime place an unfair burden on workers who are not parents.

The following articles look at this issue further.

COURTS BOLSTER RIGHTS OF WORKING MOTHERS
David Crary

David Crary is a journalist for the Associated Press agency. This article appeared in The Philadelphia Inquirer *in July 2004.*

YES

Meeting the demands of both job and family can be daunting for any working mother—or father.

However, recent court rulings are sending a strong warning to employers: Don't assume such juggling acts will lower workplace performance.

"It's not appropriate to disadvantage women because they're mothers," law professor Joan Williams said. "In the past, people were very dubious these cases could win in litigation, but now it's clear they can."

The Program on WorkLife Law is "dedicated to decreasing the economic vulnerability of parents and children by restructuring workplaces around the values people hold in family life." Go to http://www.wcl.american.edu/gender/worklifelaw/ to find out more.

"The maternal wall"

Williams, director of American University's Program on WorkLife Law, contends that many working women eventually bump up against what she calls "the maternal wall"—career roadblocks arising from employers' assumptions that motherhood will prevent a woman from being fully dedicated to her job.

"Discrimination against parents and other caregivers in employment is becoming a new battleground," Williams said. "An increasing number of employees are suing their employers because they lost their jobs, were passed over for promotion, or were treated unfairly based on their responsibilities to care for children or others."

Landmark opinion

Williams' arguments were echoed forcefully in April by a federal appeals court in New York, which ruled that workplace stereotyping about mothers can qualify as gender discrimination.

Back claimed that, after taking a three-month maternity leave, she was asked by a supervisor how she was "planning on spacing her offspring." She also said that the supervisor asked her "not to get pregnant until I retire." Back was later fired from her probationary appointment.

In what women's-rights advocates depicted as a landmark opinion, the court said school psychologist Elana Back could proceed with a lawsuit against two superiors—both women—who denied her tenure in Hastings-on-Hudson, N.Y.

Overturning a lower court's decision to quash the lawsuit, Judge Guido Calabresi said Back could proceed without having to prove that fathers were treated better than mothers by the school district.

The judge wrote: "It takes no special training to discern stereotyping when someone claims that a woman cannot be a good mother and work long hours or be in a job that requires a strong commitment if she has little ones at home."

No trial date has been set yet, but Back said in a message e-mailed to the Associated Press that she hoped her case helped women nationwide.

"There are millions of working mothers who are successful at both career and family, yet their careers suffer due to gender-biased thinking by their employers," she wrote. "I look forward to my day in court to carry the banner for working moms."

Do you think it is necessary for employees to work long hours to prove that they are committed to their jobs? See Topic 12 Is there a culture of overwork in the United States?

Other successful cases

According to the Program on WorkLife Law, there have been about 40 recent cases in which employees successfully argued that they were discriminated against because of their roles as parents or caregivers.

Several cases involved men—including one seeking to care for his ailing wife, and another for his elderly parents.

However, Jocelyn Samuels of the Washington-based National Women's Law Center said mothers were the predominant victims of such discrimination.

"Women who are on the fast track can find themselves derailed when they decide to have children," she said. "There's still an automatic presumption that women will put their child-rearing responsibilities before their employment commitment."

While there are no reliable figures on the number of working mothers, women represent 49 percent of the nonfarm workforce, according to the Bureau of Labor Statistics. In both New Jersey and Pennsylvania, women are 47 percent of the workforce.

Commentators point out that workers have responsibilities beyond caring for their children. According to a 2002 study by the Families and Work Institute (www.familiesandwork.org), 35 percent of Americans had significant care responsibilities for elderly relatives during the previous year, and more than a third of workers with these obligations were forced to take time off work or reduce their work hours to provide care. Do you think parents of young children and carers of elderly relatives should receive equal treatment in the workplace?

Juggling home and work

The federal Equal Employment Opportunity Commission, which handles job discrimination complaints regarding gender and other grounds, does not specifically track allegations of parenthood-related bias. But it could press gender bias charges against any company that treats working mothers worse—or better—than working fathers.

Dianna Johnston, the commission's assistant legal counsel, suggested that employers concerned about a parent's ability to juggle home and work should follow the approach recommended in dealing with a disabled worker.

A 2002 study by the WorkLife Law Program found that an increasing number of fathers are suing their employers if they refuse to extend parental leave programs to men. What do you think has prompted this trend?

COMMENTARY: California Paid Family Leave insurance program

On July 1, 2004, California introduced a program that may help millions of Californians spend more time with their families. The California Paid Family Leave insurance program will, estimates say, allow around 13 million workers in the state to take six weeks' leave at 55 percent of their salary in order to bond with a newborn child or to take care of an ailing family member. The move has been both praised and criticized by observers, some of whom claim that it is just another example of the state's unrealistic welfare programs. Others counter that California is showing other U.S. states the way forward in creating a more family-focused society.

What the program does

The Employment Development Department is charged with running the program. It has estimated that around 300,000 people will apply for leave in the first year and receive roughly $600 million. This sum has been raised through worker contributions of 0.08 percent of their salary (an average of $27 per worker per year), paid through the state disability fund. Critics are worried that the state has seriously underestimated the numbers of people who will apply for leave. Martyn Hopper, the California director for the National Federation of Independent Business, says, "No one knows how many people will take advantage of paid family leave. No one knows if there will be enough money." He argues that most employers understand that workers need time off to spend with their families, but it is an employer–employee issue, not a concern of government. Advocates, however, insist the program will benefit millions.

Every year Working Mother magazine (www.workingmother.com) publishes a list of the 100 best companies to work for, as judged by their approach to work and life issues. What do you think makes a "family-friendly" workplace, and what might be the advantages for employers that have family-friendly policies?

"You should not assume that because somebody has a disability, they can't perform the job," Johnston said. "You tell them what the job requirements are, and ask them, 'Can you do that?'"

Organizations representing employers recommend that businesses strive to help all their workers, parents or not, attain a satisfying balance between job and family through flexible schedules and other options.

Campbell Soup Co. has had a child-care center at its headquarters in Camden, N.J., for 20 years, spokeswoman Juli Mandel Sloves said. The center, attended by 81 children age six weeks to six years, is operated by Bright Horizons Family Solutions Inc. The cost averages $7,500 per year per child.

General Mills Inc., one of the major companies often praised for effective family-friendly policies, has options available for all employees. One feature at its Minneapolis headquarters that is particularly prized by working mothers is an onsite infant care center.

Advocates for women in the workplace say mothers' job status would improve if more fathers started pressing for and using paternity leave and other programs enabling them to share more child-care duties. Only 15 percent of U.S. companies offer paid paternity leave, according to the Society for Human Resource Management.

Drug manufacturer Eli Lilly & Co. is one of those that does, but spokeswoman Joan Todd said it took several years for fathers on the workforce to overcome fears that using the benefit would damage their careers.

The author suggests that men are reluctant to take paternity leave out of fear that their bosses and coworkers will view them negatively. Do you think their views would change significantly if paid paternity leave were more widely available? Reports in the United Kingdom in 2004 showed that only one in five fathers was taking advantage of the new paid paternity leave entitlement. Does this indicate that men are overly influenced by "macho" culture?

Antidiscrimination policies

Cynthia Calvert, a lawyer who works with Williams at the Program on WorkLife Law, has been advising employers how to avoid lawsuits of the sort filed by Back, the school psychologist. Calvert recommends expanding corporate antidiscrimination policies, and giving supervisors updated training to make clear that bias related to parenting or other caregiving is unacceptable.

Williams acknowledged that a fear of lawsuits might prompt some employers to be more cautious about what they say to working mothers, without actually changing their inner bias toward them.

"But even that would be an improvement," Williams said. "Now, people think it's perfectly OK to use maternity against women in very open ways. If they felt embarrassed, that would be a step forward."

BREASTFEEDING MOTHERS NEED WORKPLACE SUPPORT
Tamara W. Wilson

Tamara W. Wilson wrote this article for Moms Voice (www.momsvoice.com), a site aimed at helping mothers.

NO

Working and nursing don't mix? With 2000 census data showing 55% of children under the age of 6 have mothers in the labor force, this question must be addressed. Continuing to breastfeed after returning to work outside the home has many benefits. Many women encounter difficulties breastfeeding, but mothers who work outside the home face unique challenges. The payoff for perseverance can be advantageous not only to the nursing pair and their family but to employers as well. What can companies do to accommodate and encourage breastfeeding? What role can you and other individuals play in facilitating attitudes and policies regarding breastfeeding?

Go to www.breastfeeding.com/all_about/all_about_more.html to find out more about the advantages of breastfeeding.

A baby's perfect food is breast milk. The American Academy of Pediatrics recommends breastfeeding exclusively for the first six months of life. The Academy also advises that breast milk remain the primary source of nutrition until twelve months and continue as long as is mutually desirable. The advantages of breastfeeding for mothers and their babies are well documented. Mothers who work outside the home face long hours separated from their babies. Breastfeeding can help maintain a valuable link between the two of them. Breaks taken to pump or nurse are a great way to reinforce a mother's role in the middle of a busy workday. Nuzzling together at the breast after a long day of work is a comforting way for the mother and child to reconnect. Hormones released while breastfeeding help the mother relax and relieve tension, aiding her ability to deal with the inevitable stress of juggling her duties as mother, wife, and employee.

An aid to productivity

But what are some of the values of breastfeeding for employers? Employers can expect breastfeeding mothers to experience less absenteeism upon their return to work, be more productive, and suffer from less guilt and separation anxiety. A 1996 study of lactation programs run by Los Angeles Department of Water and Power (LADWP) and the Aerospace Corporation showed that after initiating lactation

Lactation programs include prenatal breastfeeding education classes and return to work classes. See http://lactation.od.nih.gov/ for more information.

programs, parents were 28% less likely to miss work. The Economic Research Service of the U.S. Department of Agriculture found that at least $3.6 billion in health care costs could be saved if levels of breastfeeding were raised to the Surgeon General's recommendation of 50% at 6 months old. Unfortunately, many mothers who work outside the home are faced with breastfeeding obstacles.

If the workplace is not supportive enough of most working mothers, is it fair that fathers should complain about the parental rights they are given by their employers?

A survey conducted by the Washington Business Group on Health in 1996 found that 55% of working mothers breastfed, but only 10% continue until their babies are six months old. Twenty-four percent of stay-at-home mothers nursed for the same length of time. Why don't more mothers who work outside the home continue to nurse their babies?...

Overcoming embarrassment

Attitudes toward breastfeeding can severely hinder a mother's efforts to combine nursing and working. Talking to a boss about breastfeeding can be difficult and embarrassing, but understanding the benefits can make it easier. You can assure them that expressing milk at work helps you be more productive and dependable. Many people view breastfeeding as a lifestyle that women choose as opposed to a health concern. Employers may not understand why mothers would refuse to use what appears to be the much more convenient formula-feeding method. Another commonly encountered attitude felt by bosses and co-workers can be implied criticism of mothers who did not breastfeed. These feelings may make mothers feel guilty about their breastfeeding success, therefore undermining their resolve to continue nursing while working. The best way to combat these attitudes is for companies to implement policies on breastfeeding in the workplace and to educate managers about the benefits. ... Nursing mothers need strong support from their employers, families, medical professionals, and community to ensure a good breastfeeding relationship.

Should this be more of a priority for companies than paternal leave?

What allowances need to be made for mothers in the workplace? Adequate time and facilities to nurse or pump are of greatest importance. Employers may not realize that in order to maintain an adequate milk supply, a nursing mother must express milk at least every three to four hours while separated from her baby. In limited cases, mothers are told they cannot express their milk on their regular breaks. Some companies do not offer a clean, comfortable, and private place appropriate for milk expression. Mothers at these companies must pump in a bathroom, which feels unsanitary and uncomfortable. Even if a place is available, many

While this may be practical for large companies, do you think small companies could bear the cost of providing private rooms for nursing mothers?

employers do not offer schedules flexible enough to allow time for milk expression. Because of the benefits employers can reap if their employees breastfeed, they should be motivated to remove these obstacles that working mothers face. Chris Sofgue pointed out that even though her company in Washington, D.C. had a great lactation program, meetings presented another difficulty:

> *In my job, the hardest thing was pumping around my meeting schedule. People don't really understand the need, and it is embarrassing to speak up sometimes. I finally just would say I was sorry, but I had to run to another "meeting" and would be back as soon as possible.*

Employers' checklist

... The Department of Health and Human Services (HHS) published a *Blueprint for Action on Breastfeeding* that included provisions recommended for workplaces. Those recommendations include:

There are around 2.2 million male single parents in the United States, many of whom have babies. Do you think that offers of flextime, compressed hours, and extra breaks should be offered to all parents irrespective of their gender?

- Prenatal lactation education specifically tailored for working women.
- Adequate breaks, flexible work hours, job sharing, and part-time work.
- Private "Mother's Rooms" for expressing milk in a secure and relaxing environment.
- Coordination with on-site or near-site child care so the infant can be breastfed during the day.
- Support groups for working mothers with children.

Since this means that nursing mothers would spend at least one hour less working each day, is it likely that employers would accept this shortfall without comment? Might other workers be put under pressure to make up the extra time? Would this cause resentment?

In addition to conforming to the federal recommendations listed above, the states of Oregon and Texas have implemented "Mother-Friendly Workplace" initiatives. The Texas' program requires breaks of 30 minutes every 3–4 hours. The Oregon Health Division advises including a comfortable chair, low table, nursing stool, and changing table in the breastfeeding area. Many companies are reporting huge success with their workplace lactation programs. Amway headquarters in Ada, Michigan provides an electric, multi-user pump in their lactation room for which mothers provide their own flanges, tubing, and bottles. Aetna, Cigna Corporation, and LADWP have piloted programs that include on-site lactation consultants and breastfeeding classes. Both Aetna and LADWP have reported a nearly 3-to-1 return on their investment in breastfeeding....

Building support

... As women break through the glass ceiling and reach for equal footing with their male counterparts, it is much more important for their reproductive rights to be protected. Although people are making great strides toward addressing the concerns of breastfeeding in the workplace, far too many women face embarrassment, disgrace, and discouragement. Lactation programs ensure the health of mothers, babies, companies, and society at large. With proper education, every member of the labor force can support nursing mothers, resulting in more productive workers and healthier children.

Many people believe that if women must be treated equally in every sector of life, so must men. This extends to paternal rights in the workplace. Would it be more fair for states to introduce programs along the lines of the California Paid Family Leave insurance program (see page 66), which would give working mothers and fathers the opportunity to spend more time with their newborn children?

Summary

There is much debate over the issue of rights for parents in the workplace. In the first article journalist David Crary reports on court decisions in the United States that have bolstered the rights of working parents. A federal appeals court in New York ruled that a woman could proceed with a discrimination lawsuit against her former supervisors without having to prove that the employer treated fathers better than mothers: The court decided that the use of stereotypes of motherhood was in itself gender discrimination. Crary quotes law professor Joan Williams, who contends that there is a growing trend among parents and other caregivers to sue for unfair treatment at work. Crary describes how some companies are adopting more family-friendly policies. However, he reports that men are still reluctant to take paternity leave even when it is paid. He concludes by quoting Williams, who concedes that even though employers are becoming more cautious in their treatment of working mothers, their biased views about them might not change.

The second article, by Tamara W. Wilson, is taken from Moms Voice, a Seattle-based website. Wilson looks at the lack of rights for mothers in the workplace, focusing specifically on the issue of breastfeeding. The author argues that studies show that breastfeeding is best for babies. She suggests that employers should install crèches and private rooms where women can express milk. Wilson also suggests implementing flexible working hours to help young mothers spend more time with their newborn babies. Similarly, offering part-time work and more breaks would help improve young mothers' rights, she claims.

FURTHER INFORMATION:

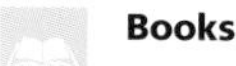

Books:

De Graaf, John (ed.), *Take Back Your Time: Fighting Overwork and Time Poverty in America.* San Francisco, CA: Berrett-Koehler, 2003.

Heymann, Jody, *The Widening Gap: Why America's Working Families Are in Jeopardy and What Can Be Done about It.* New York: Basic Books, 2000.

Useful websites:

www.globalworkingfamilies.org
"The Work, Family, and Equity Index," a report published by the Project on Global Working Families.

www.nationalpartnership.org
The National Partnership for Women and Families promotes family-friendly policies in the workplace.

www.paidfamilyleave.org
The California Paid Family Leave insurance program.

The following debates in the Pro/Con series may also be of interest:

In this volume:

Topic 7 Is stress taken seriously enough as a health issue in the workplace?

Topic 9 Do women make better managers than men?

Topic 12 Is there a culture of overwork in the United States?

DO PARENTS HAVE ENOUGH RIGHTS IN THE WORKPLACE?

DO PARENTS HAVE ENOUGH RIGHTS IN THE WORKPLACE? KEY POINTS

EQUALITY OF OPPORTUNITY
Do both parents need to spend time with babies in the early stages of their development?

YES: Research has shown that every child benefits from having two parents present from the start of his or her life

NO: Fathers do not really matter to a child in the early months of its development; mothers are, however, essential

PATERNAL SUPPORT
Do fathers have enough support from their employers and colleagues?

YES: Most employers are extremely sympathetic to fathers, especially single parents. Men are now able to take paternity leave, can work flextime, and they are afforded other benefits by their companies.

NO: Employers need to reeducate themselves and other workers to understand that wanting to spend more time with one's children does not reflect badly on a man

JOB IMPLICATIONS
Do employers treat working mothers as still committed to their careers?

YES: The glass ceiling has been broken, and women are now treated in the same way as men, irrespective of whether or not they have children

NO: They will never be seen as fully committed to the corporate cause because they will have divided loyalties

WOMEN'S RIGHTS
Does acknowledging paternal rights in the workplace help women's rights?

YES: It acknowledges the increased importance of women in the workplace and of fathers in the nursery

NO: It further undermines women's rights. Working mothers are still fighting for more rights in the workplace; fathers fighting for more parental rights just cloud the issue.

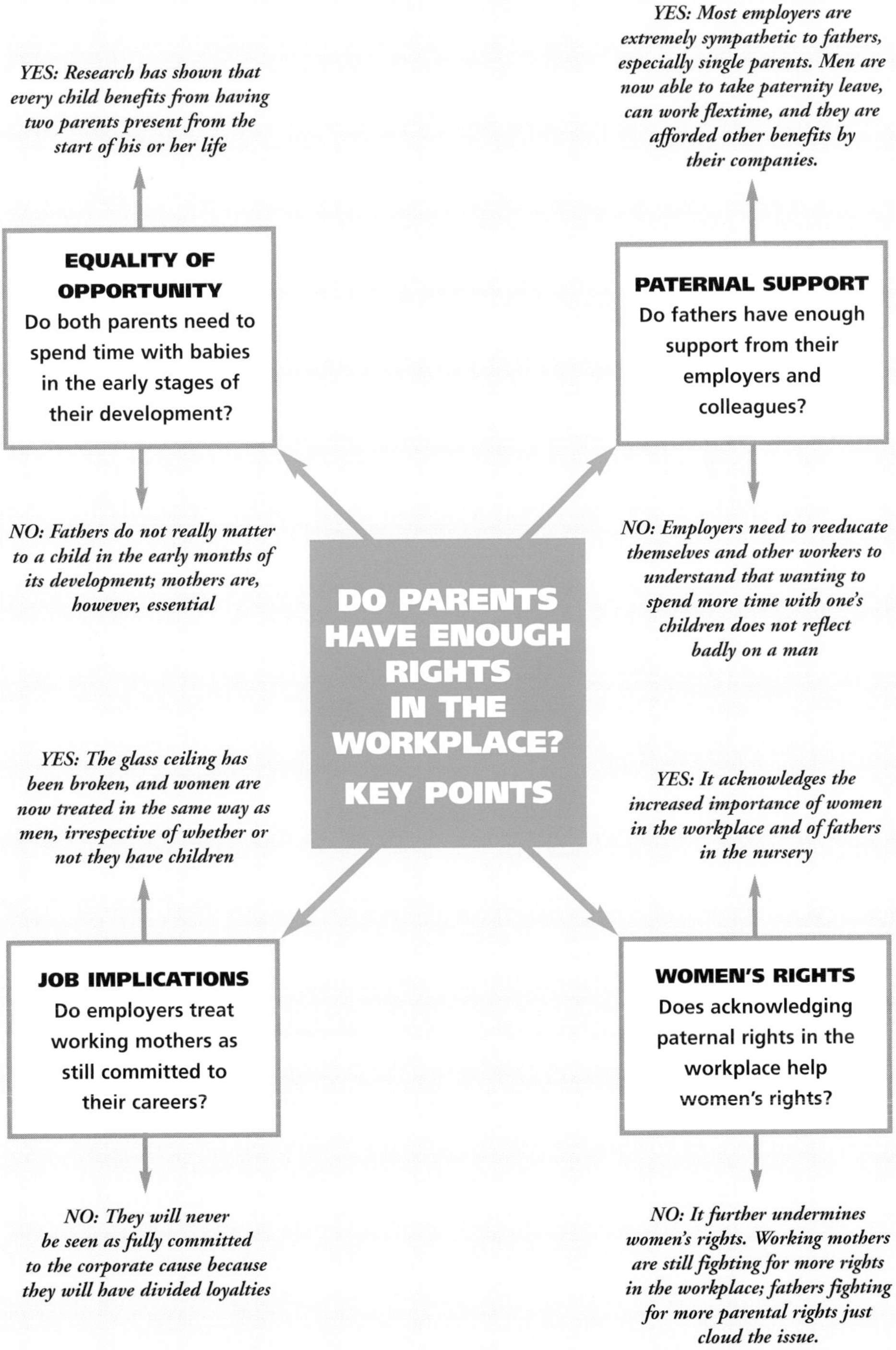

Topic 6
SHOULD THERE BE A MANDATORY RETIREMENT AGE?

YES
"CBI WARNS AGAINST SCRAPPING RETIREMENT AGE"
NOVEMBER 3, 2003
MANAGEMENT-ISSUES WEBSITE

NO
"SHOULD RETIREMENT BE MANDATORY?"
THE GLOBE AND MAIL, DECEMBER 29, 2003
REGINALD STACKHOUSE

INTRODUCTION

In recent years there has been much discussion about whether a mandatory retirement age—the set age at which a person is obliged to stop work—is necessary.

In the United States since the implementation of the Age Discrimination in Employment Act (ADEA) of 1967 and its amendments in 1978 and 1986, it has been unlawful for most employers to force their workers to retire on reaching a certain age. The only exceptions are airline pilots, air traffic controllers, and some law-enforcement and public safety officers, all of whom are required to retire at a specified age. Although compulsory retirement has also been scrapped in Australia and New Zealand, a "normal" retirement age still exists in some countries, including the United Kingdom, Japan, and some Canadian provinces. In recent years, however, western nations have been moving toward the abolition of mandatory retirement. A European Union directive will prohibit age discrimination in the workplace by October 2006, and member states are considering whether compulsory retirement amounts to one such form of discrimination.

Many employers believe that having an agreed age when most people must retire is a good idea. Their views are based chiefly on the notion of expense: Older, highly paid workers can be "pensioned off," allowing younger employees to be taken on at a fraction of the cost. This benefits not only employers but also the state since it leads to a reduction in the numbers of unemployed people claiming social security payments.

Employers further argue that younger workers bring fresh blood, enthusiasm, and innovative ideas into professional occupations. In nonprofessional occupations, too, younger employees tend to be better qualified and less likely to suffer long-term sickness than older staff. Companies also voice concern that without mandatory retirement, they will have to retain elderly, less capable workers for fear of expensive lawsuits if they were forced to leave their jobs.

Labor unions often favor a fixed retirement age. They argue that without such a provision, employees will literally work themselves to death: Mandatory retirement allows people to leave work at a reasonable age and prevents them from having to endure undignified assessments of age-related competence. They point out that a conflict-free retirement from a stressful or physically demanding job is also likely to be better for a person's health.

> *"Age is only a number … A man can't retire his experience."*
>
> —BERNARD M. BARUCH (1870–1965), FINANCIER

For many other advocates of a compulsory retirement age an employee's competence to continue performing a job is an important issue. Policymakers commonly assume that there is a causal relationship between aging and declining ability. A mandatory retirement age can be seen as the average age above which employees are thought to be more likely to suffer physical or mental problems, and, supporters claim, it can therefore serve to protect society against the effects of mistakes made by elderly professionals such as judges, surgeons, or airline pilots.

Critics argue that in professions such as law and medicine, safeguards already exist to identify incompetence. Such cases are best dealt with on an individual basis according to a person's fitness to do his or her job, they claim, rather than preventing all who want to work longer—including healthy, capable individuals—from continuing in work. Moreover, many commentators contend that older workers bring valuable expertise and experience to their jobs—qualities that their employers can benefit from in the long term. Research also indicates that there is no significant pattern of decline in the skills of older employees, at least up to the age of 70, they argue.

Economists maintain that legislation must be altered significantly to reflect changing demographics. Aging populations and corresponding declines in the ratio of workers to dependents in western countries mean that there will be more old people relying on state pensions and fewer workers to support them through paying money into pension funds. When pensions and mandatory retirement policies were introduced in the last century, most men did not live long after they retired. Today, experts point out, people live on average 20 years more after retirement, and they must put away more in savings if they are to enjoy a reasonable standard of living throughout old age. Critics of mandatory retirement assert that women are at a particular disadvantage since they typically earn less than men, are more likely to have taken a career break to rear children, and on average outlive men by seven years.

The articles that follow examine issues in this debate with regard to Britain and North America.

CBI WARNS AGAINST SCRAPPING RETIREMENT AGE

Management-Issues Website

This article appeared on the Management-Issues website (www.management-issues.com) in November 2003.

The CBI is one of the United Kingdom's most powerful lobby organizations, representing companies from different business sectors. Go to www.cbi.org.uk for more details.

Do you think employers, rather than the state, are in a better position to decide what is best for the individual worker?

The EU's Employment Directive for Equal Treatment in Employment and Occupation (2000) requires member states to implement laws prohibiting discrimination at work on the grounds of age, sexual orientation, religion, and disability.

YES

✓ Plans to scrap the UK's mandatory retirement age at 65 risks "embittering the retirement process" and could lead to a costly surge of employment tribunal cases, according to the Confederation of British Industry (CBI).

Ministers are considering scrapping retirement at 65 as part of a package of proposals on age discrimination that are due to take effect in 2006.

In its submission to the government's consultation, the CBI argues that unfair discrimination based on age is unacceptable but says that the current retirement system enables individuals to retire with dignity rather than in conflict.

Normal retirement age

Under the new rules, the state pension will continue to be paid from 65. The CBI argues that this should be matched by a "normal" retirement age, with a review of retirement arrangements in five years.

In the absence of a normal retirement age, employers will have to assess whether an individual is capable of performing a job, which some employees may find uncomfortable. And the employers' body warned that this could lead to bitter employees seeking compensation under age discrimination rules.

Digby Jones, CBI Director-General, said: "Both employers and employees need flexibility to reach a consensus on retirement. Neither party should have to maintain an employment relationship longer than they want to. The world of work has changed and everyone needs choice.

"UK firms already have the third highest participation of older workers in the EU and removing the normal retirement age would go far beyond the retirement arrangements of many European countries."

Unfair discrimination

The CBI said that while unfair discrimination based on age is unacceptable—such as specifying age ranges in job

James Garner, Tommy Lee Jones, Donald Sutherland, and Clint Eastwood play astronauts who come out of retirement for one last mission in Space Cowboys *(2000).*

advertisements—some forms of discrimination based on age are necessary. Examples include international aviation agreements that prohibit pilots over the age of 60 entering foreign airspace and rules that bar those aged under 21 from driving heavy goods vehicles.

Given that people in industrialized nations are staying healthier longer, how fair do you think it is to impose an age limit of 60 on pilots? Are such agreements discriminatory?

The introduction of age discrimination legislation in 2006 is widely expected to increase tribunal cases. Employment tribunals cost UK business £163 million each year and the CBI says that research from the USA shows that over 50 per

COMMENTARY: Tenure: A job for life?

People who work beyond normal retirement age usually fall into two categories—low-paid (and often female) workers who have insufficient savings to retire, and highly educated workers. Members of the latter group are typically financially able to retire at age 65 or earlier, yet many want to continue working because of the interesting nature of their jobs. This has led some critics to question whether such a desire is in the best interests of employers and younger colleagues.

Under a special Age Discrimination in Employment Act (ADEA) exemption enacted in 1986 U.S. universities were permitted to enforce mandatory retirement for their faculty staff who reached the age of 70. This exemption expired at the end of 1993, and today retirement in academia is entirely voluntary. Nonetheless, many faculty members and others believe that a compulsory retirement age should be reintroduced.

At the center of the debate is the issue of tenure—a traditional practice whereby the most talented, respected, and in some cases longest-serving academics at a university or college are awarded a permanent post. The main function of tenure is to protect the independence of a faculty, its teaching, and research. Some argue that in the absence of mandatory retirement, tenure amounts to granting an academic a job for life. Given the limited office and laboratory space of most higher education institutions, coupled with limited funding for salaries and research, such a situation can only mean reducing the prospects for the hiring and promotion of younger faculty members and researchers.

Depreciating intellectual capital

According to University of Chicago professors Richard A. Epstein and Saunders MacLane, "intellectual capital depreciates in the face of general advances of scholarship and the creation of new fields...." They assert that people find it harder to keep up with changes in their chosen disciplines as they get older. Productivity and creativity decline with age, while the "lifeblood" of a university—its creativity and innovation—depends on a constant input of young academics. Some observers claim that this input is being increasingly curtailed by a backlog of elderly academics remaining in their posts—positions that no one can legally ask them to vacate.

By July 2000, 70 percent of U.S. universities and colleges had some sort of retirement incentive program in place. While there may be arguments for the retention of older faculty members in teaching and mentoring positions, the majority of higher education institutions prefer to keep their research departments young, vibrant, and at the cutting edge of their disciplines. Increasingly in the United States they are no longer legally able to do so, and critics claim that they are losing out competitively to research institutes in countries where mandatory retirement policies remain in place.

cent of age discrimination claims there fail to produce any evidence of company wrongdoing.

"Age discrimination is more difficult to define than other forms of discrimination and the government must not fan the flames of the compensation culture with unclear or unworkable legislation," Digby Jones added.

"A surge of employment tribunal cases will cost companies dear, hit smaller firms especially and end up harming the employment prospects of the very people that need protection."

Do you think attitudes toward older workers would change with the introduction of antidiscrimination legislation?

SHOULD RETIREMENT BE MANDATORY? Reginald Stackhouse

Reginald Stackhouse is principal emeritus and research professor at Wycliffe College, University of Toronto. This article first appeared in the Canadian newspaper The Globe and Mail *in December 2003.*

A seniority clause is a provision in a contract of employment that specifies that, in a situation in which employees have to be selected for layoffs, preference is given to the longest-serving employees over all other considerations.

Social security in the United States provides a regular income to retired and disabled workers and the unemployed. It is funded by a compulsory payroll tax called Federal Insurance Contributions Act (FICA) tax, which employers withhold from workers' paychecks and send directly to the government. In 2000, 135 million people were enrolled in the social security system.

NO

Prime Minister Paul Martin's call for a debate on ending mandatory retirement is on track with the times. Retirement as we knew it in the late 20th century will not last long in the 21st. We will still have retirement, but it will not be mandatory, rigid and total. It will be voluntary, flexible and partial.

Workers who burn out in physically intensive jobs can still take their pensions and head for Florida. But they will be a minority.

Most other workers are already in service jobs. If they are still producing, they will be free to choose to stay on the job. That freedom will include negotiating whether they will work seasonally or year-round, full-time or part-time. Gone will be the one-size-fits-all mentality that assumes a guillotine must crash down on a career at age 65.

Retirement will be tailored to the individual, but not so much so that productivity will be sacrificed. Employers will enjoy the freedom to tell ineffective workers it's time to take their pensions and go. Tenured professorships, executive contracts and seniority clauses will be restricted by term limits.

How can we be sure these sweeping changes will happen? The simple fact is, mandatory retirement is out of date. Economics, demographics and ethics tell us this. Consider the facts:

Economics

The end of mandatory retirement will be economically imperative because not all pension funds can be counted on to finance people adequately for the protracted retirements the late 20th century taught workers to take for granted.

The number of retirees taking from pension funds is escalating, while the proportion of younger people contributing to them is sliding. When most pensions funds were designed, the opposite was the norm. In 1935, when social security was initiated in the United States, there were nine workers for every American at the age of eligibility. By 1990, the ration had become 3.3 to one. In a few decades, it will be two to one. The same trend is true of Canada.

Paul Martin, Canada's prime minister (2003–), has spoken out in favor of ending mandatory retirement in the country.

Otto von Bismark (1815–1898) was the leader of Germany for 19 years from 1871.

As well, retirees now live longer. When Germany's Chancellor Otto von Bismarck introduced the world's first national old-age pension plan in 1889, 65 was a practical age of eligibility because few people lived long after it. Now, the assumptions of that era are as outdated as Bismarck's horse-drawn artillery.

Do you think that the phrase "fully financed permanent vacation" is a fair way to describe retirement?

So are the pension assumptions of that time. The assumption that every worker at 65 can have a fully financed, permanent vacation cannot go on. So, some people will stay on the job longer. Some will work part-time after taking their pensions. It will have nothing to do with ideology, just numbers.

Demographics

According to Statistics Canada, the federal statistical agency, Canada's fertility rate in 2002 was an average of 1.5 births for women age 15 to 49, compared to 2 births for women in the United States. Go to http://www.statcan.ca/Daily/English/040419/d040419b.htm for details.

This century will see the graying of Canada. That, combined with a our low fertility rate, means there will soon no longer be long lines of bright, young people eager to push older workers out of the way. This will change our thinking about older people in the workplace as no philosophical or political debate could do. When there is no surplus of young people lined up at human resources, employers may find themselves clutching at their "old reliables."

Already, companies are organizing "job banks" to arrange for retired workers to return seasonally or on "flex hours." At the executive and management levels, companies are contracting with retirees to work as consultants. Experience shows this can take some finessing to satisfy legal and union requirements. But it is being done, and not because anyone is forced by law to do it, or because anyone is being cheated out of a pension, but because some men and women need—or just want—extra income. Some also enjoy getting out of the house, or find they really don't want to play golf every day. Many covet the chance to do work to which they had devoted much of their lives.

By "Freedom 55" the writer is refering to a series of commercials for a Canadian life-insurance company. The commercials suggested that if viewers invested wisely, they would be able to retire at 55 with no financial worries.

Yes, some lines of work have to be abandoned because of the toll time takes. But there's a dramatic difference between the labour of a mill hand and the agenda of a research worker. So, for some, "Achievement 65" easily trumps "Freedom 55."

Ethics

Is the freedom to choose when you retire more important than the right to be able to retire at a reasonable age?

Social and corporate ethics must respect the freedom to choose as much when people are older as when they were younger. For many men and women, work is an essential part of identity. When they are deprived of their work, they lose part of themselves. No pension can make that up. No limitless leisure can either. Why should people be denied the freedom to be themselves as long they as they can remain effective?

The word retirement, unintentionally but irresistibly, implies a person has been marginalized and is no longer a participant. It means being on the sidelines rather than on the field. What's wrong with that? Nothing if a person chooses it, or is not capable of more.

What if a man or woman prefers the other choice? Canada now has a Prime Minister who, at 65, is not automatically disqualified by the calendar, so why should any other worker be? If the only standard for judging a prime minister is his record, why should that not be the sole criterion for anyone else?

Mandatory retirement is a form of legalized age discrimination. It has no place in a country whose people are proud of their Charter of Rights and Freedoms.

Paul Martin became prime minister of Canada in 2003 at age 65. He has said he does not believe in mandatory retirement, arguing, "If you're rooted in the past, well then you could be 45 or 35 and you shouldn't be prime minister." Do you think there should be an age limit for politicians?

The Canadian Charter of Rights and Freedoms, part of the Canadian Constitution, was enacted in 1982. It guarantees certain rights for Canadian citizens. Go to http://laws.justice.gc.ca/en/charter to find out more.

Summary

In the first article the Management-Issues website reports on opposition by the Confederation of British Industry (CBI) to the British government's proposal to scrap mandatory retirement at age 65. The CBI believes that it would fall to employers to assess the capabilities of individual workers, which could lead to employees seeking compensation under new age discrimination legislation. The CBI maintains that some forms of age discrimination are essential, such as an age limit for pilots. The article concludes by drawing attention to a likely surge in employment court cases: Although evidence from the United States shows that more than half of age discrimination claims do not produce proof of company wrongdoing, the CBI predicts that such cases will prove a huge financial burden for small companies.

In the second article Reginald Stackhouse uses a speech by the Canadian Prime Minister Paul Martin as the starting point for arguing that mandatory retirement should end. Stackhouse believes that retirement will become voluntary, flexible, and partial instead of mandatory, rigid, and total. He argues that fixed retirement is out of date for economic, demographic, and ethical reasons. First, the number of retirees is increasing, while at the same time the proportion of younger people contributing to pension funds is falling. Second, because the fertility rate in Canada is low, there will not be enough young workers to replace retired employees. Stackhouse finally points out that in a country that prides itself on its Charter of Rights and Freedoms, the freedom for people to choose when they retire is an important consideration.

FURTHER INFORMATION:

Books:

Jackson, William A., *The Political Economy of Population Ageing*. Northampton, MA: Edward Elgar, 1998.

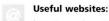

Useful websites:

http://www.cbc.ca/news/features/mandatory_retirement.html
"Retiring Mandatory Retirement" by Martin O'Malley.

http://www.debatabase.org/details.asp?topicID=66
Discussion with pros and cons of mandatory retirement.

http://www.eeoc.gov/types/age.html
Age discrimination information from the U.S. Equal Employment Opportunity Commission.

http://www.thescientist.com/yr1994/apr/goodman_p1_940418.html
Article about mandatory retirement in universities and colleges published by *The Scientist*.

The following debates in the Pro/Con series may also be of interest:

In this volume:

Topic 12 Is there a culture of overwork in the United States?

Topic 13 Do labor unions have too much power in the United States?

In *Poverty and Wealth*:

Topic 4 Should people have to look after their elderly relatives?

SHOULD THERE BE A MANDATORY RETIREMENT AGE?

SHOULD THERE BE A MANDATORY RETIREMENT AGE? KEY POINTS

ECONOMIC SENSE
Does mandatory retirement make economic sense?

YES: Mandatory retirement frees up jobs; consequent reductions in unemployment benefits allow more funds to be put into pension funds

NO: Populations are aging, and the burden of dependents on the state and on those in work is set to increase

COMPETENCE
Are people physically and mentally less able to perform their jobs over the age of 65 or 70?

YES: There is an average age above which it is more likely that employees will experience physical- or mental-health problems; older workers are more likely to suffer long-term sickness

NO: There is no medical evidence supporting the idea that people over a particular age are likely to be either infirm or incapable

BUSINESS SENSE
Does mandatory retirement make good business sense?

YES: Mandatory retirement allows younger employees to progress in their careers and brings in new talent and fresh ideas to jobs and professions

NO: Older workers are highly proficient at their jobs and bring the advantage of valuable experience to a workplace

SAVING TO RETIRE
Are people able to put aside enough savings to provide a reasonably comfortable retirement?

YES: Most people have 40 to 45 years of work before they retire; this is more than enough time to save for retirement as long as they are prudent

NO: People live longer and so need more retirement savings than ever before; low-paid and female workers are at a particular disadvantage

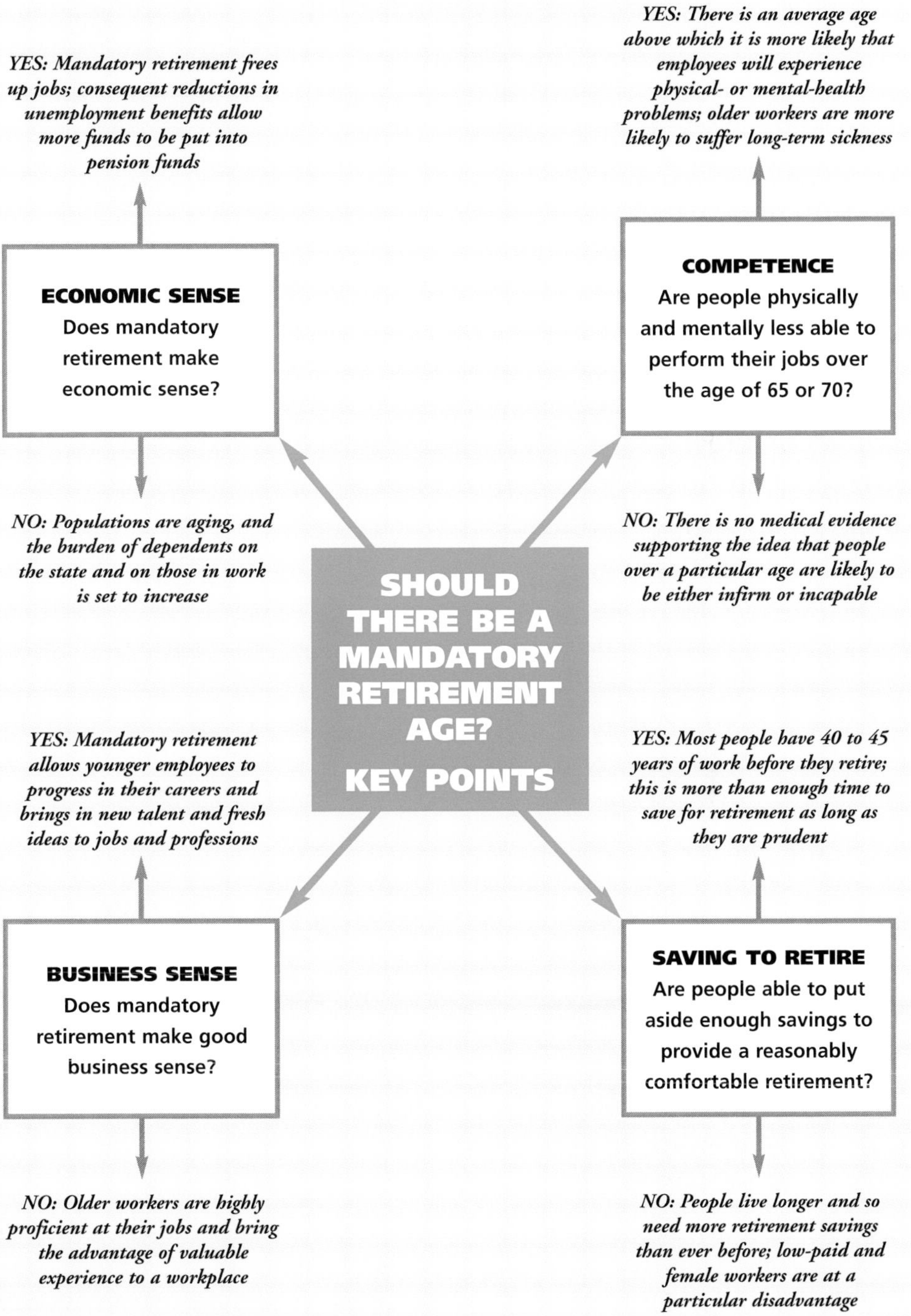

PART 2
WORK CULTURE

INTRODUCTION

As people spend increasingly long hours in the office, work culture has come under scrutiny. The study of office dynamics, the methods by which people get certain jobs, how they behave once they are in the workplace, and reasons for discrimination, among other things, have all fascinated sociologists for years. The following debates examine key work culture issues.

Work practices

Prior to the mid-19th century work in the United States and European nations such as Britain and France was not incessant. Before the industrial revolution people were predominantly employed seasonally in agriculture—busy during planting and harvesting but more relaxed during the winter months. Even in the workshops and stores where craftsmen and women worked, employment was not constant: Changing demands due to the seasons, a varied availability of raw materials, and poor transportation and communications contributed to interruptions in the flow of work.

Nonetheless, a culture of hard work was still prevalent, particularly among America's recent European immigrants, who approached the task of building a new world in what many referred to as the "wilderness" with determination and sweat, blood, and tears. U.S. colonists viewed this Puritan or Protestant work ethic as a "calling," a sacrifice that demonstrated moral worthiness.

Industrialization had a dramatic effect not only on work but also on people's attitudes toward it. Home and workshop trades were replaced by mass production in factories; craftsmanship, skill, and individual control over personal production was replaced by machine manufacture, division of labor, discipline, and anonymity. The idea of work as a calling was replaced by the concept of public usefulness—based on the notion that the country would fall into poverty and decay if people failed to be industrious.

Postwar trends

In the wake of World War II and the decades of unprecedented economic growth and prosperity that followed during the 1950s and 1960s, demand for labor was high, unemployment low, and human relations became an important issue as managers began to turn their attention to finding ways to make jobs more fulfilling for workers.

People in the mid- to late-20th century also experienced tremendous cultural and social shifts with the advent of the information age. Since 1956 blue-collar, manual jobs in U.S. goods production, construction, trades, and so on have become increasingly outnumbered by white-collar positions in technical, managerial, and clerical work and in the service sector. By 2004, some 35 percent of the U.S. workforce was deskbound. Many jobs in manufacturing and industry also became more technical, involving more skill, discretion, and decision making. Employees at the start of the 21st century are more likely to enjoy their jobs, to find their work interesting and fulfilling, than their peers of 100 or 50 years before. However, at the same time, many have suffered the effects of downsizing—a popular trend during the 1980s of reducing the size of a firm, mainly by shedding staff as a means to cut costs. This has often led those still employed to feel insecure in their jobs; many are expected to do the work of two or more people for the same pay in the same amount of time, and this has led to an increase in work hours. Consequently workers are finding themselves increasingly stressed by their work environment, and critics claim this has effected their health and productivity. Some employers have recognized this problem and have introduced programs to help their employees destress; others argue that stress is not an issue. Topic 7 examines this issue.

Periods of rising unemployment, as seen in the 1980s, can throw a spotlight on unconventional or unethical recruiting practices—for example, when positions are awarded not on merit but to friends or relatives of the owners or managers of firms or of people in public office. Although some historians argue that America's economy is based on family-run businesses, several states and countries have introduced antinepotism laws. Topic 8 discusses nepotism.

Among the other issues discussed when examining work culture are how gender and sex affect the workplace. In 1900, for example, women made up just 18 percent of America's paid workers. By 1990 this had risen to nearly 50 percent, at which it has remained.

Many people believe that so-called "female" characteristics and attitudes make women more popular with employers for particular types of work—in the "caring" professions, for instance, but also for white-collar and service-sector jobs, which continue to grow in western countries. The suitability of women over and above men for certain types of work is explored in Topic 9. The presence of women combined with longer worker hours has led to a boom in the number or sexual relationships between work colleagues. The appropriateness of such cases is discussed in Topic 10.

The final topic examines sexual orientation in the workplace. Evidence show that gays and lesbians are sometimes discriminated against by their bosses and their peers, although legislation exists to protect them.

"By working hard eight hours a day, you may eventually get to be a boss and work hard twelve hours a day."

—ROBERT FROST (1874–1963), AMERICAN POET

Topic 7
IS STRESS TAKEN SERIOUSLY ENOUGH AS A HEALTH ISSUE IN THE WORKPLACE?

YES

FROM "EMPLOYERS SEEK TO RELIEVE STRESS, DEPRESSION"
AUSTIN BUSINESS JOURNAL, MAY 15, 2000
JENNA COLLEY

NO

FROM "JOB STRESS, BURNOUT ON THE RISE"
MSNBC NEWS, SEPTEMBER 1, 2003
JANE WEAVER

INTRODUCTION

According to the National Institute for Occupational Safety and Health (NIOSH)—the federal agency responsible for conducting research and making recommendations for the prevention of work-related illness and injury—of the 550 million workdays lost annually in the United States through unscheduled absenteeism, 20 percent can be attributed to stress. Stress is defined in this context as psychological tension arising from real or imagined threats that can cause depression or chronic illness.

The problem is global and, observers believe, most acute in developed nations: In Britain, for example, the Health and Safety Executive estimates that industry loses 13.4 million workdays a year because of stress. Some estimates give stress a role in an even higher proportion of lost workdays. Figures from Ireland and Canada, for instance, cite it in 50–60 percent of all absences. This highlights a major problem in talking about stress: Apart from the direct psychological pressure itself stress can be interpreted as a causal factor in a wide range of illnesses and conditions—including depression, musculoskeletal disorders such as back pain, gastrointestinal problems, and heart disease and strokes. According to some reports, people who suffer from stress for most of their working lives are 25 percent more likely to suffer a fatal heart attack; they also have a 50 percent greater chance of dying from a stroke. This has led workers' rights analysts, among others, to claim that employers are simply not taking stress seriously in the workplace.

Part of the reason for this may be that there is not enough evidence to prove that there is a causal link between work, stress, and illness—people who work may fall sick, but it is difficult to prove that their jobs are directly responsible for their ailments. Most studies are based on self-reporting; others draw on carefully worded questionnaires; neither method produces results that satisfy everyone as being conclusive.

Some critics believe that greater demands on the labor force have resulted in what some sociologists call a "culture of overwork." In 2003 the Organization for Economic Cooperation and Development estimated that the average U.S. working year lengthened by 50 hours (3 percent) between 1979 and 1999. This may have to do with smaller workforces doing the jobs once carried out by several more people or the same numbers carrying a much greater workload than before in many industries. Others also do several jobs, often on casual or short-term bases in order to make ends meet. This constant multitasking, combined with the attempt to balance work with childcare and reduced job security, has caused a huge increase in the sources of stress.

> *"The process of living is the process of having stress imposed on you and reacting to it."*
>
> —STANLEY J. SARNOFF, PHYSIOLOGIST (1963)

Some psychologists, however, claim that stress can have a positive influence on people's working lives, actually increasing their job satisfaction. In one study, as many as 46 percent of workers interviewed said that time seems to pass more quickly when they are under pressure, while only 7 percent reported slowing down when they felt stressed. This "positive" stress may, however, be closely linked to the work being done: The pressure of meeting a deadline when the task is a creative and stimulating challenge can be stressful and positive at the same time. However, the stress involved in much blue-collar work—from being required to do a dull and repetitive task more quickly or for longer hours in an environment over which the worker has little control—is much less likely to give satisfaction and is much more likely to be a factor in illness.

Many employers have reached the conclusion that they can no longer ignore the problem. Increasing numbers have introduced systems designed to identify stress and take preventive action against its ill effects. They collect details of stress-related illnesses and may even have a codified stress policy. They offer confidential counseling and may, in certain circumstances, reduce hours, workload, or specific tasks to help employees who display or report stress symptoms. Since such measures were unheard of 50 years ago, there is little doubt that more is being done to combat stress in the workplace. What is less clear is whether it is enough.

Some countries have tried to address the problem through legislation, but most of the laws have been ineffective. In Britain the 1974 Health and Safety at Work Act stops companies from causing unnecessary stress at work, but as of 2003 there were no prosecutions. As in the United States, most stress cases come to court as civil claims for compensation, but critics say that far too few are successful.

The following articles look at the question in more detail.

EMPLOYERS SEEK TO RELIEVE STRESS, DEPRESSION
Jenna Colley

The author, Jenna Colley, is a Texas-based business journalist. She writes regularly for both the Houston Business Journal *and the* Austin Business Journal.

National Research Corporation (www.nationalresearch.com) carries out satisfaction and performance studies for the U.S. health-care industry.

The WHO lists depression as the second-greatest contributor to the global tally of "years of productive life lost to disability" for 15- to 44-year-olds. See http://www.who.int/mental_health/management/depression/definition/en/ for more details.

The NFBR was founded in 1989 to increase "scientific ... understanding of the brain in health and disease." See http://www.brainnet.org/index.php?lid=about for more details.

YES

✓ Austinites trumpet the Capital City's extraordinary quality of life at every turn. They cite parks, lakes and live music as outlets for healthy social outings.

But Austin's prosperous, competitive economy still prompts many employees to spend long hours at work under sometimes tremendous stress.

Separating work issues from personal issues proves difficult for many—problems that arise in an employee's personal life often surface on the job. Such stress often leads to depression, a major cause of lost productivity and general workplace malaise.

A nationwide study done last year by the National Research Corp. found the Austin area ranked third in the country for the percentage of people reporting depression or anxiety orders. Austin was at 17 percent; the national average was 13 percent.

Address depression, increase national wealth

"If we could address just the depression issue—which the World Health Organization recognizes as the number two health issue—we would probably have a different GNP and GDP," says Leonard Sperry, a professor of psychiatry at the Medical College of Wisconsin and chairman of the American Psychiatric Association's committee on psychiatry in the workplace.

"ASA has a determined effort to address depression as an important issue in the workplace because it makes a significant difference in the overall productivity and level of well-being of corporate America," he says.

Depression costs the United States about $44 billion a year in lost productivity, according to a National Foundation for Brain Research survey of human resources professionals.

Employers increasingly recognize the importance of mental health programs and stress-reducing techniques in maintaining employees' productivity and happiness, especially in light of Austin's tight labor market, says Sandi Aitken, manager of premier employee services for Motorola

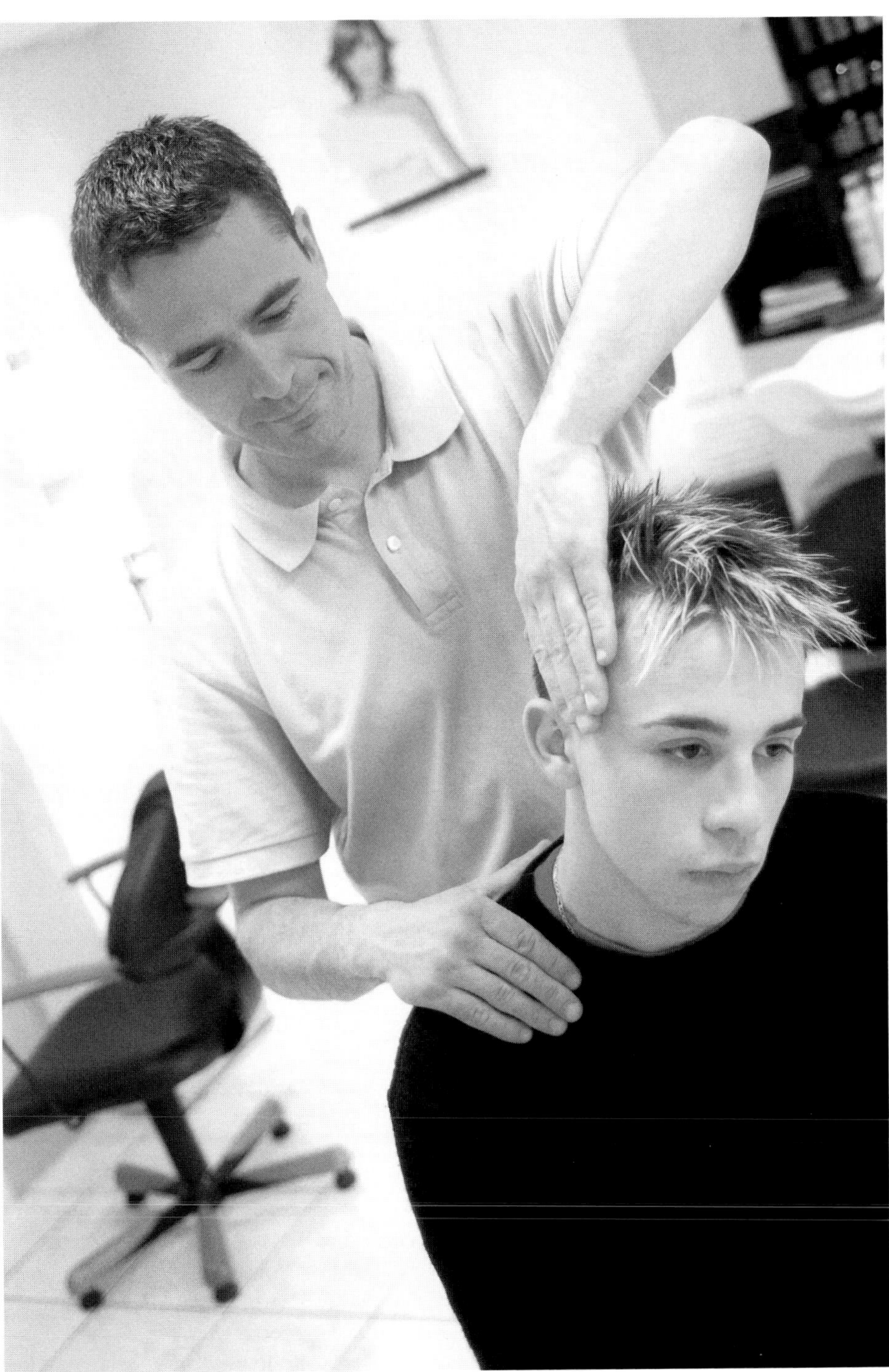

Shiatsu, or head massage, is used to relieve stress. Some employers bring in out-of-house masseurs to help their employees.

Semiconductor Products Sector, which has 10,000 full-time workers.

"We reinforce taking control and at the same time letting go," Aitken says. "With unemployment at a low [rate], from a company perspective, it's logical that employee loyalty is reinforced if they work for a company that cares and recognizes that workers are more than employees—they are people with unique and special needs."

Motorola is a transnational corporation that can afford such measures. Are people working for small companies more likely to be stressed in the workplace?

Motorola provides employees with a concierge service to cut down on stress caused by daily errands; an activity center; and a child development center operated by Bright Horizons Family Solutions, in addition to an employee assistance program, on-site therapists for employees and family members, and a mental health component in its health care package.

A growing and emerging issue

Of the more than 400 human resources professionals surveyed by the National Foundation for Brain Research, 80 percent reported depression was a problem at their workplaces and 56 percent reported the problem was significant enough to harm productivity.

Depression is "an issue that is continuing to grow as people become more aware of it," says Mark Finger, vice president of human resources for Austin's National Instruments Corp., which employs about 2,100 employees worldwide, 1,500 of them in Austin. "What once may have been called a 'bad attitude' now may be related to a medical reason."

"National Instruments spends a significant amount of money via medical plans to help with these issues."

This year, NI made *Fortune* magazine's annual list of "100 Best Companies to Work for in America."

NI offers an employee assistance program and mental health coverage as well as sand volleyball courts and a fitness center, which are designed to provide a physical outlet for releasing stress and reducing depression....

See http://www.utexas.edu/student/cmhc/booklets/depression/depress.html for a resource page on the causes, symptoms, and treatments for depression. Is it treated seriously enough as an illness?

Defining depression

Depression is an illness that disturbs a person's emotional well-being. Although many people periodically experience mood shifts, people who consistently find themselves in depressed moods every day over a period of two weeks or more might be experiencing depression. Stressful life events, such as a death in the family or financial problems, can trigger depression.

"We demand a lot of people's time," says Eric Webber, a spokesman for GSD&M Advertising. "When people experience stress, they are not as productive. We want people to be healthy and happy."

In addition to mental health provisions in its health care coverage, GSD&M provides employees with a family room where they can bring their children to work. The firm also promotes a liberal work-from-home policy.

Working at home can remove sources of stress such as difficult colleagues and provide an environment associated with comfort and security. However, it can also add to stress by depriving workers of a sense of their home as a refuge from work, as well as the stimulation of social interaction with colleagues.

Webber says: "Our philosophy is that as long as you're getting the job done...."

Although 98 percent of companies responding to the Brain Research Foundation's survey offer employees health insurance—most of which covers treatment of mental illness—the study authors note "there are often limitations and restrictions to such coverage."

What HR professionals are doing

When asked what they do when they suspect a worker is depressed, 60 percent of the human resources professionals questioned say they refer the worker to an employee assistance program, and about half encourage the worker to seek counseling. About 20 percent spoke to the worker's supervisor; 11 percent spoke with co-workers. Six percent say they don't take any action.

Should it be the responsibility of human resource personnel, with no medical training, to make these kinds of judgments? Is it better to leave affected workers to seek help themselves?

Austin-based Whole Foods Market Inc. ... intends to use an employee assistance program that's connected to its health care provider so that referrals from the program to therapists will be easier.

"There is a potential disruption factor when the EAP is not coordinated with the managed care provider," Bearden says.

Whole Foods also made *Fortune* magazine's annual list of "100 Best Companies to Work for in America." Whole Foods employs about 17,000 people nationwide.

A key for Gay Warren Gaddis, president of local advertising agency The Think Tank [T3], is making sure that as her company grows, employees are clued into the goings-on of the company, which has 72 employees.

"As companies grow, the left hand often doesn't know what the right hand is doing, and that can create stress."...

T3 holds 15-minute meetings once a week for staffers to fill each other in on their personal and professional lives. Gaddis also emphasizes a family environment by encouraging employees to bring children and pets to work—something she thinks lowers the stress level.

Do you think this is sensible? What health and safety implications might this have? Do you think it might affect company insurance?

"It's not just a casual nod to company culture; it's a way of life that is real important to me," Gaddis says.

JOB STRESS, BURNOUT ON THE RISE
Jane Weaver

The author, Jane Weaver, is a journalist and the health editor of MSNBC. See http://msnbc.msn.com/id/3168830 for the "How We Work" series of articles.

NO

✗ You're doing the work of three people at your job. Some weeks you spend more time at work than at home. You missed your child's soccer game … again. In the morning, you feel more exhausted than rested….

With mass layoffs, pay cuts, seemingly endless workdays and disappearing vacations, Americans are coping with an enormous amount of job stress. … [U]nable to keep up with the demands of their jobs, many are reaching burnout levels.

Is it fair that workers should be subject to increased levels of stress for someone else's profit? Would it be better if work hours were limited by law? See http://www.brook.edu/dybdocroot/fp/cusf/analysis/workweek.htm for discussion of the 35-hour limit in effect in France.

In its series on "How We Work: Punching the Clock in the New Economy," MSNBC.com has chronicled Americans who are toiling longer and harder at their jobs. While fewer people working longer days may be good for profit-minded corporations, those increases in productivity can come at a price for individuals.

"As the workforce has shrunk, people are overloaded and stress is the result," says Ronald Downey, Kansas State University professor of Industrial and Occupational Psychology. "If the stress keeps on unending, then they're in trouble."

Stress without end

Trouble starts when employees take on more job responsibilities, but lose their sense of control over their work. Working excessively long hours begins to take a heavy toll on family life and social relationships, adding to the stress level, researchers say.

It's well-known that stress can lead to hypertension, cardiovascular disease, heart attacks and other physical ailments, research indicates.

Early signs of job stress are headaches, short tempers, trouble sleeping and low morale, according to the National Institute for Occupational Safety and Health (NIOSH).

See http://www.cdc.gov/niosh/stresswk.html for further information on NIOSH and its recommendations on reducing stress in the workplace.

And it's not just physical health. An estimated 60 percent of work absences are from psychological problems—at a cost of over $57 billion yearly—according to the American Psychological Association.

"People don't have enough time to do the things they're being asked to do," says Dr. Ron Restak, an expert in brain function and author of *The New Brain*.

Too much multi-tasking leads to distraction and a loss of concentration.

"You cannot accomplish two things at the same time as efficiently as you would ... separately. A lot of accidents and a loss of efficiency can occur from that," says Restak.

In fact, health costs are almost 50 percent greater for workers who report high levels of stress, according to the *Journal of Occupational and Environment Medicine*.

"Body systems start to fail," says Downey. "Then you have stress syndrome and you break down."

If stressful workplaces impose greater costs on health care, should medical insurers offer discounts to employers who offer reduced-stress working environments?

A fatal work ethic

In Japan, it's known as "karoshi," or death from overwork.

The Japanese government has reported 10,000 cases a year of managers, executives and engineers who have died from overwork, a fallout of the country's prolonged economic slump.

See http://www.workhealth.org/whatsnew/lpkarosh.html for more background on the karoshi phenomenon.

It's hard to say whether it's reached that extreme in the U.S., but the number of full- or part-timers who report high job stress rose to 45 percent in 2002, up from 37 percent the year before, according to a NIOSH study. An estimated 40 percent of U.S. workers reported their job was very or extremely stressful, with 25 percent calling their jobs the number one stress factor in their lives, the organization reported.

Everyone reacts to stress in different ways and recognizing when you're reaching burnout levels can be difficult, says Dr. Jeffrey Kahn, clinical associate professor of psychiatry at Cornell.

"The most stressed-out ones don't know they're having problems," says Kahn, who is also president of WorkPsych Associates, a New York executive and corporate consulting firm. "They don't realize that things are getting to them."

Increased absenteeism isn't always a giveaway

The new buzzword is "presenteeism" which happens when people are too afraid to call in sick. Instead they show up, but are still too stressed-out to be productive, says Dr. Richard Chaifetz, chairman and chief executive of ComPsych, a Chicago firm which provides human resources services.

See http://www.stressbusting.co.uk/articles/news_present.asp for a description of "presenteeism."

"A lot of people realize it's better to show up and be less than 100 percent productive," says Chaifetz. "But if they're not focused, their performance will go down."

Much of the problem comes from the blurring of the lines between work and home life, with workers tethered to their jobs through cell phones, pagers and e-mail, researchers say.

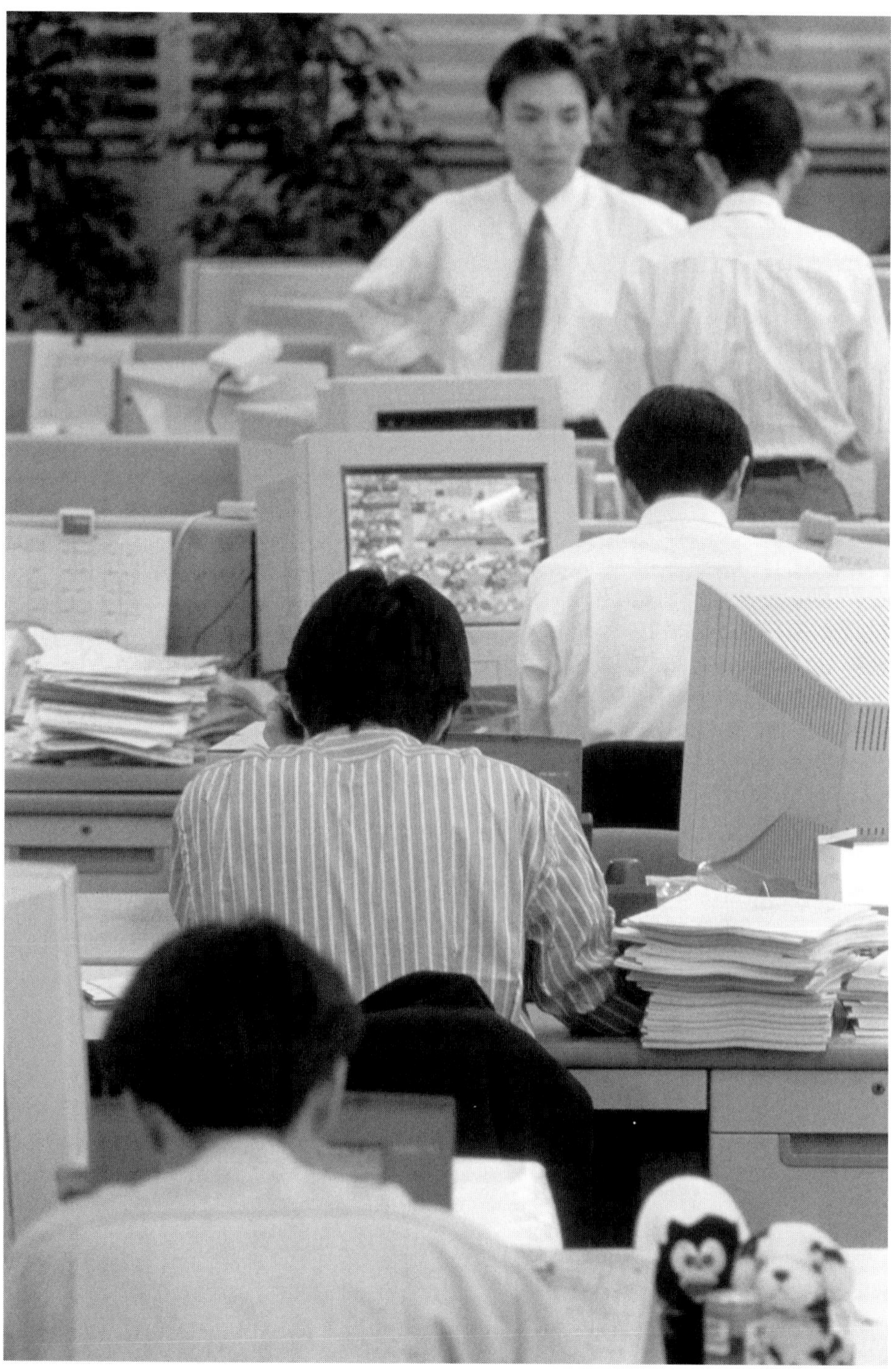

Long commutes on packed trains, formal and hierarchical workplaces, long work hours, and short vacations make Japanese workers among the most stressed in the world.

An estimated 70 percent of more than 1,500 participants felt they don't have a healthy balance between their work and their personal lives, according to a May [2003] survey on work/life balance by online job board TrueCareers.

"There are no clear demarcations anymore," says Restak. "When people left work for the day, that was it. Employers were reluctant to call them at home. Now people don't feel like they're ever off duty."

With more people working at home at least part of the week, the divide between workplace and home is difficult to make. Would having a separate telephone line and e-mail address, for example, help reinforce this distinction?

Household with two working parents or single parent households are especially vulnerable to burnout from work overload, says professor Downey.

"Before, men didn't have to worry about meals or their kids and it relieved pressure," says Downey. "Now men and women are worried about their children if they're sick and how to get to games."

Not all job-related stress leads to burnout. For some workaholic types, boasting of burnout is an ego-booster, a macho way to feel indispensable in an otherwise bleak jobs market, say experts.

Is this argument convincing? Why might people find it an ego boost to boast of burnout?

For them, "it's almost a badge of courage," says Dr. Rosch, president of the American Institute of Stress in Yonkers, N.Y.

"Some people thrive in a pressure cooker and doing many things at once," he says.

Desk slaves, free yourselves

Even as American workers are putting in more hours, a genre of anti-work ethic books has emerged, including such publications as *Work to Live: The Guide to Getting a Life*, by Joe Robinson and *The Importance of Being Lazy: In Praise of Play, Leisure and Vacations*, by Al Gini.

Meanwhile, some corporations are making efforts to alleviate overwork by offering paid sabbaticals or on-site classes in meditation to help employees deal with long days.

"The consequence of burnout is that productivity begins to slip," says Chaifetz. "The smart organizations are the ones that can balance the needs for increased productivity with appropriate employee morale."

Productivity is typically measured as the value created for the company for each hour worked, so the most productive companies are those that get a high value out of each hour of their employees' work. Simply increasing the number of hours worked, therefore, decreases productivity since the final value must be divided by a greater number of hours.

Jeffrey Pfeffer, professor at the Graduate School of Business, Stanford University, says American companies who want to compete in a global economy should follow the European model of shorter workweeks and month-long vacations.

"There is no evidence that excessive hours are necessary for competitive success," says Pfeffer. "But somehow we've gotten in our minds that to succeed in this world is to work yourself to death."

Summary

In the first article Jenna Colley reports on a nationwide survey, conducted in 2000, which found that the workers in Austin, Texas, are among the most stressed in the United States. Employers there have been motivated to take this problem seriously because the local job market is "tight." Since there is low unemployment, workers who get sick or resign due to stress are hard to replace, so firms have to nurture their existing workforce. The author describes some of the specific stress-combating measures taken by some of Austin's major employers. They include the provision of on-site childcare facilities, counseling referrals through the human resources department, mental health care on demand, the freedom for many staff to work from home, and weekly ideas meetings at which colleagues can discuss their work. One firm even encourages staff to bring their pets to work.

Jane Weaver, in the second article, examines some of the ailments that have increased over the last 20 years and are believed to be caused by stress in the workplace. She describes some of the early-warning signs, including "presenteeism"—the fear of taking vacations or calling in sick—but claims that those most at risk often do not realize that anything is wrong. According to Weaver, the problem is caused partly by the downsizing of many businesses. Such rationalization has resulted in many individuals being required to perform tasks that would formerly have been the work of several people. Weaver comments that the need to juggle work and childcare leads to loss of concentration, and the resulting lack of control is a classic cause of stress.

FURTHER INFORMATION:

Books:

Jex, Steve M., *Stress and Job Performance: Theory, Research, and Implications for Managerial Practice*. Thousand Oaks, CA: Sage Publications, 1998.

Levine, Daniel S., *Disgruntled: The Darker Side of the World of Work*. New York: Berkley Boulevard, 1998.

Maslach, Christina, and Michael P. Leiter, *The Truth about Burnout*. San Francisco, CA: Jossey-Bass, 1997.

Useful websites:

www.stressbusting.co.uk
Resource page on stress reduction techniques.

http://www.teamchrysalis.com/What%20Stress%20Costs.pdf
Team Chrysalis's report on what stress costs business.

www.workhealth.org
The Job Stress Network resource page.

The following debates in the Pro/Con series may also be of interest:

In this volume:

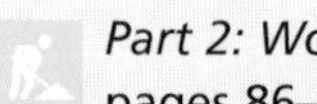

Part 2: Work culture, pages 86–87

Topic 12 Is there a culture of overwork in the United States?

Topic 13 Do labor unions have too much power in the United States?

IS STRESS TAKEN SERIOUSLY ENOUGH AS A HEALTH ISSUE IN THE WORKPLACE?

IS STRESS TAKEN SERIOUSLY ENOUGH AS A HEALTH ISSUE IN THE WORKPLACE? KEY POINTS

COMPANY POLICY
Do firms do enough to alleviate stress?

YES: New measures, such as massage and counseling, are being introduced all the time

NO: Firms act only when they have no alternative source of labor; they are concerned about stress only when there is low unemployment

CAUSE AND EFFECT
Is the link between work and stress too weak to be convincing?

YES: People may be stressed by their private lives, and that can carry over into their jobs; the work itself, however, does not give them their condition

NO: Increasing numbers of studies are being conducted into this problem. Figures show that large numbers of workers are taking time off due to work-related stresses.

NOT JUST AN EMPLOYER PROBLEM
Are employees ignoring the problem of stress?

YES: In many working environments any admission of stress is taken as a sign of weakness or failure; some people boast about how hard they work

NO: Increasingly workers' organizations are fighting to make sure that employers make work environments as stress-free as possible

THE WAY FORWARD
Does legislation adequately protect against stress-related problems?

YES: Worker legislation is very extensive, and health and safety are a big issue. Legislation already adequately protects employees should they need it.

NO: Stress is a difficult condition to prove under law. Governments have to do more to study the condition, its causes, and its effects, and also to make sure that the law protects those who suffer from it.

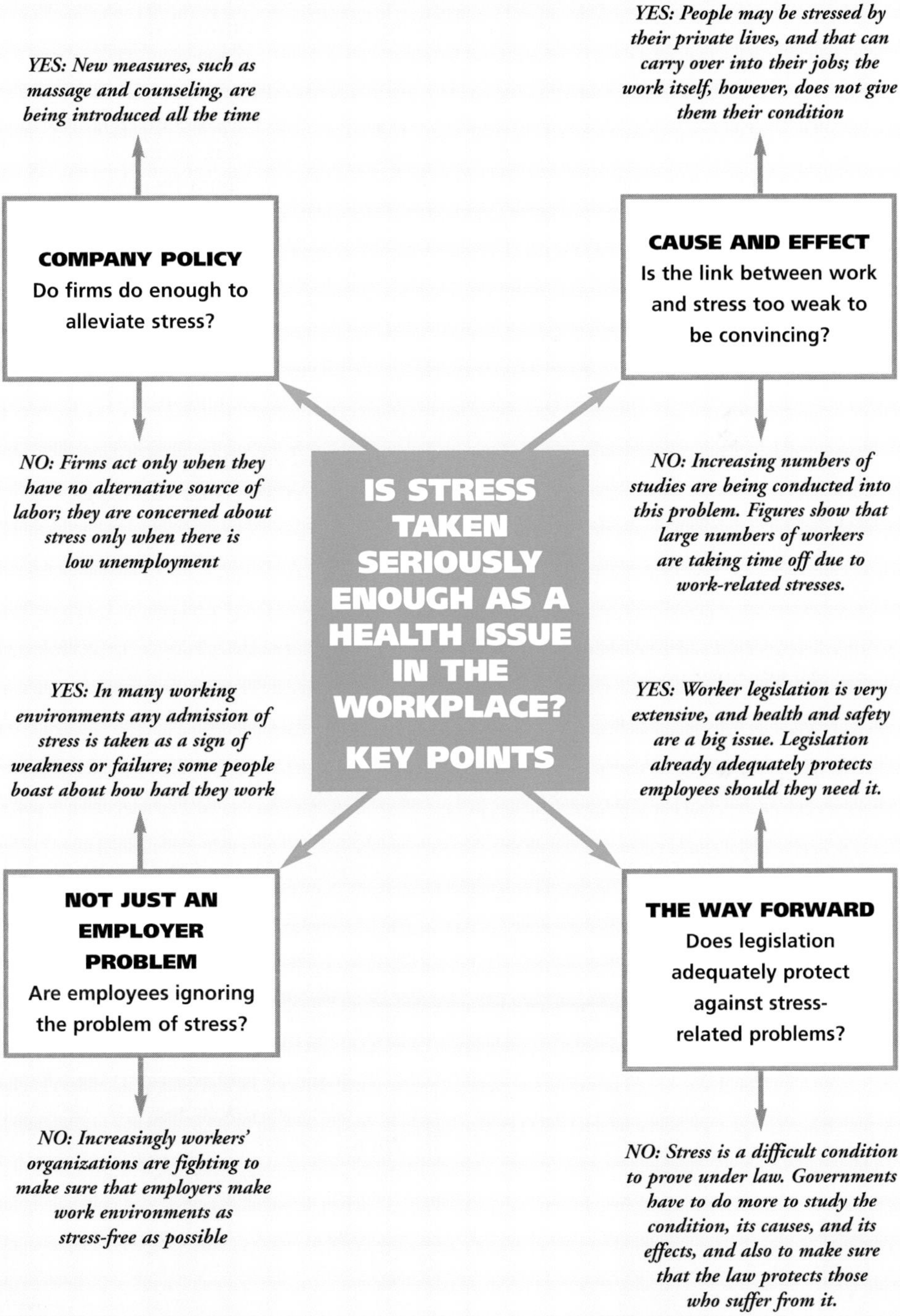

Topic 8
IS NEPOTISM IN THE WORKPLACE WRONG?

YES

"GOOD TIMING"

PHILADELPHIA CITYPAPER.NET, JANUARY 10–17, 2002

JENN CARBIN

NO

FROM "IN PRAISE OF NEPOTISM: AN INTERVIEW WITH AUTHOR ADAM BELLOW"

HTTP://WWW.FAMILY-BUSINESS-EXPERTS.COM/NEPOTISM.HTML

FAMILY BUSINESS EXPERTS

INTRODUCTION

In 2001 journalist Helen Thomas wrote an article highlighting the "staggering" number of relatives of officials who had gained employment in the administration of President George W. Bush. "It's as if other applicants were found unqualified simply because they ... didn't have the right family connection," she claimed. Some people say that Thomas's concern about nepotism—favoritism shown toward relatives in the appointment of a job—in politics applies equally to other sections of society. However, while critics view nepotism as an unjust and immoral practice, some observers believe that it is a fact of life, and that there is nothing inherently wrong with it. They point out that many economies were founded on small, family-run companies, and even in business today, they say, nepotism is to be expected.

The word "nepotism" derives from the Latin *nepos*, meaning nephew. "Nepotismo" was a pejorative term used during the Renaissance to refer to the papal practice of appointing relatives—often illegitimate sons ("nephews")—to church positions. The use of public office to grant favors to relatives or to advance their careers remains a widely condemned form of nepotism today. In order to prevent corruption, most state governments enforce antinepotism laws that prohibit officials from appointing relatives to governmental positions.

Some commentators point out, however, that nepotism in public life can be a moral gray area. For example, Robert Kennedy owed his position as attorney general to his brother, President John F. Kennedy (1961–1963). The controversial appointment led to restrictions on the employment of relatives of public officials in federal government, yet Robert Kennedy is widely thought to have performed his job well. Critics might argue that Senator Edward Kennedy and President

George W. Bush owe their political positions to their family names, but both were nonetheless elected through a democratic mandate.

Observers claim that nepotism in business similarly poses moral issues. A 2003 survey by the Raymond Institute for Family Businesses estimated that there are more than 24 million family-run businesses in the United States. For people who have founded and built up their own company, passing ownership to their son or daughter at retirement or death is not nepotism; it is a matter of continuing a family tradition, or at the very least, simply the inheritance of property.

Less clear-cut, however, are the ethics of giving a close relative a position of employment or executive control in a company. While some might consider it laudable to give a relative an entry-level position from which he or she can advance on merit, many say that it is hard to justify either the promotion of a relative above a more qualified candidate or the appointment of a family member to a senior position.

> *"Nepotism is one of those practices that people love to hate."*
>
> —ADAM BELLOW, *THE WALL STREET JOURNAL* (2003)

Aside from ethical questions, critics say that there are other reasons why nepotism should be discouraged in the workplace. One argument is that people often react emotionally toward their relatives, and resulting tensions can affect morale within a company. Some companies have antinepotism policies prohibiting relatives, including spouses, from working together. Other staff may feel that they cannot act or speak freely in the office for fear of any criticism being repeated to the management by relatives. Critics also point out that nepotism can lead to talented people leaving a company if they believe they are being overlooked for promotion.

Some commentators argue, however, that nepotism can have a positive effect on a business. For example, in his book *Good to Great* (2001) author Jim Collins found that companies that outperformed their peers in relation to shareholder profit over a number of years were mostly led by CEOs descended from the company founders. Collins argued that such CEOs are more driven to win long-term benefits for their organization than those who have no family ties. Similarly, some observers believe that businesses prefer to hire relatives of existing employees because they tend to be more committed and have a greater desire to prove their worth. Some companies run internship programs for family members of their staff, and in a bid to lower recruitment costs, others offer employees rewards for referring a relative to fill a vacancy.

Observers have also identified a trend toward relatives of famous or successful people following them into careers in areas such as entertainment, sports, and the arts. Often they use their relations' contacts to obtain their first job. Even if they do succeed in the long term, this does not alter the fact that they got their first break through family connections, critics argue.

The following articles examine in more depth the issue of whether nepotism is wrong in the workplace.

GOOD TIMING
Jenn Carbin

Jenn Carbin is a freelance journalist based in Philadelphia. This story was written for the Philadelphia CityPaper *in January 2002.*

YES

The timing seems almost magical: [Philadelphia] Councilman Michael Nutter introduces an anti-nepotism bill on Dec. 20 [2001], and one week before the bill gets a hearing, it comes to light that Mayor Street's wife, Naomi Post, is up for the $130,000-per-year position of deputy managing director for social services. How much did Nutter know?

"It had nothing to do with that," Nutter maintains of his amendment. "Generally, just like other people, I was surprised."

In Philadelphia the city controller is responsible for auditing the city's financial dealings. Saidel has filled the post since 1989, winning a fourth term in 2001.

Nutter says it was in fact the recent travails of City Controller Jonathan Saidel and his "conflict-of-interest problems" that led to Nutter's introducing the legislation. Since 1995, Saidel has been paid a total of $515,000 by two law firms that won (or sought) legal work for the city. Nutter, after reading a newspaper account of that story, was looking at case law and ordinances as they would relate to such a situation when he came across a certain chapter of the city code called "Standards of Conduct and Ethics," which deals with "personnel action" and conflict of interest. In his pile of research also lay a court opinion from the late '80s that states that the same Philadelphia code is "not as clear as it could be" regarding the who and what of hiring relatives.

Making the law consistent

Struck by the fact that the lack of clarity was "unresolved and no change had been made since the court opinion," he says he decided to make the city code "consistent with the federal statute on the same issue.... I thought I'd be able to craft a piece of legislation ... that was clearer if not more definitive.

See http://www.seventy.org/resources/Philadelphia-Home-Rule-Charter.pdf for Philadelphia's City Charter (1951). Article X states: "No councilman shall ... benefit by ... any contract ... for the supplying of any services to be paid for out of the City Treasury."

"Some people seem to be confused, or confused on purpose, over the language of the code or the spirit of the law."

The current code defines relatives as "Immediate Family. A spouse residing in the individual's household and minor dependent children." Nutter's version uses the word "relative" and includes spouses, parents, children, siblings, aunts, uncles, nephews, nieces, in-laws, step-relatives, and life partners,

Kate Hudson is one of a generation of Hollywood stars who have famous parents. Some people argue Hudson would not have done so well as an actor if she had not been Goldie Hawn's daughter.

COMMENTARY: Nepotism and U.S. politics

Nepotism in politics has received a lot of attention in recent years. During the 2000 presidential election campaign much was made of the fact that both candidates came from political dynasties: Al Gore was the son of Senator Albert Gore of Tennessee; George W. Bush was the son of former President George H.W. Bush (1989–1993). Jim Hightower, formerly Texas commissioner of agriculture, once suggested the senior Bush was "a man who was born on third base and thinks he hit a triple"—a description some people thought more fitting for his son, who had never quite matched his father's achievements. After George W. Bush became president in 2001, critics argued that his administration fast became a family affair.

Dana Milbank wrote in *The Washington Post* that "in the Bush administration governing is a family matter.... [B]loodlines begin at the top and flow through the rank and file." Milbank was commenting on the administration's apparent habit of giving out government appointments to relatives of leading Republicans. Among those benefitting from this practice were: Michael Powell, the son of Secretary of State Colin Powell, who became chairman of the Federal Communications Commission; Elizabeth Cheney, daughter of Vice President Dick Cheney, became a deputy assistant secretary of state, while her husband became the chief counsel for the Office of Management and Budget; Elaine L. Chao, wife of Senator Mitch McConnell (R–Ky), became secretary of labor, and her chief labor attorney was Eugene Scalia, son of Supreme Court Justice Antonin Scalia.

Although there are restrictions on the employment of relatives of public officials in the federal government, there was nothing illegal about these appointments. All members of a presidential administration except the president and vice president are appointed, not elected. In a parliamentary system such as in Canada or the United Kingdom, by contrast, every member of the cabinet is a member of parliament with his or her own democratic mandate from the voters.

Has anything really changed?

Many people believe the trend toward nepotism in U.S. politics is not new. During the Civil War, for example, the federal payroll included at least one family member of each of President Abraham Lincoln's cabinet. Some observers even argue that voters actually prefer political dynasties such as the Kennedys and the Bushes because they believe that family members provide a sense of continuity and can be trusted to follow through on policies that their relatives have promoted. On the other hand, Andrew Sullivan commented in *The New Republic* that George W. Bush, as the son of a former president, should have been more circumspect in appearing to "foster a culture of nepotism." He said, "All this nepotism is a worrisome sign that America's political class is becoming increasingly insular."

among others. His law prohibits not only hiring but recommending relatives for positions.

Nutter disagrees with the idea that anti-nepotism laws discriminate against qualified relatives of public officials such as Naomi Post. And there should be no conflict for the mayor in understanding his role, he explains: "There are certain privileges and certain responsibilities with being in public office. Along with the privileges, such as getting good tables in restaurants, come certain things you can't do.... If you're going to take the perks, you have to take the responsibilities."

Do you agree that relatives of public servants should be ruled out of the running for public jobs on principle, no matter how well qualified they are? Does the importance of guarding against corruption outweigh the infringement of individual freedom?

Nutter wants to make it clear this isn't personal. "I have the utmost respect for Mrs. Street, for her work ethic and for her work," he says. "She is very accomplished and has clearly made her own mark as an individual on this city.... And it is very uncomfortable for me to engage in conversation about some job prospect [involving her]. This [proposal] is across the board; it's not targeted at anyone, it's not about who has what qualifications.... Government officials should not hire family members."

Councilman Jim Kenney would agree. "Regardless of the qualifications," Kenney says, "I don't think public officials should have the ability to unilaterally appoint relatives to high-paying government positions. It gives the public the impression that you need political connections to succeed in this government."

In some situations people who have a connection with a candidate leave the room when that person is being interviewed or discussed, or they remove themselves from the selection process altogether. Could that approach be used in cases such as that of Naomi Post, or would problems still remain?

Mayor must be involved

Nutter says though he didn't plan this around the seemingly imminent Naomi Post appointment, he's not disappointed with the timing. "I think that if this issue hadn't come up now, there wouldn't have been the kind of discussion [that's happening regarding the bill]. It was an important public issue on Dec. 20 when I introduced it, now it's even more crystal clear."

Meanwhile, Mayor Street's been characteristically mum on the issue. Luz Cardenas, his spokesperson, says, "[City Managing Director] Estelle Richman has said she will make appointments this week; maybe this will be one of them. We will find out then.... These are her appointments."

Kenney isn't buying it. "I think the mayor's attempt to say he has nothing to do with the hiring is extremely transparent and weak," he says. "The [City] Charter says that the mayor signs off on the appointments of the managing director.... I don't think the city needs this controversy. I think he should stop pursuing it."

On January 16, 2002, a few days after this article was written, Naomi Post withdrew her candidacy for the position. Post, president of the child advocacy organization Philadelphia Safe and Sound, said it was "painful and unacceptable to have the public think I am receiving something I do not deserve."

IN PRAISE OF NEPOTISM: AN INTERVIEW WITH AUTHOR ADAM BELLOW
Family Business Experts

NO

Adam Bellow (1957–) is the son of the novelist Saul Bellow (1915–). Adam Bellow was educated at Princeton University and works as an editor.

FBE: Tell us what influence your father had on your choice of vocation?

BELLOW: I didn't grow up with my father because my parents divorced when I was two. So he served more as a model than someone who was hands-on and personally involved in my learning to write. He did have a powerful influence on me, and I was clearly drawn in his direction at an early age. He had nothing to do with my getting into publishing, however … at least, not directly. That was more of an accident after I ran out of other options. I was thirty and just married and went to see a friend of my father for advice. He directed me to Erwin Glikes, publisher of The Free Press, who hired me as an editor. Over the course of my career I have not benefited at all as the son of Saul Bellow, even though my entry was definitely facilitated by the connection. I'm a good example of what I refer to in my book as the "new nepotism."

Like Rob Reiner (mentioned below), Bellow seems to be an example of someone who has benefitted from an initial break gained from a connection of his father's. Such connections are common even when the parent is not famous. Given that it does not involve corruption or unearned promotion to a high level, does this deserve to be called nepotism?

FBE: What does that mean?

BELLOW: New nepotism is not the same kind of nepotism that people generally think of. It's not the same as we have defined in years gone by. There are important differences. With the new nepotism, parents no longer pick up the phone and pull strings. Instead, it's the children themselves who decide this on their own and they find their own way to exploit those connections.

Rob Reiner is a good example. He's one of the most respected and talented people in Hollywood. But his father Carl was famous before him and Rob grew up in that milieu. His father's friends were Mel Brooks and Norman Lear, who would come to the Reiner house for dinner. So Rob grew up in this world and it was clear that he wanted to be like his dad, but his father never lifted a finger to help him. He didn't have to. Rob was cast by Lear in *All in the Family* and has gone on to great success. Nobody uses the term nepotism for

In this case the writer and producer Norman Lear was hiring someone he already knew socially. Do you think it is more acceptable for an appointee to be a friend rather than a relative?

Carl Reiner (1922–) has had a long and successful career as a movie director, writer, actor, and producer. His friends in Hollywood helped give his son Rob Reiner his start in the industry.

Rob. But you do hear that when people talk about Tori Spelling, daughter of Aaron Spelling. She wasn't a very good actor and never achieved much after she was cast in her first role.

Tori Spelling (1973–) was cast in the TV series Beverley Hills 90210 *but has not found success in feature films. Is it fair to say we only consider it nepotism if the result is judged a failure and ignore it if it is a success?*

On the other hand, Sofia Coppola was cast by her father and therefore tarred with this (nepotism) brush, but to her credit she became serious as a director. She eventually put out some modest and well-crafted movies and received praise from the critics. Now she has a movie that's wildly praised and won an Oscar for best screenplay. So she wiped out the

Sofia Coppola, daughter of director Francis Ford Coppola, wrote and directed Lost in Translation *(2003), starring Bill Murray and Scarlett Johansson. She won an Academy Award for Best Screenplay. See pages 112–113.*

stain on her past in the only way possible, by buckling down and putting herself through an exhaustive apprenticeship. Of course, when she accepted her Award the first thing she did was thank her father, who is a wonderful teacher. The Coppola's operate on the old system, and they really are like the Corleone family. But they are also very talented.

FBE: Your book received a few harsh criticisms, probably because you "praise" nepotism even though you're the son of a famous author.

In Praise of Nepotism *(2003) was Bellow's first book as an author. As an editor he worked on Dinesh D'Souza's* Illiberal Education *(1992) and David Brock's* The Real Anita Hill *(1993), which its author later disowned.*

BELLOW: I've been a professional book editor for almost 20 years, and as it happens I've published a number of controversial books that cut against the grain of majority opinion and sentiment. I got a reputation in the 90's for doing this, so I've had an opportunity to observe how challenging ideas are received. My book is radical in the strict sense of looking at a phenomenon from the roots. Most people don't examine the roots of their own ideas and float along on the surface of popular opinion. When you challenge people to rethink their basic assumptions, it's literally painful and people react defensively. I've seen this before but never experienced it directly....

FBE: It seems you may have hit a nerve with some of your readers.

What do you think Bellow means by describing nepotism as a "fault-line issue"?

Bellow sees nepotism as almost any kind of help from family or relatives. Do you agree, or is it something more specific?

BELLOW: Nepotism is a fault-line issue, especially in America where our practices are at variance with our principles. That's why we want it left alone. People don't want to acknowledge how much nepotism plays a role in their own lives. We want to think of ourselves as self-made men and women. People in other parts of the world don't understand that. They ask why Americans put parents in old folks homes and children move thousands of miles away and allow our families to fall apart.

FBE: How does that relate to your concept of new nepotism?

BELLOW: What we're experiencing is a swing of the pendulum away from radical individualism and back to the family. For the last several decades we've focused on the entrepreneur as the ideal businessman. He's a Lone Ranger figure, with maybe a loyal Tonto at his side, but certainly no relatives. He hacks out a homestead, fights off the Indians. He's independent in the image of John Wayne. That's the ideal, but it's not really the American way, which is in actuality the family business tradition. You see it in the Westerns, where so many of the ranchers were Irish immigrants and very family oriented....

FBE: How did nepotism earn its bad name?

BELLOW: The old nepotism was discredited by the Crash of '29 and the Depression. People began to feel that the American business elite was too nepotistic, they had gotten rich and given out partnerships to sons and sons in law, they allowed family interests to outweigh business rationale. It was the subtext of the Depression, and it had a powerful and lasting effect on our view of nepotism and family management in general. After World War II, American business went global. There was a boom in the economy, and a new era of corporate management and governance was introduced. Along with that came efficiency, meritocracy, etc. It was the era in which [anti-]nepotism rules were instituted in big corporations and government. And that was a good thing. It's not my purpose to say that nepotism should be left alone, because what you get then is what you see in Nigeria, India and Brazil....

"Meritocracy" refers to a system in which the most talented people are chosen and promoted on the basis of their achievement.

FBE: ... You say the children are returning to their family business roots.

BELLOW: There is a swing back the other way. People don't want to work in the corporate environment. They want to be part of a family enterprise and build something to leave for their children. The family business is perhaps the only way to leave something for your heirs and the best reason to stick around instead of moving to LA.

Do you agree that people want to be "part of a family enterprise"? Where does this leave competent and ambitious workers who are not related to the owners of the companies they work for?

FBE: So how are the new nepotistic heirs faring? At FBE, we deal with inner-family struggles that affect the business side.

BELLOW: There's nothing wrong with sibling rivalry. It may give people some comfort to see family dynamics as disruptive, and many think that they force the business to be counterproductive. But the opposite is true. History shows that these are powerful forces and they often supply the motivation and drive that gets people to strive for excellence and give that last ounce. If George W. Bush feels he has to finish his father's work in Iraq and prove that he's the legitimate heir, so much the better for the U.S.

Some people believe that President George H.W. Bush should have ousted the Iraqi dictator, Saddam Hussein, from power in 1991 when a U.S.-led coalition force drove Iraqi occupying forces out of Kuwait. In 2003 critics accused President George W. Bush of trying to finish off his father's job when a U.S.-led coalition force invaded Iraq.

Summary

Nepotism in the workplace has received a lot of attention in recent years. In the first article journalist Jenn Carbin looks at this issue with regard to politics. She focuses on the case of Philadelphia Councilman Michael Nutter, who tried to introduce an antinepotism bill just before the wife of the mayor was due to be interviewed for a job in social services. Nutter said the timing was coincidental and that his bill was prompted by the lack of clarity in the existing Philadelphia code of ethics on the hiring of relatives. Carbin reports Nutter's argument that public officers should accept the responsibilities of public office as well as the perks, and this includes not being able to hire family members. Carbin also cites another councilman, Jim Kenney, who criticized the mayor for remaining silent on the controversy.

The second extract is from an interview with Adam Bellow, son of writer Saul Bellow and author of a book called *In Praise of Nepotism*. Bellow states that his father did not actively help him in his work but that he was able to use his father's contacts simply through being exposed to them when he was growing up. He claims this is an example of what he calls "new nepotism." Bellow says, "With the new nepotism, parents no longer pick up the phone and pull strings. Instead, it's the children themselves who decide this on their own and they find their own way to exploit those connections." He believes that this is a healthy development because it acknowledges the role that families, and the connections they bring, play in building up businesses and passing wealth on from one generation to the next. He cites some examples of people who have used this "new nepotism" to succeed, including Rob Reiner, son of the director Carl Reiner.

FURTHER INFORMATION:

Books:

Bellow, Adam, *In Praise of Nepotism: A Natural History.* New York: Doubleday, 2003.

Collins, Jim, *Good to Great: Why Some Companies Make the Leap and Others Don't.* New York: HarperBusiness, 2001.

Hatfield, J.H., *Fortunate Son: George W. Bush and the Making of an American President.* New York: Soft Skull Press, 2001.

Useful websites:

http://www.afrboss.com.au/magarticle.asp?doc_id=23261&listed_months=1
Article on the "new nepotism" in Australia.

http://www.oag.state.tx.us/AG_Publications/pdfs/98traps.pdf
State manual on avoiding nepotism in public office.

http://prorev.com/family.htm
A listing of family connections in U.S. politics.

The following debates in the Pro/Con series may also be of interest:

In this volume:

Part 2: Work culture, pages 86–87

Sofia Coppola: A case of successful nepotism?, pages 112–113

IS NEPOTISM IN THE WORKPLACE WRONG?

IS NEPOTISM IN THE WORKPLACE WRONG? KEY POINTS

PEJORATIVE TERM
Is nepotism a pejorative term?

YES: Nepotism implies favoritism and unfair awards to people who have done nothing to deserve them

NO: Nepotism is sometimes used to describe the handing down of a family business from one generation to the next. In this sense the term is associated with tradition and continuity.

BAD PRACTICE
Is nepotism inherently bad practice?

YES: Nepotism undermines meritocracy, a system in which the best possible candidate gets the job

NO: Relatives are often more committed to achieving success for a company than those with no family connections

BUSINESS SENSE
Does nepotism make bad business sense?

YES: Nepotism promotes people because of their relationship to other people, not their worth. People appointed in this way are often unqualified to do their job properly.

NO: Family-run businesses have traditionally helped economies flourish. Many successful companies today are still family based.

WORKING RELATIONSHIPS
Does nepotism lead to difficult working relationships?

YES: People appointed or promoted through nepotism are resented by their peers. Tensions can also arise between relatives working together.

NO: People appointed through nepotism usually go out of their way to prove their worth to other colleagues

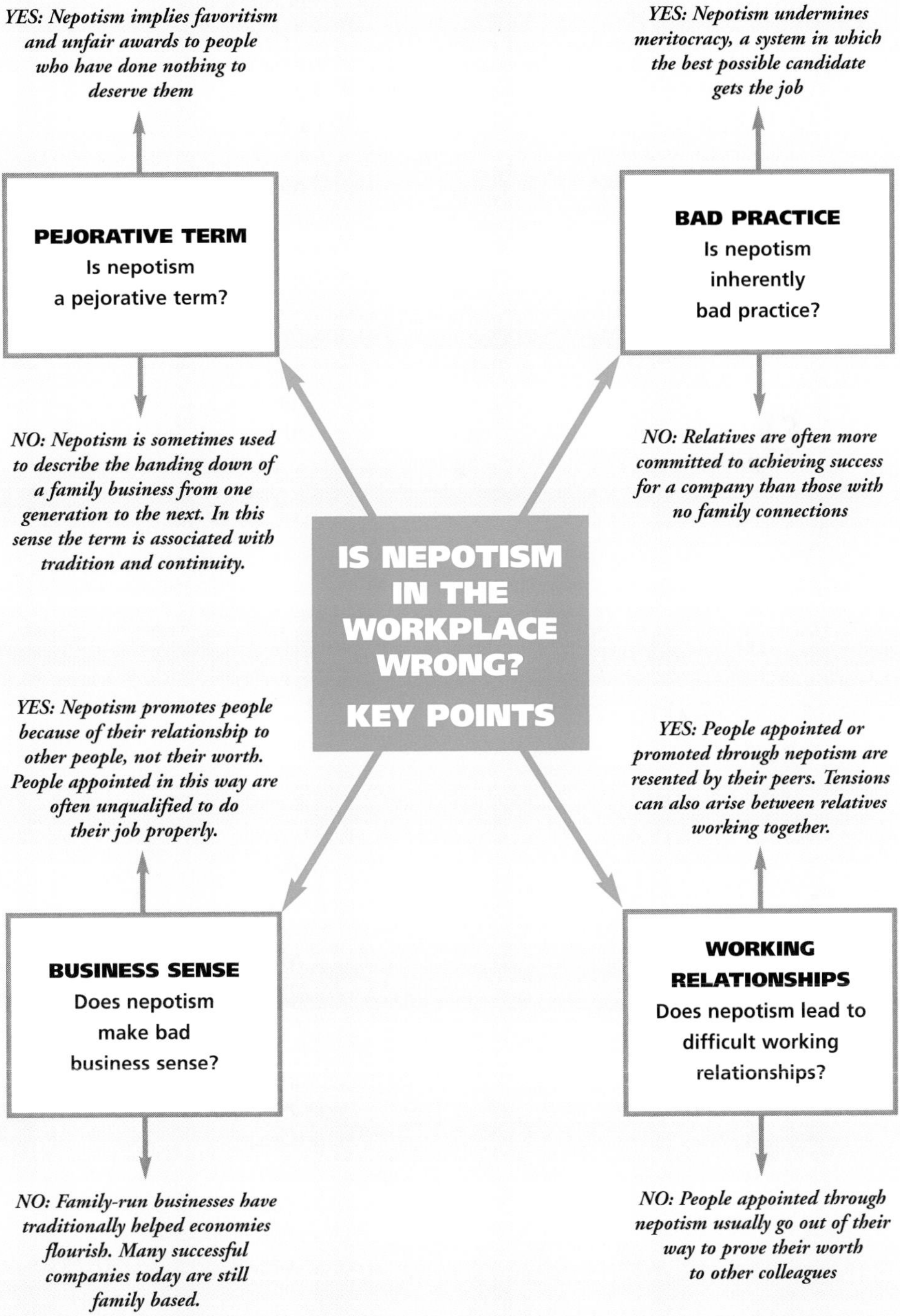

SOFIA COPPOLA: A CASE OF SUCCESSFUL NEPOTISM?

"Is it nepotism? Sure, I'll call it and say it's nepotism; no matter how talented Coppola is (and make no mistake she's very talented), she'd never get the chance to make this film if not for her revered pop. But does it matter?"

—JOSH BELL, *LAS VEGAS WEEKLY* (2003)

Sofia Coppola is the daughter of the acclaimed film director Francis Ford Coppola. One of a generation of children of famous people who have been criticized for trading on their family name, Coppola was once severely ridiculed by critics for her stilted performance in *The Godfather III* (1990), the final movie in her father's critically acclaimed trilogy. Coppola was written off by many critics as yet another example of nepotism gone wrong—until, that is, she was nominated for the best director Academy Award for her film *Lost in Translation* (2003). Although she did not win the award, she did win the Oscar for best original screenplay for the film, leading her supporters to claim that she had had the last laugh.

A career in nepotism?

Sofia Carmina Coppola was born in 1971 and spent her childhood on and around her father's film sets. Francis Ford Coppola is renowned for giving his family and friends jobs in his movies, and Coppola received her first screen role when she was just a few weeks old, appearing as the baby boy in the climax of *The Godfather* (1972); the film also featured her aunt, Talia Shire, and her late brother, Gian-Carlo. She played a small child in *The Godfather II* (1974) and took roles in Francis Ford Coppola's *Rumble Fish* (1983), *The Outsiders* (1983), *The Cotton Club* (1984), and *Peggy Sue Got Married* (1986)—the latter also starred Coppola's cousin Nicolas Cage. While Francis Ford Coppola's habit of employing his relatives in his films has always provoked some comment, many critics believe that he went too far when he cast his daughter as Mary Corleone in *The Godfather III.*

The Godfather III: The kiss of death or a new lease of life?

The actress Winona Ryder had originally been cast to play the central role of Mary, the daughter of Michael Corleone (Al Pacino), in the long-awaited final part of *The Godfather* trilogy. Ryder was a well-known and popular actress, and the role was a significant one. When Ryder had to step down from the movie because of fatigue, there were many young actresses who would have been only too happy to step into her shoes. Instead, Francis Ford Coppola gave the role to his daughter. Unfortunately, while fitting the role physically, Coppola lacked both the training and the talent to carry the role off. Her wooden performance, California accent, and general lack of spark prompted one of the most vicious criticisms of a movie performance in film history. Francis Ford Coppola was also vilified for his blatant use of nepotism. Some commentators, however, argue that few actresses could have carried off the role, cast against such movie heavyweights as Al Pacino and Diane Keaton. The film also had a lot to live up to: Both *The Godfather I* and *II* were film legends. Others believe that her father did Coppola a favor—as a result of the criticism she received, Coppola focused her talents in other directions.

Nepotism for success

Coppola set up Milk Fed, a line of designer clothing, and hosted a tongue-in-cheek lifestyle and celebrity focus television show called *Hi-Octane*. She was very well connected and was a regular face in fashion and gossip columns as a noted figure in the New York and Los Angeles club scenes. She appeared in music videos, including Madonna's "Deeper and Deeper" and the Chemical Brothers' "Elektrobank." The latter was directed by Coppola's then boyfriend, Spike Jonze, whom she later married. Although now estranged, Jonze and Coppola were once viewed as one of the most talented young couples in Hollywood.

While Jonze achieved considerable fame as director of the 1999 cult movie *Being John Malkovich*, Coppola made her name for directing and writing the screenplay for the critically acclaimed film *The Virgin Suicides* (2000). Some observers argued that she had yet again traded on her connections: Her father was a producer of the film, and her brother Roman also worked as second unit director. Actress Kathleen Turner, who played the mother in the movie, had also played the main role and Coppola's older sister in Francis Ford Coppola's *Peggy Sue Got Married*. Actor James Woods, however, who played the father in the film, challenged the critics: "Now the joke is going to be on everyone else.... So all the naysayers, who slammed her when she was a teenager because her father put her in a movie, will finally get to shut up."

For many, Coppola really did astound her critics with her next critically acclaimed film, *Lost in Translation*. Focusing on the relationship between a has-been film actor (Bill Murray) and an emotionally lost young woman (Scarlett Johansson) in Tokyo, the film was nominated for several international awards. Even then rumors abounded that Francis Ford Coppola had spent two weeks helping his daughter out by working alone on the film in the editing room. Others believe that such stories are just sour grapes: Many people simply do not want Sofia Coppola to be the successful, talented filmmaker that she appears to be, preferring instead to believe that she has traded on the success of her father and her family. Others claim that even if Coppola got her break through her father, she has more than proved her worth. Like Norah Jones, daughter of sitar virtuoso Ravi Shankar, Sean Lennon, son of singer and songwriter legend John Lennon, and actor Kate Hudson, daughter of actor Goldie Hawn, Sofia Coppola has shown once and for all, her supporters assert, that nepotism is not such a bad thing.

Topic 9
DO WOMEN MAKE BETTER MANAGERS THAN MEN?

YES
"WHY WOMEN MAKE BETTER MANAGERS"
MARKETING INTELLIGENCE, WWW.BCENTRAL.COM
JOANNA L. KROTZ

NO
"MY BOSS, THE BITCH"
THE AGE, FEBRUARY 26, 2004
MICHELLE HAMER

INTRODUCTION

A 2002 Gallup poll indicated that while an unprecedented number of women are becoming managers, most American workers, irrespective of gender, preferred to be managed by a man rather than by a woman. Some observers believe that this attitude reflects the fact that workers are simply not used to having a female boss. As more women move into management roles, they say, there will be greater acceptance of female managers. Moreover, they insist that men and women are equally likely to make good bosses. Other people argue, however, that such surveys prove that genuine differences in skills and traits exist between the sexes when it comes to managing staff.

According to the Labor Department, more than 21 million women worked in managerial and professional occupations in 2002, compared to 14.7 million in 1992. In 2003 Catalyst, a nonprofit organization that works to advance women in business, reported that women held about 16 percent of corporate officer positions in the 500 largest U.S. companies, up from 9 percent in 1995.

While many people praise the steady progress that women are making, others claim that most female managers tend to specialize in certain areas, such as personnel management, which are unlikely to lead to the most senior management positions. A 1997 report "Breaking through the Glass Ceiling," published by the International Labour Organization, concluded that females worldwide were still largely barred from top levels of management. It revealed that although women constituted almost half the managerial workforce in the United States, they held less than 3 percent of the highest management jobs. In 2004 *Fortune* magazine also stated that only eight of the nation's 500 largest companies had female chief executives.

Many people maintain that attitudinal and organizational prejudices remain the biggest obstacle to women reaching top management positions. Given the opportunity, they say, women prove to be as good, if not better, than men. As evidence they cite the results of studies that have analyzed the skills of men and women in similar managerial posts. A 1998 evaluation of midlevel managers by the Management Research Group in Maine, for example, found that men and women tended to approach their jobs in different ways but were judged equally competent leaders by their own bosses. A study of senior managers by the California-based Hagberg Consulting Group in 2000 suggested that women managers actually rated far higher than their male counterparts in a majority of management skills such as mentoring employees and setting goals.

"Women in key leadership positions become a magnet for talented women and men."

—SHEILA WELLINGTON, PRESIDENT, CATALYST (2003)

However, some commentators regard the lack of women in senior jobs as an indication that women lack the qualities often associated with successful managers: Decisiveness, assertiveness, competitiveness, and the ability to take risks, for example, are all qualities that are traditionally considered to be male. In contrast, other qualities, such as empathy and creativity, are seen as inherently female. Some observers suggest that women should consciously imitate the "male" management style and abandon their "natural" traits in order to succeed as good managers.

While other people agree that women may have different emotional and intellectual qualities than men, they feel these traits actually make women better managers. They point out that today the business environment is built on communication and trust rather than on authoritarian principles. Women are more suited to modern management techniques, observers argue, because they tend to be good communicators who listen well, encourage openness, and act with diplomacy.

Some critics believe, however, that it is patronizing to both sexes to make assumptions about gender-specific skills and character strengths. A 1999 study of women's workplace advancement at Harvard University found that most women managers questioned thought there was no predominant "female" style of leadership. Researchers at Stanford Graduate School of Business are among those who say that praising "female" management traits can actually be discriminatory. They contend that a woman manager who feels she should be good at nurturing her staff is being forced to conform to a stereotype. Other people suggest that if a woman manager defies preconceptions and acts assertively, for example, she is often perceived as being too aggressive by both male and female colleagues. They argue that a male manager behaving in a similar way would not attract criticism and might even be admired. Ultimately, critics say, people's opinions of who makes a good manager should be determined not by gender stereotypes but by competence alone.

The two articles that follow address this debate in greater depth.

WHY WOMEN MAKE BETTER MANAGERS

Joanna L. Krotz

Joanna L. Krotz is a business writer and journalist. She is also president of Muse2Muse Productions, a New York communications company.

YES

Before getting to the point of this provocative headline, here's a disclaimer: Prepare to consider widely accepted generalizations.

Translated, that means, "Included in this article are some sweeping statements presented as general truths but based on limited or incomplete evidence."

Let me add this: Remember, too, that being equal does not mean being the same. Now, let's proceed.

Figures from the Census Bureau indicate that in 1997, 26 percent of nonfarm businesses were owned by women. Go to http://www.dol.gov/wb/factsheets/wbo02.htm for details.

As women gained traction in the workforce, gender differences among senior and junior staffers turned up in every workplace, from offices to factory floors to fighter planes. Now that women are pulling up chairs at boardroom tables and launching their own companies—the number of women-owned firms has increased by 103% in the past 10 years—those differences are increasingly playing out in executive suites, too.

Studies show that both male and female styles of leadership can be effective. But when compared side by side, "female" has the edge.

Biology and upbringing

Gender differences stem from nurture and nature alike. It's not only socialization that shapes men and women. It's also biology.

The part of the brain that controls rational functions, the cerebral cortex, has two halves, or hemispheres. The theory is that the left hemisphere is verbal and analytical, and the right hemisphere is visual and intuitive.

Researchers are discovering physiological variations in the brains of men and women. For example, male brains are about 10% larger than female brains. But women have more nerve cells in certain areas. Women also tend to have a larger corpus collusum—the group of nerve fibers that connects left and right hemispheres. That makes women faster at transferring data between the computational, verbal left half and the intuitive, visual right half. Men are usually left-brain oriented.

As girls and boys grow up, of course, they're also molded by differing sets of social rules and expectations. Gender obviously colors behavior, perception and just about everything else.

Gender matters

Typically, when comparing managers, the dialogue is framed as men's command-and-control style versus women's team-building or consensus approach.

"Women managers tend to have more of a desire to build than a desire to win," says Debra Burrell, regional training director of the Mars-Venus Institute in New York. "Women are more willing to explore compromise and to solicit other people's opinions." By contrast, she says, men often think if they ask other people for advice, they'll be perceived as unsure or as a leader who doesn't have answers.

The Mars-Venus Institute was set up to teach workshops based on the writings of John Gray, author of Men Are from Mars, Women Are from Venus *(1992), the controversial bestselling book about gender differences.*

Other female leadership strengths:

- Women are better than men at empowering teams and staff.
- Women encourage openness and are more accessible.
- Women leaders respond more quickly to calls for assistance.
- Women are more tolerant of differences, so they're more skilled at managing diversity.
- Women identify problems more quickly and more accurately.
- Women are better at defining job expectations and providing valuable feedback.

Are the author's comments too general? Would her argument be more convincing if she used research and statistics to support the points that she makes?

Men tend to be more speedy decision-makers, compared to women. Male managers are also more adept at forming what management psychologist Ken Siegel calls "navigational relationships," or temporary teams set up to achieve short-term goals.

Women are better communicators

Big deal and surprise, surprise, right? So women typically outperform men at communications and interpersonal skills. You're probably thinking: Those are "soft skills," not the hard tools and analysis demanded to grow a business into consistent profitability.

How do such "female" traits translate into better business management?

In today's lean workplace, when employees have multiple jobs and fleeting loyalty, when technology enables even tiny companies to compete in global marketplaces, the ability to make staff feel charged up, valued and individually recognized is a definite competitive edge.

"Some companies succeed while others don't," says Jeffrey Christian, CEO of Christian & Timbers, a well-known Cleveland search firm. "It's not about production, it's about talent. Whoever has the best team wins."

Do you agree with Christian's assertion that success is influenced more by talent than by production? Is good management about teamwork, or is it about getting results?

Money is not the primary reason talented people stay on the job or jump. Rather, they stay predominantly because

Do you think that workplace relationships are more important than, for example, money or promotion prospects? For what other reasons might a person stay in a particular job?

of relationships. "Women get that," says Christian, whose firm placed Carly Fiorina at Hewlett-Packard, among other high-level hires.

Generally, women delegate more readily and express their appreciation for hard work more often. "Women ask questions, men tend to give answers," says author, consultant and career coach Terri Levine. By communicating company goals more readily and expressing appreciation more often, women tend to be better at making staffers feel valued and rewarded. That translates into cost-effective recruiting and being able to operate with stable, loyal employees—or, as Christian puts it, the best talent.

But no drop off in "hard skills"

Which of these propositions do you think is more likely—that women have always had "male" skills, or that they have acquired them over the years?

Besides generally being credited with better communications and relationship skills, women are lately demonstrating higher levels of traditional "hard" or "male" skills as well. Some investigators suggest that many women workers had such skills all along, but that male bosses either overlooked or misperceived them. Others think that the cumulative years of experience for women are broadening their skills.

One influential study in 1996, conducted by management consultant Advanced Teamware … analyzed a database of 360-degree assessments for more than 6,000 managers. Such assessments include anonymous reviews from a manager's peers, supervisors and subordinates. The study by Michael R. Perrault and Janet K. Irwin looked at a range of managerial behavior, including problem solving, controlling, leading, managing self, managing relationships and communicating.

The results:

- "… Previous studies showed that women excelled in interpersonal skills (right brain), not in intellectual skills (left brain). Our study demonstrates that women are considered better performers in both right- and left-brain skill areas."
- "Women received higher evaluations than men in 28 of the 31 individual behaviors, representing 90% of items."
- "The most problematic factor for women is managing self.… The worst rated of the 31 behaviors is coping with one's own frustrations."

More glass ceilings to break

Every year Fortune *magazine compiles a list of the 500 largest companies in the United States based on the last year's revenue. In 2004 women headed only eight* Fortune 500 *companies. Go to http://www.fortune.com/fortune/500archive for the current list.*

Obviously, there are still very few women running *Fortune* 500 companies and, in the corporate VP ranks, roughly three men to every woman. So if women have the managerial edge, how come you don't see more of them in positions of power?

Here's my speculation: Men are used to running the show and, for the most part, don't reward "female" style management because they see it as weak. Women have had to prove that their way of managing works, over and over again. Then, too, women have only gained the independence and skills to ascend in the latter half of the last century. No doubt, their rise will continue.

Can you think of other reasons why male bosses might not promote women managers?

For owners of small and midsized businesses, being able to keep staffers and stakeholders enthusiastic as you steer the company forward may be the most important factor in building success. "You want to delegate outcomes, not tasks," says Ken Siegel, whose Los Angeles firm, the Impact Group, works with executives to develop leadership. "You must have the ability to let go. Women can do that better than men because their self-esteem is multifaceted," he says. "Men's self-esteem is based on what they do, it's uni-dimensional."

One possible explanation why women's self-esteem may be multifaceted is that traditionally women have had other roles in society in addition to or instead of being wage earners. Do you think this is likely to change as more women climb the corporate ladder?

The upshot for chief executives should be to move over to the "female" side of management, whether you're a thoroughgoing left-brainer or a woman manager who may be trying to manage "male." Turns out, girls do it better.

MY BOSS, THE BITCH
Michelle Hamer

Michelle Hamer is a journalist who writes for the Australian newspaper The Age, *where this article first appeared in February 2004.*

NO

Over four years, Angela Timms's happiness and self-esteem were systematically stripped away. The 57-year-old suffers depression, posttraumatic stress disorder and anxiety and has been under the care of a psychologist for the past two years after enduring workplace bullying.

We've all heard such shocking stories before, but what makes Timms's case unusual is that the abuse was perpetrated by two female bosses who led a group of younger women to erode Timms's self-esteem, hamper her ability to perform her role, to socially isolate and ridicule her and eventually contribute, along with a bullying male boss, to her nervous breakdown.

Studies show that women are the primary targets of both male and female bullies in the workplace. See http://www.workdoctor.com/home/research.html for a roundup of reports on workplace bullying in the United States, Canada, and the United Kingdom.

Bullying in the office

"When I started at the job the girls in the office were bullying this (male co-worker)," Timms says. "There were about six or seven girls. The office was run by a lady who led the bullying against him. I wouldn't be involved in it. They would shout at him, intimidate him and belittle him. I couldn't believe the shouting, it was just awful. I saw him almost crying a few times.

"I said to one girl of about 19, 'Why are you doing this to him, it's upsetting him so much?' and she said 'I enjoy it'." Eventually the bullying was directed toward Timms after she was made a supervisor above the other women.

"They ignored me, wouldn't speak to me. The worst thing was how they isolated me and how they would ignore me if I asked them to do something. I couldn't do my job because of that.

"I went to management, I even emailed the CEO, but nothing was done, and in the end I was the one who had to leave, I just broke down."

Timms said one female boss would question her about taking toilet breaks and made sarcastic remarks to the rest of the office whenever she did take a break.

"The impact (of the bullying) has been just devastating. They take away all your happiness. I just want to be doing my job, bringing home some money and enjoying life, but instead my health is wrecked, I have a WorkCover claim on my record and I've lost my job."

The Victorian WorkCover Authority provides compensation to employees who suffer work-related injury or illness in the Australian state of Victoria.

It's a little-known fact that a woman can be as severe a bully in the workplace as a man, and according to experts, such behaviour among women is increasing.

Evelyn Field's website on bullying at www.bullying.com.au has information about her strategies for dealing with bullies.

Melbourne psychologist Evelyn Field says women bully just as much as men do, "but because more bullies are managers and more managers are male, more bullying is done by men. But you certainly get a lot of bullying from women and sometimes they behave more aggressively than males."

Field, author of *Bullybusting*, a self-help book for children faced with bullying, is also writing a book on workplace bullying. According to information she has gathered from interviews for her new book as well as her own observations (speaking to groups of women), women often feel pressured to adopt male behaviours in the workplace to get ahead.

"Women will copy the patterns and behaviours of males, so that they become really quite aggressive," Field says.

At least half workplace bullies are female

In the United States the Workplace Bullying and Trauma Institute at http://bullyinginstitute.org offers advice and information on workplace bullying. According to the institute, 58 percent of workplace bullying in 2003 was done by women.

Prominent British anti-bullying campaigner Tim Field said that at least half of 3000 bullying reports made to the UK National Workplace Bullying Advice Line involved a female serial bully (who had bullied several co-workers). No such figures exist on the gender of Australian workplace bullies, but local experts estimate Australian figures would reflect Britain's.

In 2001–02, 1148 claims of workplace bullying were reported to the Victorian WorkCover Authority, compared with 1107 in the previous year.

In her recently released book, *Catfight*, which explores female competitiveness, U.S. author Leora Tanenbaum found that "working women are expected to be aggressive and masculine. Worried about being perceived as a mediocre or incompetent worker, many women go out of their way to prove they are not too emotional or passive, and can be more aggressive and demanding than any man."

She points to groundbreaking research undertaken in the '70s, which she says is still relevant today. The researchers—psychologists Graham Staines, Carol Tavris and Toby Epstein Jayaratne—coined the term "Queen Bee" to describe a token woman at a high level in a corporate environment.

Can you think of any female public figures who have the characteristics of a "Queen Bee"?

Based on questionnaire responses from 20,000 women, they found that "the Queen Bee who is successful in a male-dominated field identifies with the male colleagues who are her reference group, rather than with the diffuse concept of women as a class … (she) thereby disassociates herself from the fundamental issues of equality for women, while reassuring her male colleagues that she is not of that militant ilk."

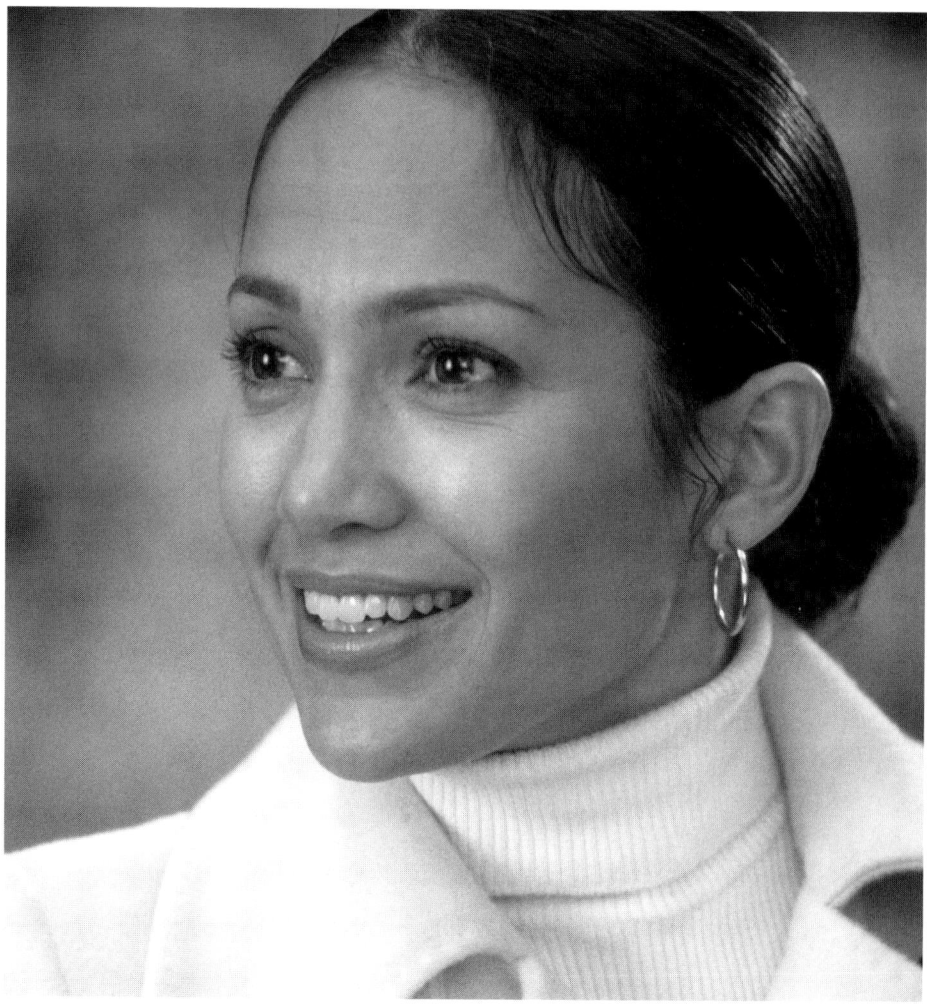

Jennifer Lopez plays a hotel maid with aspirations to move into management in the 2002 movie Maid in Manhattan.

What do you think would be the most common complaints about male supervisors?

Go to www.bullyonline.org for more information about Tim Field's antibully campaign.

Tanenbaum also found that professional women were often hardest on their own sex.

"Many professional women confess they prefer male rather than female supervisors. They complain that women at work refuse to share power, or withhold information, or are too concerned about receiving credit for every little thing they accomplish, or are cold toward underlings (male and female alike). In such complaints they use the word 'bitch' a lot"...

Tim Field believes the stereotypical view of men as aggressive and women as nurturing often prevents the female serial bully from being seen for what she is: "A sociopath in a skirt."

Research shows workplace bullying is also an expensive problem for Australia with the Workplace Bullying Project Team at Griffith University estimating it costs employers between $6 billion to $13 billion annually. This is based on a conservative estimate of 3.5 per cent of workers experiencing bullying.

These figures are in Australian dollars. At 2004 exchange rates these figures were roughly the equivalent of U.S. $4–9 billion.

Evelyn Field says applying the more-accurate estimate of 15 per cent of workers being bullied increases the employer costs to between $17 to $36 billion. (A recent Worksafe survey found that one in seven Victorian workers were bullied in the past six months and almost a quarter knew a colleague who was being bullied.)

WorkSafe is responsible for promoting and improving workplace safety in the Australian state of Victoria.

It's all too familiar to Angela Timms who believes bullying is entrenched in our community, and through the Victims of Workplace Bullying support group which she attends, she has heard more stories of female bullying.

"It seems to be everywhere, in places you wouldn't expect it, and time and again I hear of females doing the bullying."

Subtle techniques of the female bully

Evelyn Field said female bullies were often more subtle in their behaviour than their male counterparts. "Women are usually less physical, they would use techniques such as excluding others, over-supervising and controlling and verbal abuse."

Ricky Nowak, a workplace communications training specialist and head of the company Confident Communications, says women's bullying is "often quieter, behind closed doors, over the phone, via curt emails, or through giving their staff a sense of ... (being overwhelmed), for example: asking women with families to stay behind when they don't really have to do so."

Nowak runs leadership groups for professional women and says she has had many disclosures from women admitting they had bullied their colleagues.

"It was behaviour such as intimidating others, standing over them, giving colleagues the silent treatment and so on."

Some observers suggest that the way in which girls are socialized has a big effect on the way many women bully. Girls are often taught not to express anger verbally, for example, so women may use the silent treatment as a form of bullying. Can you think of some other examples to support this theory?

Evelyn Field describes bullying as a problem for everyone. "The micro level is the individual target who can be affected emotionally, physically, socially, career-wise, financially, family-wise over a long-term basis and many of them have severe health problems," she says.

"The onlookers also get affected—20 per cent of onlookers will leave the job, others will have sick days and suffer poor morale. And the cost to industry is enormous—bullying is everyone's problem."

Summary

Some observers say women make better managers because they have qualities that male managers lack. Detractors say women are hampered by an unwillingness to take risks. Others argue that there are no proven gender-specific differences. The preceding articles consider aspects of the debate.

In the first article Joanna L. Krotz claims that although both male and female management styles can work, women have the edge because they are better communicators with superior interpersonal skills. The ability of female managers to make staff feel valued and recognized gives companies a definite competitive edge, she says. Krotz suggests that women have recently shown they have the "hard" skills more often attributed to men, but it is unclear whether women have always had these skills or whether such skills were overlooked or misinterpreted by male bosses. She speculates that the reason so few women make it to positions of power is that male bosses fail to reward the "female" management style because they see it as weak.

The second article focuses on female bullies at work. Australian journalist Michelle Hamer interviews a female victim of workplace bullying and several experts. She quotes psychologist Evelyn Field, who says women bully just as much as men do. Field believes that some women adopt aggressive male behaviors to get ahead, and U.S. author Leora Tanenbaum says that working women are often expected to be masculine and aggressive. Communications specialist Ricky Novak and Field both claim that female bullies are often more subtle in their bullying behavior, and Field asserts that "the cost to industry is enormous—bullying is everyone's problem."

FURTHER INFORMATION:

Books:

Helgesen, Sally, *Female Advantage: Women's Ways of Leadership*. New York: Doubleday, 1995.

Powell, Gary N., and Graves, Laura M., *Women and Men in Management* (3rd edition). Thousand Oaks, CA: Sage Publications, 2003.

Rosener, Judy B., *America's Competitive Secret: Women Managers*. New York: Oxford University Press, 1997.

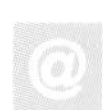

Useful websites:

http://www.businessleader.com/bl/may99/women.html
"Women Managers: The Myth of Male Leadership" by Thomas Walken.

http://www.usatoday.com/careers/news/newsusa2.htm
"Female Managers Get Less Respect" by John Eckberg.

The following debates in the Pro/Con series may also be of interest:

In this volume:

Topic 4 Is workplace sexual harassment legislation adequate?

Topic 10 Should sexual relationships in the workplace be allowed?

In *Individual and Society*:

Topic 3 Are women still the second sex?

DO WOMEN MAKE BETTER MANAGERS THAN MEN?

DO WOMEN MAKE BETTER MANAGERS THAN MEN? KEY POINTS

OPPORTUNITY
Do women have enough management opportunities?

YES: Labor Department statistics indicate an increase in the number of women starting and managing businesses

NO: Male networks and role models mean that men still appoint men at the higher levels of corporate management. Recent statistics show that only a small percentage of top-level managers are women.

TRANSFERABLE SKILLS
Do women bring special skills to management?

YES: Most women are better communicators than men and have superior interpersonal skills. The ability to make staff feel rewarded and valued gives a definite competitive edge.

NO: Women managers are unwilling to be assertive and take risks, and they can become too close to their staff, "nurturing" rather than providing the authority necessary for good management

MOTIVATION
Are women motivated to succeed in management?

YES: Women are no different from men in their ambitions. Traditional obstacles to women's advancement may even have made them more determined to succeed.

NO: Women are unwilling to take risks, which prevents them from succeeding at senior management positions

TEAM-BUILDERS
Are women better at leading people?

YES: Women managers have strong skills in diplomacy, empathy, and communication—all invaluable modern management techniques

NO: Surveys on gender and management have found no conclusive evidence that such skills are defined by gender

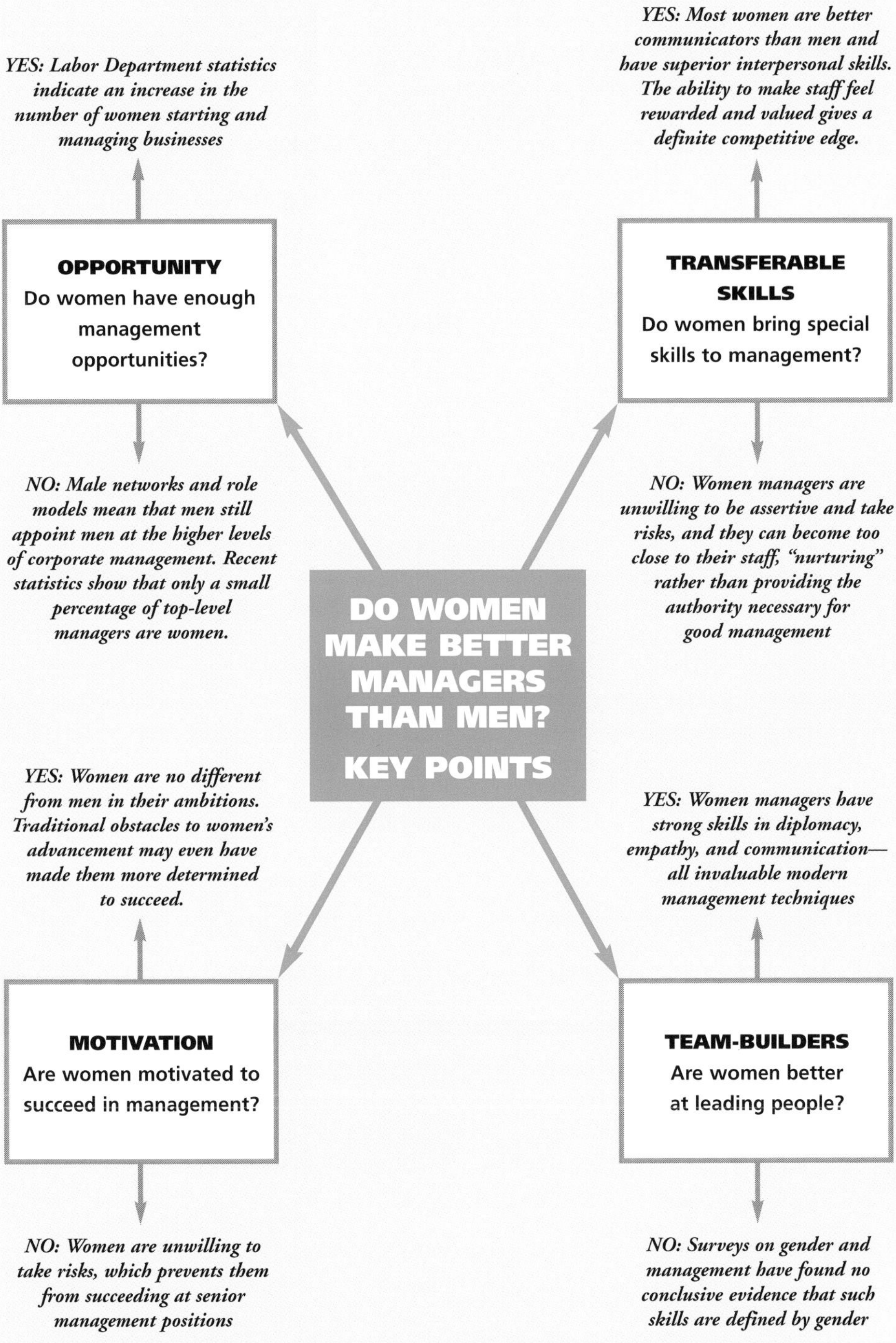

Topic 10
SHOULD SEXUAL RELATIONSHIPS IN THE WORKPLACE BE ALLOWED?

YES

FROM "STRETCHING THE MEANING OF SEXUAL HARASSMENT"
ST. PETERSBURG TIMES, MARCH 8, 1998
ROBYN E. BLUMNER

NO

FROM "DANGEROUS LIAISONS"
FORTUNE SMALL BUSINESS, FEBRUARY 14, 2004
ELLYN SPRAGINS

INTRODUCTION

In 1998 research by the Bureau of National Affairs found that the workplace is now the most likely place for Americans to meet a romantic partner. In fact, it stated that workplace romance is so common that about one-third of all relationships begin at work. However, some people question whether sexual relationships in the workplace should be allowed at all. Mindful of rulings that have established employers' liability in the lawsuits that can arise if romance turns sour, many U.S. companies have strict policies on relationships at work.

As businesses increasingly demand longer working hours from their employees, the workplace has become the focus of social contact for many people, replacing college, bars, and clubs as the the best place to meet others with the same background, education, and interests. Observers also point out that there are more women in the workforce than ever before.

Many workers regard flirting with colleagues as harmless fun. A 2001 European survey of 1,000 workers conducted by the Italian Gestalt Institute found that office flirting was considered good for relieving work anxiety and stress. Statistics indicate that most workers also see no reason to inform their employer if a relationship develops. Many suggest there should be no problem with office romances as long as couples are open about their relationship, behave professionally, and one of them is not the direct supervisor of the other. They argue that being secretive and having to hide relationships actually does more harm than good by fueling gossip and promoting a culture of fear and repression—and possibly even leaves people vulnerable to blackmail.

Some companies, however, go to great lengths to regulate workplace relationships. In an attempt to ward off sexual harassment charges and revenge-motivated complaints, some employers advocate the use of so-called "love contracts," which typically spell out that a relationship is consensual, that couples are aware of the company's sexual harassment policy, and that they agree to settle any dispute through arbitration rather than a lawsuit. Employment attorneys warn that these types of agreement must be signed voluntarily by the parties involved and should be used only sparingly to avoid the appearance that companies sanction such relationships. Other companies impose an outright ban on any sexual relationship at work.

> *"Although Freud said happiness is composed of love and work, reality often forces us to choose love or work."*
>
> —LETTY COTTIN POGREBIN, AUTHOR OF *FAMILY AND POLITICS* (1983)

Many workers view the idea of such a ban as an infringement on their right to privacy and claim this kind of policy results in low morale and reduced productivity. A 2001 poll conducted by recruitment agency America At Work found that 62 percent of workers said that romantic relationships at work are none of their employer's business. Employees often resent any attempt by a company to dictate their behavior outside of work. Many point out that it is impossible to legislate against love.

However, according to a 2002 study by the Society for Human Resource Management, 20 percent of U.S. firms have policies on office romances, while 81 percent of human resource bosses said such relationships were dangerous. Some people argue that sexual relationships in the workplace can waste valuable resources if the two coworkers involved are furthering their romance during the company's time by flirting or indulging in e-mail correspondence. Relationships between a superior and subordinate can result in favoritism toward the subordinate and a conflict of interest—and even if they do not, critics point out, other employees may perceive that they do.

Relationships between coworkers often end acrimoniously, resulting in an uncomfortable workplace atmosphere. While in European countries such situations are usually dealt with on an informal basis or by internal disciplinary procedures, in the United States they often lead to lawsuits both against individuals and against employers. By some counts 50 percent of U.S. sexual harassment lawsuits arise out of workplace relationships that started out as consensual. In 1998 the U.S. Supreme Court made two landmark decisions—in the cases of *Faragher v. City of Boca Raton* and *Burlington Industries, Inc. v. Ellerth*—which ruled that employers are liable for supervisors' sexual misconduct toward a subordinate employee. Many believe that companies' fear of this liability, and the consequent threat of lost profits through claims for damages, is the key to understanding why U.S. employers are increasingly concerned about office romances, leading more and more firms to look for ways to limit sexual relationships in the workplace.

The following two articles look at these issues in greater depth.

STRETCHING THE MEANING OF SEXUAL HARASSMENT
Robyn E. Blumner

Robyn E. Blumner is a Florida-based journalist specializing in workplace and privacy issues. This article appeared in the St. Petersburg Times *in March 1998.*

YES

Catharine MacKinnon is on a roll. Twenty years after the radical feminist author and University of Michigan law professor wrote the book *Sexual Harassment of Working Women*, most of the legal reforms she sought have been realized. Now the question is: How much further does she want the law to go in regulating sexual discussions, material and relationships at the workplace?

A recent conference at Yale law school gives us a chilling glimpse at the answer.

Catharine MacKinnon is a U.S. lawyer and legal theorist. In the 1980s her work concentrated on attempts to ban pornography; in the 1990s she focused on sexual harassment law.

At the late-February [1998] conference celebrating the 20th anniversary of MacKinnon's book, speakers expressed dissatisfaction with current law prohibiting sexual harassment at work because the law only makes employers liable for "unwelcome" harassing work conditions. In fact, an entire panel was devoted to the question of unwelcomeness, with subtitled questions asking: "Should sex have to be 'unwelcome' to be recognized as actionable? Should relations of hierarchy be enough? Should context—education, work, military—matter?"

Not surprisingly, nearly every speaker on the panel objected to the legal requirement that a woman expressly indicate that sexual advances or language are unwelcome in order to make a harassment case. To this, MacKinnon uttered not a peep of protest.

Sex must be presumed unwelcome

It appears that this is the next legal frontier. Militant feminists in the legal, sociological and activist communities would like to push sexual harassment law to a place where any sexual discussions or materials at work are presumed to be unwelcome and the burden would be on the speaker to prove otherwise.

Does this seem a reasonable idea? Or does it reverse the fundamental legal principle that it is the prosecution's responsibility to prove guilt, not the defendant's responsibility to prove innocence?

Imagine if this idea were imported into tomorrow's workplaces. Workers would have to sign consent forms before the next intern-in-the-White-House joke could be told. Sadly, today's interpretation of sexual harassment law has employers so scared of being sued that most

Jack Lemmon plays "Bud" Baxter in Billy Wilder's film The Apartment *(1960). Lemmon is in love with elevator operator Fran Kubelik, played by Shirley MacLaine, who in turn is having an affair with Lemmon's boss.*

See http://www.eeoc.gov/policy/docs/currentissues.html for the Equal Employment Opportunity Commission's discussion of how "unwelcomeness" is evaluated in court cases.

large workplaces have already adopted similar zero-tolerance policies.

But MacKinnonite feminists want the law to stretch further. They argue that the "unwelcomeness" requirement is unfair to women because it reinforces the status quo in the workplace, traditionally a patriarchal institution. It presumes that women are available sexually at work, giving the harasser one free approach. Only after a woman had rebuffed a co-worker's advances or lurid discourse does subsequent conduct become harassing.

These radical feminists would like to strip the workplace of any potential romance. Many would like a summary rule forbidding sexual relationships between a supervisor and an underling. They say that as long as women are not equals at work, even consent to a sexual relationship is not truly freely given.

Tell that to my maternal grandparents who were once boss and secretary.

Do you agree that women can give informed consent to a relationship? Or is today's society too unequal for that to be possible? If so, who is to decide when relationships are equal enough for consent to be meaningful?

Victimhood infantilizes women

Wholesale rules against sexual relationships at work insultingly imply that women need to be protected from their own decisions. Often there are substantial economic power differentials in couples, but that doesn't negate the consent given by the "weaker" adult. Coerced sex, which may occur more frequently when one partner has economic power over another, should be prohibited, but consensual sex among colleagues should in no way interest the law.

At the conference, University of Illinois psychology professor Louise Fitzgerald argued that the explicit unwelcomeness requirement should be dropped because, according to her research, fewer than one in five harassed women will tell the perpetrator to stop. Instead, women employ coping mechanisms to show unwelcomeness, like changing the subject, ignoring the harasser and going along.

How would an employer know in practice if one employee was harassing another unless there had been some complaint?

According to this rationale, an employer should be held liable to pay damages to a woman when sexual discussions at work create a hostile work environment, even if the only clues the employer got that the conduct was unwanted was that the victim "went along with it."

The current law at least encourages women to speak up if they are feeling harassed. It provides some notice to the employer that someone is uncomfortable at work, allowing for the opportunity to adjust the workplace environment. But these feminists would like to see that changed. And they are carefully watching a case out of Florida before the Supreme

Court this term that challenges the requirement that employers have notice of hostile work conditions before they can be successfully sued.

At the conference, professor Jane Larson of the University of Wisconsin law school took the harassment debate to the next extreme. She suggested that the employer should be liable even if the sexual conduct is explicitly welcome. Larson explained that the legal question should focus on the "objective reasonableness" of the conduct—whether the average woman would find it harassing and not whether it was welcome by the woman to whom it was directed. This ... would protect workplaces from being sexualized by those women who accept and even enjoy sexual banter at work, or as she technically called them: "the least resistant women."

So now, not only must employers police the workplace of unwanted flirting, but that which is invited as well.

This case is Faragher v. City of Boca Raton *(1998); see page 52, and go to http://supct.law.cornell.edu/supct/html/97-282.ZS.html for the Supreme Court's opinion. The court held that employers can be liable even if no complaint was registered, but only if they did not take "reasonable care" to prevent harassing behavior. In this case the court found that the supervisors "were granted virtually unchecked authority," and that the plaintiff was "completely isolated from the city's higher management."*

Plausible denial?

In the Feb. 23 [1998] issue of *The New Yorker*, MacKinnon angrily responded to an article by Jeffrey Toobin on sexual harassment in the workplace. MacKinnon summarily denied that she promoted the idea that all sex at the workplace constitutes sexual harassment. Instead, she insisted that she has always supported the proposition that workplace sex has to be "unwelcome" in order to be considered harassing.

In Feminism Unmodified *(1987) Mackinnon describes "prostitution, marriage, and sexual harassment" as being "indistinguishable." Do you think this is consistent with her reply in* The New Yorker *that "All sex is not sexual harassment. Nothing in my work implies that it is"?*

But MacKinnon and her disciples' private leanings belie her public protests. Maybe even MacKinnon understands the extremism of her views and doesn't want to show her hand until she has pushed the law incrementally to where there's no turning back.

What this comes down to is a group of militant feminists who have declared war on men and their sexual desires. To them, intimate acts and conversations on sex are only benign when initiated by women who are financially, socially (and probably physically) their partner's equal. They want the law to codify this view.

Although their demands seem absurd, in the last 20 years since MacKinnon's book, much of what the author sought has found its way into federal sexual harassment jurisprudence. It's hard to say where the madness will end.

DANGEROUS LIAISONS
Ellyn Spragins

Ellyn Spragins is a health care reporter for Newsweek *and the author of* Choosing and Using an HMO *(1998). This article appeared in* Fortune Small Business *magazine in February 2004.*

NO

In a perfect world, romance would never show its spaniel-eyed face at your company. Who needs the emotional dramas, the public displays of affection, or the breakup angst that can spread through an office faster than the flu? Love in the office "is always disruptive," says Marc Ostrofsky, 41, a serial entrepreneur and investor based in Houston. "The only upside is during that period when things are peachy keen between a couple and both are willing to come to work early and stay late."

Ostrofsky's view is one widely held among employers large and small, yet office romance is becoming more and more accepted. Corporate paranoia about harassment lawsuits has given way to a tolerant, keep-it-professional attitude. Policing workers seems futile in an increasingly laissez-faire society—and faintly ridiculous when often it's the boss who's making kissy faces at work....

These are the estimated figures for the number of new workplace relationships starting each year, not a cumulative total. They are based on research carried out for U.S. News & World Report *in 1998 and statistics from the Labor Department and the Bureau of National Affairs for 2003.*

Romance on the rise

Those who study the subject say office romance is on the rise and—apart from boss-employee relations and extramarital affairs—is becoming more respectable.... Workplace relationships [in the United States] rose to about ten million last year [2003], up from eight million in 1998, estimates Dennis Powers, a business-law professor at Southern Oregon University and author of *The Office Romance: Playing With Fire Without Getting Burned*....

Reasons why relationships within the same chain of command are often banned include temptation for the supervisor to exploit the position for sexual ends, inability of the supervisor to review the employee's work impartially or to discipline the employee, and the possibility that the supervisor might cover up poor work by the employee.

Employers are justified in relaxing their fraternization policies, says Powers, because, at least in the aggregate, failed love affairs rarely come back to haunt companies.... Even so, most firms wisely ban fraternization between people in the same chain of command to avoid sexual harassment suits, says attorney Daniel Blake, a labor partner in Epstein Becker & Green's Boston office. Experts advise against general bans on office romance, which might invite invasion-of-privacy lawsuits. So far, though, workers have filed only a handful of such suits, and none have held up in court....

Love affairs don't have to generate lawsuits to be disruptive, of course, and the smaller the business, the greater the impact. In a one-office company with a handful of employees it's more likely that everyone has overlapping duties and less likely that you can transfer a love-struck worker to a different department or boss, which is one of the most effective ways to deflect a sexual harassment suit. Some employers ask co-workers in a dating relationship to sign a "love contract," or consensual-relationship agreement, in which both parties acknowledge that they are willing participants. Generally, says Blake, the agreements are used as a defense in sexual harassment suits [against the company] more than anything else. Blake, whose office specializes in entrepreneurial clients, instead recommends that bosses monitor the situation to ascertain that no-one's work performance is suffering and that there are no negative repercussions in the workplace.

See http://www.sfgate.com/cgi-bin/article.cgi?f=/c/a/2001/12/02/AW129618.DTL for background on the circumstances in which "love contracts" are imposed and a sample wording.

How much trouble is it worth?

But what, exactly, is a tolerable level of disruption? To retain valued employees, company owners sometimes live with intrigue and grievances unless a serious problem develops. "My personal pet peeve is all the rumor and innuendo that goes on around a relationship at work," says David Rippe, 45, CEO of Celestia International, a five-employee marketing and communications firm in Cincinnati. At Dia Interactives, a marketing company with 44 employees that he dissolved in 2001, he witnessed several romances among staffers, ranging from a one-night liaison involving a married man, to an on-again, off-again long-term relationship between two single people. "There would be days when a couple weren't talking to each other, and you could feel the negative energy. You get pulled in," he recalls. Apart from asking the romantic partners to look beyond their emotions in performing their work, Rippe did not intervene in the relationship involving the single people, even when the rumor mill was in overdrive. He reasoned that if a serious problem developed, they would mention it to him. But when he got complaints that the married man "started hitting on every woman in the office," he says, he told him to stop, and the problem ended. Rippe has taken a similar approach at Celestia.

Is it fair for employers to have different standards of behavior that they will tolerate according to how much they value employees? Is this a form of discrimination?

Indeed, love flourishes at many small companies without causing problems....

But keeping a lid on love is sometimes tough. The founder and CEO of a computer-refurbishing company near Sacramento with $2.4 million in annual sales has been struggling with a female warehouse manager who has twice had affairs with computer technicians who reported to her. A few months ago the CEO ... spoke to the manager about

One of these situations could be described as the normal ups and downs of a romantic relationship; the other was behavior bordering on harassment. Was the employer right to intervene in one case and not in the other?

This and all the remaining examples in the article refer to relationships between people in the same chain of command. Are any of their lessons relevant to people in other situations?

how her latest relationship could make his company vulnerable to a lawsuit from her boyfriend. "She got a little defensive and said she didn't think there would be any difficulty," says the CEO.

But he thinks the relationship has compromised her judgment. Recently the technician began grousing after the CEO denied him the opportunity to install a new computer network. The CEO had several discussions with him, explaining that he lacked the necessary skills and then asked the warehouse manager to handle the problem. Instead, she defended her boyfriend. "It became clear that she had no real ability to be objective," says the CEO.

Another dilemma: The warehouse manager protects her boyfriend whenever he makes a mistake. The blame is turned back onto other technical-support employees, causing resentment and frustration. Because the warehouse manager is otherwise a good employee and the couple recently announced their engagement, the CEO is living with the problems until the technician leaves the company in order to join the Army, a plan he recently announced.

Some observers argue that it is justifiable to have different rules for supervisors and owners of companies because their jobs place them in a position of trust in relation to an employee like that of a doctor to a patient or an attorney to a client. Do you agree with this analogy?

The boss's dilemma

Does it all sound like a nightmarish rerun of your high school's dating scene? Well, consider that the headaches of managing lovers seem minor compared with what an entrepreneur can encounter when he or she falls for an employee. Paul Lewis, 38, CEO of P.G. Lewis & Associates, a data forensics firm in Whitehouse Station, N.J., with $2 million a year in sales, readily admits that his office romance of a decade ago "was the biggest mistake I made in my professional career." Then the CEO of MC2, a computer systems integration company in Warren, N.J., with $1.5 million in annual sales, Lewis began dating his office manager a few months after hiring her in 1993. Later she moved into his house, and they stayed together about two years.

"That decision almost sank my company. I lost respect from my employees, arguments were brought into the office from my home, and my business partner thought I was an idiot," Lewis says. He encouraged his live-in girlfriend to pursue a different career, which she did, and the relationship broke up. He sold MC2 in 1999. At his current 15-employee company, "we have a strict rule that you're not allowed to be involved with anyone at the company," he says. He's even requiring that the wife of the founder of a small company that P.G. Lewis is acquiring be terminated from her office manager job as a condition of the deal.

Is it unfair for Lewis's bad experience to be used as a reason for firing someone from her job if she has been doing it well and without causing trouble?

For Christine Carey, 33, and Jerry Golley, 38, trying to conduct both a romantic and a work relationship for five years was so stressful that their bond crumbled in both arenas. They met and began dating in the Denver office of Lipper Analytical Services, a financial firm based in New York City, in 1995. After Golley launched AMI Visions, a software firm in Lakewood, Colo., in 1996, his third hire was Carey. "We had total trust," says Golley.

For the first three or four years the couple, who were living together, maintained both a professional and a personal relationship with the help of some strict rules. Neither, for instance, was allowed to mention business once one of them changed into pajamas. Both worked hard to maintain their professionalism at the office. "It worked, but we were suppressing a great deal and creating a pressure-cooker situation," says Carey.

Does the need for such strict self-imposed rules indicate that such relationships are inherently strained from the beginning?

Driving a wedge

The strain began to show in 2000, when Carey disagreed with many of the decisions made by a new president whom Golley had promoted from within the company. Golley deferred to the executive's judgment, which he says "drove a wedge between me and Christine." Another source of tension was Golley's decision to give one share of common stock to the new president, rather than Carey, in order to obtain key-man insurance....

"Key-man insurance" is a life-insurance policy taken out on essential personnel by their company to give the company financial breathing space to recruit a replacement or to close the company in an orderly way if they should die. See http://www.slcentral.com/slf-key-man-insurance.html for more details.

By 2001 a sputtering economy added a new layer of stress. The company needed to lay off one of seven highly paid managers. Christine volunteered to step away, hoping that it would help her and Golley rekindle their feelings. Although they had gotten engaged, "we'd pretended we didn't have any passion for so long, after a while I didn't feel it," says Carey. Nor did Golley.

After Carey left, they had less time together—and less and less in common—as Jerry devoted long hours to AMI. In the summer of 2002, Carey moved out and they stopped seeing each other. Both say they feel they sacrificed a unique romantic bond so that AMI could survive and grow. "Sexual passion and work life should absolutely be separated," says Carey. "I would never again date somebody I work with." Though his business is again stable and thriving ... Golley agrees: "Even if it works well, you're creating issues and complexities in your relationship." And like many entrepreneurs who've discovered the hazards of office romance, he'd prefer, when he's behind his desk, to concentrate on the complexities of business.

If you were in that situation, which would you prefer to save—the company or the relationship?

Summary

Should sexual relationships in the workplace be allowed? In the first article Robyn E. Blumner argues that they should. She says that genuine sexual harassment is already legislated against, and that consensual sex among colleagues should in no way interest the law. She blames, as she sees it, a hidden agenda by radical feminists to declare "war on men and their sexual desires" as being behind a move to toughen sexual harassment legislation. She points out that at the time of writing, employers must be told of a complaint before they can be sued, which, she argues, encourages the woman to speak up and gives the employer a chance to rectify the situation. However, a Supreme Court judgment announced shortly after made employers liable for damages (if certain conditions are met) even if there has been no complaint. Blumner argues that this will be totally unworkable and will lead to a stifling and fearful workplace. She also points out that she might not have been born had such rules existed back when her grandparents worked together.

However, Ellyn Spragins says there are many dangers in allowing sexual relationships in the workplace. She points out that love affairs in the office do not have to generate lawsuits to be disruptive. The fallout from a relationship at work can have a detrimental effect not just on those directly involved but also on many of those around them: Rumor and innuendo, favoritism, misplaced blame, loss of objectivity, and negative energy can all be damaging in the workplace. Spragins's article also details how the pressures of work are liable to damage relationships. She concludes that love life and work life should ultimately remain separated.

FURTHER INFORMATION:

Books:

Agonito, Rosemary, *Dirty Little Secrets: Sex in the Workplace*. Syracuse, NY: New Futures, 2000.

Petrocelli, William, and Barbara Repa, *Sexual Harassment on the Job: What It Is and How to Stop It* (4th edition). Berkeley, CA: Nolo Press, 1999.

Powers, Dennis, *The Office Romance: Playing with Fire without Getting Burned*. New York: American Management Association, 1998.

Useful websites:

http://www.bizjournals.com/related_articles/?story_id=848635&jst=s_rs-lk

Articles on office romance from U.S. business journals.

http://careerplanning.about.com/library/weekly/aa012598.htm

Articles on the theme "Office Romance: A Bad Idea."

The following debates in the Pro/Con series may also be of interest:

In this volume:

Topic 1 Should workers have a right to privacy in the workplace?

Topic 4 Is workplace sexual harassment legislation adequate?

Topic 11 Does sexual orientation matter in the workplace?

SHOULD SEXUAL RELATIONSHIPS IN THE WORKPLACE BE ALLOWED?

SHOULD SEXUAL RELATIONSHIPS IN THE WORKPLACE BE ALLOWED?

KEY POINTS

HARMLESS FUN
Is romance in the workplace harmless fun?

YES: Flirtation in the workplace eases stress and boosts morale. The office is a safe environment in which to meet a partner of similar background and interests.

NO: Those involved in a relationship have lower productivity levels, and coworkers become demoralized by favoritism shown toward a colleague by a manager with whom he or she is having a relationship

REPORTING RELATIONSHIPS
Should sexual relationships between supervisors and subordinates be allowed?

YES: As long as the relationship is consensual and open, there is no reason why a supervisor should not date a member of his or her staff

NO: Boss–employee relationships can lead to preferential treatment toward the subordinate. They can result in claims of discrimination and sexual harassment if the romance turns sour.

OVERREACTION
Are companies that have strict rules on relationships at work overreacting?

YES: It is insulting to suggest that employees are not able to maintain a professional attitude toward their jobs while dating someone at work

NO: Sexual relationships at work are always disruptive and usually end acrimoniously. Companies are protecting their own interests against expensive lawsuits.

LOVE CONTRACTS
Are "love contracts" a bad idea?

YES: Office romances are a private matter, not the company's business. "Love contracts" are unenforceable and constitute an invasion of privacy. They can also drive couples into engaging in secret affairs and subterfuge.

NO: "Love contracts" are useful since they establish ground rules for acceptable behavior and ensure that relationships are consensual

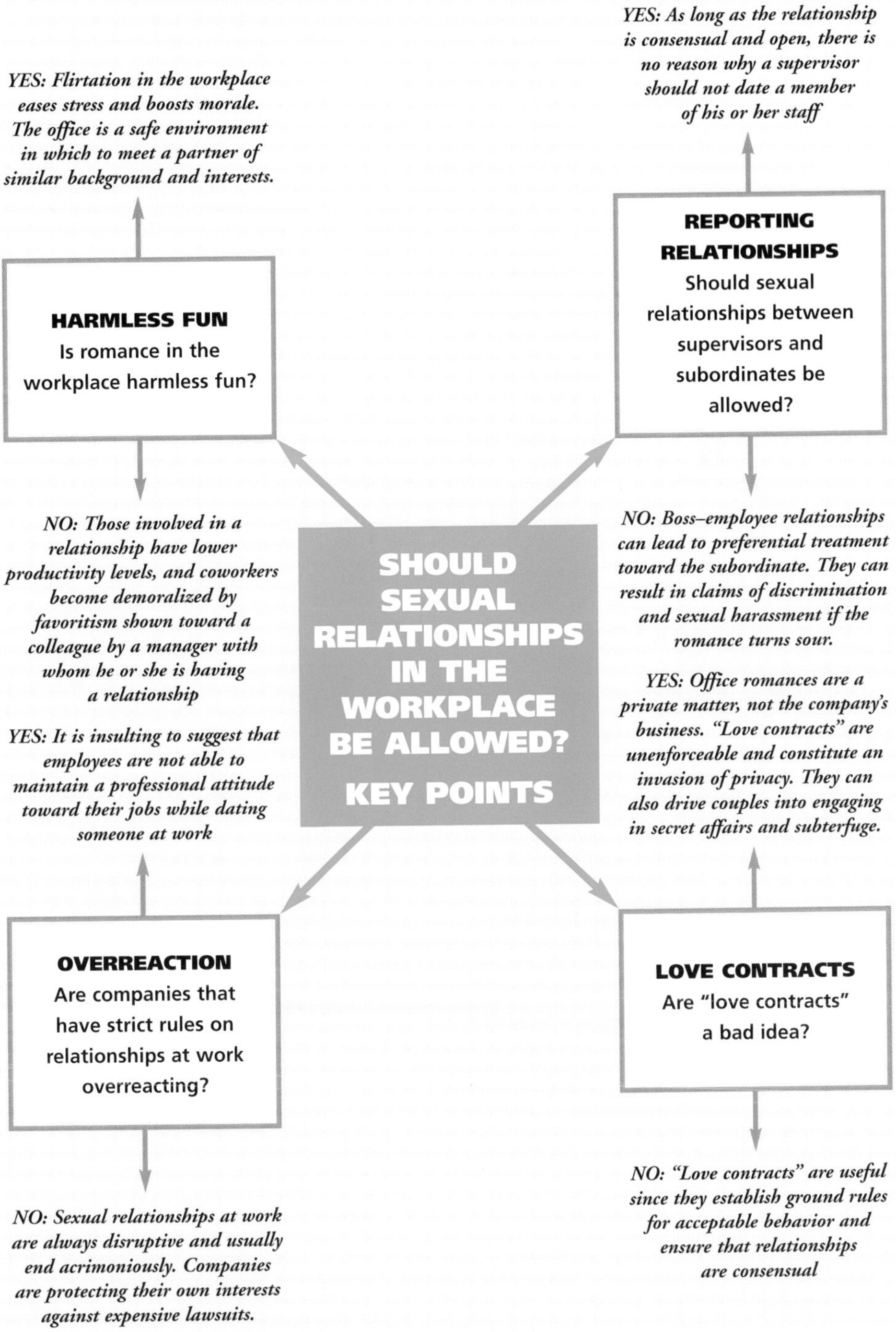

Topic 11
DOES SEXUAL ORIENTATION MATTER IN THE WORKPLACE?

YES

FROM "DON'T VIOLATE THE FREEDOM OF SPEECH AND RELIGION OF NONHOMOSEXUALS ON THE JOB"
INSIGHT ON THE NEWS, SYMPOSIUM, APRIL 1, 2002
LOUIS P. SHELDON

NO

FROM "ENDING JOB DISCRIMINATION AGAINST GAYS AND LESBIANS IS GOOD FOR BUSINESS"
INSIGHT ON THE NEWS, SYMPOSIUM, APRIL 1, 2002
WINNIE STACHELBERG

INTRODUCTION

A 2001 Gallup poll found that 85 percent of respondents in the United States favored equal opportunity in employment for gays and lesbians. However, in most U.S. states, as in many countries throughout the world, it is legal for an employee to be fired or otherwise discriminated against solely because of his or her sexual orientation.

Many people believe that this situation is unacceptable. They argue that sexual orientation in no way affects a person's ability to do a job and should not be taken into account in employment decisions. Some claim that a person has no choice over whether he or she is gay since sexual orientation is innate, like race or gender. Other observers counter that there is absolutely no scientific evidence to support this supposition, and that since people choose to be gay, it is obviously a lifestyle choice. They also believe that it would be wrong on both religious and moral grounds, among other things, to introduce a law that would give preferential treatment to gay men and lesbians.

While the 1964 Civil Rights Act prohibits employment discrimination based on race, color, religion, sex, or national origin, there is no federal law to protect against discrimination on the basis of sexual orientation. Despite this, many corporations, including over 300 of the *Fortune* 500 companies, have thought the issue important enough to include sexual orientation in their own antidiscrimination policies. By mid-2004, 14 states and the District of Columbia had also enacted laws prohibiting sexual orientation discrimination in the workplace.

The Civil Service Reform Act of 1978 also bans federal employees from discriminating against applicants and employees on the basis of conduct that does not adversely affect their performance. The federal government has interpreted discrimination based on "conduct" to include that based on sexual orientation. Some union collective bargaining agreements also protect employees against this type of discrimination.

Despite these measures, observers argue that many public- and private-sector workers face harassment and loss of employment without legal recourse on account of their sexual orientation. They point out that the United States lags behind the European Union (EU), whose Employment Directive required member states to implement legislation prohibiting discrimination on the grounds of sexual orientation by December 2003.

"Individuals should not be denied a job on the basis of something that has no relationship to their ability to perform their work."

—BILL CLINTON,

42ND PRESIDENT (1993–2001)

Proposed legislation known as the Employment Non-Discrimination Act (ENDA) would prohibit all U.S. public and private employers, employment agencies, and labor organizations from using an individual's actual or perceived sexual orientation as the basis for employment decisions such as hiring, firing, promotion, or compensation. ENDA has, however, had an arduous journey through Congress. It was first introduced in 1994, although a broader version of the bill had been suggested before. Two years later a modified version of the bill was narrowly defeated in the Senate by a 49-50 vote. Senators Edward Kennedy and Lincoln Chafee in the Senate and Representatives Chris Shays and Barney Frank in the House reintroduced the bill in 2003.

Despite this, ENDA's supporters—which range from the labor union AFL-CIO to large companies such as Microsoft—remain optimistic that it will eventually be passed. Such advocates claim that bill will simply extend to people of all sexual orientations the same federal employment protections already afforded to other individuals on the basis of religion, race, sex, age, and disability. The bill will not allow for preferential treatment of homosexuals, nor will it impose quotas on employers or compel them to collect statistics on sexual orientation, as critics seem to fear. Proponents also point out that ENDA will only apply to small businesses with fewer than 15 employees or to nonprofit religious organizations.

Among the criticisms levied at the bill is that sexual orientation is a choice, and therefore lesbians and gays should not receive the same protection afforded to other minority groups. Such views also contend that the effect of ENDA on small businesses could be catastrophic, since many could be forced out of business by lawsuits brought by people claiming discriminatory treatment by employers or colleagues.

The following articles examine the proposed ENDA legislation.

DON'T VIOLATE THE FREEDOM OF SPEECH AND RELIGION OF NONHOMOSEXUALS ON THE JOB
Louis P. Sheldon

Louis P. Sheldon is chairman of the Traditional Values Coalition (www.traditionalvalues.org), a profamily organization that is "committed to living ... by the moral precepts taught by Jesus Christ and by the whole counsel of God as revealed in the Bible." This article was published as part of a symposium in the weekly magazine Insight on the News *in April 2002.*

Sheldon argues that the question of whether homosexuality is a life choice or a genetic condition is important to this issue. Why do you think it matters to some people at all?

NARTH (www.narth.com) claims that its function is to "provide psychological understanding of the cause, treatment, and behavior patterns associated with homosexuality."

YES

The Employment Non-Discrimination Act (ENDA) is being debated in Congress again. It has been reintroduced in various forms for the last seven years by Sens. Ted Kennedy (D-Mass.) and Jim Jeffords (I-Vt.). ENDA ostensibly is designed to forbid "discrimination" against a person's sexual orientation. Currently, "sexual orientation" is defined in ENDA as "homosexuality, bisexuality or heterosexuality, whether the orientation is real or perceived."

ENDA will make it a federal offense to discriminate against any individual because of actual or perceived sexual orientation. The bill will cover any employer who is engaged in interstate commerce and who has 15 or more employees.

Underlying assumption

The primary underlying assumption of ENDA is that the sexual orientation of a person is "fixed," "normal" and "healthy" in American life. In actuality, the sexual-orientation view advanced by ENDA is closer to the idea of protecting alcoholism or drug abuse than race or gender. Sexual acts have consequences. ENDA attempts to impose a federal gag order on the crucial question about whether homosexual activity is voluntary and whether homosexual practices have negative social consequences. ENDA is based upon the faulty premise that homosexuality is normal and that individuals are born gay. This premise recently has been exposed to be a fraud by none other than homosexual researchers themselves who have admitted there is no scientific proof that a homosexual gene or brain exist.

Psychologists with the National Association for Research and Therapy of Homosexuality (NARTH) recently published "The Innate-Immutable Argument Finds No Basis in Science," which quotes homosexual researchers and philosophers on the discredited born-gay theory. In this article, NARTH quotes homosexual researcher Dean Hamer: "There is not a single master gene that makes people gay."...

Homosexuality is a behavior, a lifestyle choice. It is not genetically based, nor is it a healthy way to live. The federal government has no right to force America's businesses, labor unions and nonprofits to support a poor lifestyle choice. Yet that is precisely what ENDA will do.

Even if this is the case, why should sexual orientation affect someone's capacity to do his or her work?

ENDA places homosexuality on an equal par with heterosexuality, which has been the norm throughout human history. Behaviors such as homosexuality, bisexuality and cross-dressing are expressions of gender-identity confusion and should not be equated with heterosexuality as being normal.

A legal disaster

Labor lawyer Dudley Rochelle has thoroughly analyzed ENDA. She notes that the inclusion of "perceived" in the definition of sexual orientation in ENDA is a recipe for legal disaster for businesses. She writes: "There is no condition of sexual abnormality that may not be perceived to fall within one of these categories, including all those excluded by the ADA [Americans with Disabilities Act]—transvestism, transexualism, pedophilia, exhibitionism, voyeurism, gender-identity disorders and sexual-behavior disorders. Without containing an explicit exclusion, persons with these conditions will have a certain degree of protection under ENDA."

Dudley Rochelle is an attorney at a law firm in Atlanta, Georgia. She specializes in employment discrimination and religious harassment cases.

ENDA defines "sexual orientation" as "homosexuality, bisexuality, or heterosexuality, whether the orientation is real or perceived."

ENDA will be a trial lawyer's dream come true and certainly will benefit sexually confused individuals such as transgenders who believe they are the opposite sex.

Gender identity is not the same as sexual orientation. Most transgendered people are heterosexual. There have been calls by lesbian, gay, and bisexual groups for transgender inclusion in the ENDA bill. However, some people are concerned that adding gender identity to ENDA would lose it support in Congress, particularly among Republicans.

It will prove to be a nightmare for employers and normal employees, who will be forced to remain silent as their cross-dressing coworkers press for the right to wear dresses to work. The transgender issue also will affect a business's rest-room policies. Under ENDA, it is likely that a business will be forced to add separate rest rooms, showers and changing areas for cross-dressers, or simply allow a transgender to use whatever rest room he desires.

This already is happening. In June 2001, Ohio University designated 30 rest rooms on campus as "unisex" to appease transgender and homosexual activists on campus.

That same month, a Latino AIDS agency sued its former landlord for discrimination because the landlord was forcing a transgendered male to use the men's rest room instead of the women's rest room. The American Civil Liberties Union is defending the right of this man to use a woman's rest room because he thinks he's a woman. ENDA will result in endless litigation over rest-room facilities.

ENDA also contains a hate-crime provision that forbids "retaliation or coercion" against a person who is or is perceived to be a homosexual. The bill says: "A person shall not coerce, intimidate, threaten or interfere with any individual in the exercise or enjoyment of, or on account of such an individual's having exercised, enjoyed or assisted in, or encouraged the exercise or enjoyment of any right granted or protected by this title."

Should people be allowed to distribute religious material at work? Do you think ENDA would infringe on their right to free speech?

Religion and ENDA

An employer or employee who may express opposition to homosexual behavior can be sued under ENDA for verbalizing such beliefs in the workplace. A person with religious convictions against homosexuality can be sued if, for example, he drops an ex-gay Christian-testimony pamphlet on the desk of a practicing homosexual in the office.

Despite claims that ENDA exempts religious denominations or organizations operated by them, the truth is that this legislation will impose federal control over such nonprofit groups as Bible publishers and Christian bookstores, TV/radio stations, day-care centers, day camps and more.

Title VII of the Civil Rights Act of 1964 (known simply as Title VII) makes it illegal for an employer to discriminate against individuals because of their religion in hiring, firing, and other terms and conditions of employment. See http://www.eeoc.gov/types/religion.html for details.

ENDA only exempts an organization when it promotes a religion or is controlled by one. Interfaith groups also would be covered under ENDA.

This legislation will pit religious employees against activist homosexuals in the workplace. The employer will be caught in the middle, trying to balance issues of freedom of speech and religion with the requirements of ENDA. As Rochelle has written: "The employer will have to choose between suppressing the ability of employees to express their religious viewpoints, for which they have relatively little protection in the workplace (religious speech is far less protected than religious observances), and risking costly claims from homosexuals under ENDA's broad language. Most likely, the employer will impose a rule on the workplace that, in effect, allows no criticism of homosexual or bisexual lifestyles, even among peers."

ENDA actually could overturn antisodomy laws in states that have not yet passed pro-homosexual antidiscrimination laws. It would be discriminatory to forbid individuals to engage in sodomy under ENDA.

ENDA would not allow for quotas or preferential treatment based on sexual orientation. It would also not allow the Equal Employment Opportunity Commission (EEOC) to collect statistics on sexual orientation or compel employers to collect such statistics.

ENDA does not require quotas in hiring homosexuals but, to comply with the law, a business owner may believe he must keep statistics on how many homosexuals he hires. In addition, courts involved in ENDA lawsuits could force quotas upon businesses to make certain the firms are not engaged in a pattern of discrimination against homosexuals. If homosexuality is considered on an equal par with race or ethnicity, then quotas could be imposed by an activist court.

Economic burden

ENDA will add to the economic burden of employers. To defend a company against an individual filing a discrimination charge, the following fees are typical:

- Agency-dismissal stage: $5,000–$25,000
- If claimant files a lawsuit and the company wins on summary judgment: $25,000–$75,000
- To prevail at trial: $150,000–$250,000

Simply defending one's company from a frivolous lawsuit could bankrupt smaller businesses. Employers eventually may win these lawsuits but suffer huge financial losses and bad publicity.

The ENDA bill, like Title VII and the Americans with Disabilities Act (ADA) of 1990, exempts small businesses with fewer than 15 employees. Do you think that this fair?

Rochelle has noted the following points about ENDA's impact on businesses. The cost of defending and winning one discrimination case can be enough to break a small company. Most small companies do not have insurance that covers discrimination claims....

ENDA is broader than any federal discrimination law ever passed, both in its definition of discrimination and its protection of different categories of persons.

Employers will have difficulty defending themselves against ENDA claims because the protected class is not based on a known characteristic, may be based on a behavior one can opt into and out of and is subject to interpretation. Employers will be caught in the crossfire of claims between homosexual activists and employees with deeply held religious, moral or traditional beliefs against homosexual behavior.

In several places throughout the text the author uses the phrase "homosexual activists." What do you think is his intention in doing this?

Employers will be unable to identify and prevent hostile work environments due to sexual orientation without invading the privacy of employees.

Employees are under no obligation to discuss their sexual orientation with their employer. In what way would ENDA invade an individual's privacy?

ENDA will violate the freedom of speech and religion of nonhomosexual employers and employees; impose a homosexual/transgender agenda on businesses; and result in endless litigation that will cost companies millions of dollars to defend themselves. America's businesses must not be forced to protect a sexual behavior that frequently results in the spread of sexually transmitted diseases and death from AIDS infections. ENDA must be defeated.

ENDING JOB DISCRIMINATION AGAINST GAYS AND LESBIANS IS GOOD FOR BUSINESS
Winnie Stachelberg

Winnie Stachelberg is political director of Human Rights Campaign (www.hrc.org), an organization that works for lesbian, gay, bisexual, and transgender equal rights. This article was published in the same edition of Insight on the News *as Louis P. Sheldon's article on pages 140–143.*

NO

It is not often that business and labor, Senate Democrats and Republicans enthusiastically join together in support of legislation. But that is exactly what happened in February when these disparate groups testified in favor of the Employment Non-Discrimination Act (ENDA) in front of the Senate Health, Education, Labor and Pensions Committee.

Most people don't realize this, but it is perfectly legal in 38 states to fire a person because of his or her sexual orientation. If passed, ENDA would ensure that gay and lesbian Americans have equal rights in the job market and workplace. Specifically, it would bar employers from using a person's sexual orientation as the basis for employment decisions—including hiring, firing, promotion or compensation.

For recent statistics on Congressional support for ENDA go to http://capwiz.com/hrc/issues/bills/?bill=3674056 and http://capwiz.com/hrc/issues/bills/?bill=3629581 for the bill's status in the House of Representatives and the Senate respectively.

Bipartisan support

ENDA enjoys widespread, bipartisan support. The Senate bill's lead cosponsors are Sens. Edward M. Kennedy, (D-Mass.); Arlen Specter, (R-Pa.); Joseph Lieberman, (D-Conn.) and James Jeffords, (I-Vt.) House lead sponsors are Reps. Christopher Shays, (R-Conn.); Barney Frank, (D-Mass.); Mark Foley, (R-Fla.) and Ellen Tauscher, (D-Calif.).

ENDA would also not apply to uniformed members of the armed forces. See Volume 7, The Constitution, *Topic 8 Should homosexuals be allowed to serve in the military?*

Aside from prohibiting workplace discrimination, ENDA is supported because of what it does not do. This legislation does not cover small businesses with fewer than 15 employees. It does not cover religious organizations. And ENDA doesn't allow preferential treatment or quotas based on sexual orientation. And this legislation does not require an employer to provide benefits for the same-sex partner of an employee.

This is partly why major corporations support the bill. They also know that workers can better focus on their jobs and be more productive when they are not worrying about workplace discrimination. ENDA is simply good for business. In fact, the closer a company is to the top of the

Fortune list, the more likely it is to include sexual orientation in its nondiscrimination policy. While nearly 60 percent of the *Fortune* 500 have such policies, a full 86 percent of the *Fortune* 50 does. With such major support for equality in corporate America, it should be no surprise that 65 companies, including 29 major corporations, have endorsed ENDA.

Large corporations that have given their support to ENDA include Apple Computer, General Mills, Hewlett-Packard, IBM, Levi Strauss, Nike, Quaker Oats, and Yahoo. How do you think these companies would benefit from ENDA?

Robert Berman, director of human resources and vice president at Eastman Kodak Co., testified at the recent hearing that passing ENDA is a matter of extending fairness and equality to all citizens. "... The Employment Non-Discrimination Act is a logical extension of the fundamental value of fairness to an area that has been neglected for far too long."

FleetBoston President and Chief Executive Officer Charles K. Gifford echoed this support, testifying that passing ENDA is about promoting equal opportunity and eliminating discrimination.

"The lack of workplace protections based on sexual orientation leaves a gaping hole in America's commitment to equal opportunity and is an invitation to the perpetuation of stereotype and prejudice," Gifford told the committee. "I urge the Congress to come together and see to it that discrimination against gays and lesbians in the workplace will soon be viewed as an unacceptable relic of another time."

No increase in litigation

Some conservatives worry that ENDA might bring unwanted regulation to business. But this misguided notion was addressed at the ENDA hearing by Lucy Billingsley, a lifelong Republican and a founder of the Billingsley Co., a Texas real-estate firm that employs 30 people.

"Some might voice concern that adding federal workplace protections for gays and lesbians will be a costly burden to America's small-business owners," said Billingsley. "But actually, not doing so would be the more costly route. When people trust their employer they will be more adaptable to changing business forces," she continued. "Inclusive workplace policies can improve recruitment and lower turnover, boost productivity and lead to business opportunities." Additionally the General Accounting Office found that in the District of Columbia and in the 12 states that prohibit discrimination there has been no marked increase in lawsuits.

By mid-2004, 14 states and the District of Columbia had passed laws prohibiting sexual orientation discrimination in the workplace: California, Connecticut, Hawaii, Maryland, Massachusetts, Minnesota, Nevada, New Hampshire, New Jersey, New Mexico, New York, Rhode Island, Vermont, and Wisconsin.

Others believe this matter should not be handled at the federal level and instead be left to the states. But, historically,

Go to Volume 1, Individual and Society, *pages 34–35, to find a timeline of civil rights in the United States.*

ensuring basic civil rights has been the sphere of Congress. Imagine how detrimental it would have been to our nation if Congress had waited on all 50 states to pass civil-rights laws for other minorities. We might, in fact, still be waiting for some states to pass nondiscrimination laws based on race or religion. Another drawback to the state-by-state approach is that it hurts companies by making them sort out a patchwork of laws.

Stephen L. Miller, chairman and president of Shell Oil Co., says that ENDA would simplify administration and benefit businesses by creating a uniform national policy. "A federal law would level the playing field for corporate America with a single, straightforward policy against discrimination," explains Miller. "Currently our business has to comply with 12 differing state laws against sexual-orientation discrimination, while our employees in other states are afforded no legal protection. One uniform federal policy would ease our administrative burden."

On pages 140–141 Louis P. Sheldon maintains the opposite—that sexual orientation is a choice. Which author makes the more convincing argument?

Another line of reasoning for ENDA opponents is that since sexual orientation is a "choice," it should not be protected. First, most modern science leads to the conclusion that sexual orientation—whether gay or straight—is not a choice. Second, that argument fails when you consider that religion, which already is protected, is something that people choose.

Supporting ENDA is not the equivalent of giving approval to a person's sexual orientation. It only means that people should be judged solely on their merits....

Fundamental values

A fundamental American value holds that people who do their jobs, pay their taxes and contribute to their communities should not be singled out for discrimination. Unfortunately, gay people routinely are fired from their jobs, refused work, paid less and otherwise discriminated against in the workplace ... Antigay discrimination in the American workplace knows few bounds. It occurs in every region of the country, in large cities and small towns, on factory floors and in restaurant dining rooms. It happens in major corporations, struggling nonprofits and public agencies. It affects executives with six-figure incomes and those who clean offices at night for the minimum wage. To suddenly receive a pink slip after years of positive performance evaluations solely because of one's sexual orientation is not uncommon. The emotional and financial burdens of unexpected job loss have caused many gay Americans to lose promising careers, homes and even relationships.

Antigay discrimination often means enduring daily harassment—including name-calling, humiliation and physical threats—from coworkers and bosses alike. Some employers are unabashed in their desire to exclude gays and lesbians from the workforce. When the new head of a Midwest health-care facility realized several gay employees were on his staff, he immediately fired them and then bragged about it in the local media. When Cheryl Summerville was fired from her job as a restaurant cook in 1991, her notice said, "This employee is being terminated due to violation of company policy. The employee is gay."...

Go to http://www.10percent.org/out_at_work.html for an explanation of Summerville's case and other examples of sexual orientation discrimination in the workplace.

Discretion and discrimination

Many gay employees, justifiably worried about discrimination, use great discretion about their sexual orientation. The circumstances of daily life, however, often force them out of their protective closets. They have a picture of their partner on their desk. Their same-sex partner's parent becomes ill. They are photographed by the local newspaper while attending an AIDS memorial. They are seen in a gay neighborhood or are victims of an antigay hate crime. They designate a same-sex partner on their life insurance or buy a home together. They wear wedding rings. Simple acts that heterosexual employees take for granted are dangerous steps for many gay employees and can expose them to harassment and discrimination in the workplace.

Do you think there could be circumstances in which an employee should consider disclosing his or her sexual orientation to an employer? What if, for example, he or she is being harassed by colleagues at work? The Workplace Fairness website addresses this issue and provides further advice on sexual orientation discrimination. Visit http://www.nerinet.org/sexualorientation.php for more information.

The Civil Rights Act prohibits discrimination in the workplace based on race, color, religion, sex and national origin—but not sexual orientation. Currently, a patchwork of protection exists in several states, and an estimated 225 municipalities have laws or policies that bar antigay discrimination. The White House, federal agencies and a large majority of Senate and House offices from both parties have similar policies in place.

The courts consistently have ruled that the Civil Rights Act does not cover sexual orientation. One federal district court, disgusted with evidence of antigay discrimination and frustrated by the lack of a relevant statute, called for action. The situation in the American workplace calls for an "immediate remedial response by Congress," it said.

Go to http://www.med.uscourts.gov/Site/opinions/brody/1998/mab_1-97cv273_higgins_v_new_balanc_doc26_oct.pdf to read about the case Higgins v. New Balance Athletic Shoe, Inc., *which prompted this call for action.*

We urge Congress to ... unite our country behind the principles of fairness and equality. Each day that we wait, more hard-working, taxpaying Americans will lose their jobs simply because of who they are. Congress can use its power to put a stop to this injustice and demolish one of the last remaining vestiges of discrimination that haunts our nation.

Summary

The preceding articles both consider the proposed Employment Non-Discrimination Act (ENDA). In the first article Louis P. Sheldon argues that ENDA is based on the "faulty premise" that homosexuality is "normal," and he cites research that refutes the theory that individuals are born gay. He also quotes a labor lawyer who maintains that the inclusion of the word "perceived" in ENDA's definition of sexual orientation is a "recipe for legal disaster" for companies since it would offer protection to people with "sexual abnormalities." Sheldon expresses concern that ENDA would infringe on the freedom of speech of religious employees and could lead to courts imposing quotas on companies. He also points out that lawsuits resulting from ENDA could bankrupt small businesses. Sheldon concludes by saying that the proposed bill would impose a homosexual and transgender agenda on businesses and promote behavior that can result in disease and death.

In the second article Winnie Stachelberg claims that ENDA has widespread support across the political spectrum and also from major corporations. She cites evidence that there has been no obvious increase in lawsuits from those states that currently have laws prohibiting sexual orientation discrimination. Stachelberg argues that sexual orientation is not a matter of choice, whereas religion is. Supporting ENDA does not equate to giving approval to a person's sexual behavior, she points out; it means that people would be judged only on their merits. She concludes by urging Congress to pass ENDA and remove "one of the last remaining vestiges of discrimination that haunts our nation."

FURTHER INFORMATION:

Books:

Herek, Gregory, M. (ed.), *Stigma and Sexual Orientation: Understanding Prejudice against Lesbians, Gay Men, and Bisexuals.* Thousand Oaks, CA: Sage Publications, 1998.

Winfeld, Liz, and Susan Spielman, *Straight Talk about Gays in the Workplace* (2nd edition). New York: Harrington Park Press, 2001.

Useful websites:

www.eeoc.gov
U.S. Equal Employment Opportunity Commission site.

http://www.hrc.org/Template.cfm?Section=Employment_Non-Discrimination_Act
Information on ENDA from Human Rights Campaign.

www.lambdalegal.org
Lambda Legal campaigns for full recognition of the civil rights of people of all sexual orientations.

The following debates in the Pro/Con series may also be of interest:

In this volume:

Part 1: Worker rights

In *Individual and Society*:

Topic 4 Should the constitutional "right to privacy" protect homosexual conduct?

In *The Constitution*:

Topic 8 Should homosexuals be allowed to serve in the military?

DOES SEXUAL ORIENTATION MATTER IN THE WORKPLACE?

DOES SEXUAL ORIENTATION MATTER IN THE WORKPLACE? KEY POINTS

EXISTING PROTECTION
Are employees adequately protected against sexual orientation discrimination?

YES: Some states and local authorities have enacted laws on sexual orientation discrimination to protect employees, and many companies have nondiscrimination policies

NO: There is currently no federal law to prevent an employer firing an employee solely on account of his or her sexual orientation. Many employees have to conceal or lie about their sexuality.

EQUAL TREATMENT
Is it wrong to treat sexual orientation with the same importance as race or gender?

YES: Some people argue that homosexuality is not a natural state; sexual orientation is a lifestyle choice rather than innate like race or gender

NO: All workers should be protected from prejudice on the grounds of their sexual orientation, which has nothing to do with their ability to do their job

NEW FEDERAL LAW
Will the proposed ENDA legislation hinder more than it helps?

YES: If passed, the ENDA legislation is likely to lead to positive discrimination for gay, lesbian, and bisexual people, and could result in expensive lawsuits that will bankrupt small businesses

NO: The proposed act expressly prohibits preferential treatment or quotas based on sexual orientation. It does not apply to businesses with fewer than 15 employees or to religious organizations.

FREEDOM OF SPEECH
Will the proposed legislation prevent freedom of speech?

YES: Those people disapproving of homosexuality on religious grounds would not be able to voice their views at work for fear of prosecution

NO: If sexual orientation discrimination were illegal in the workplace, employees would be free to express their sexuality without fear of harassment or victimization

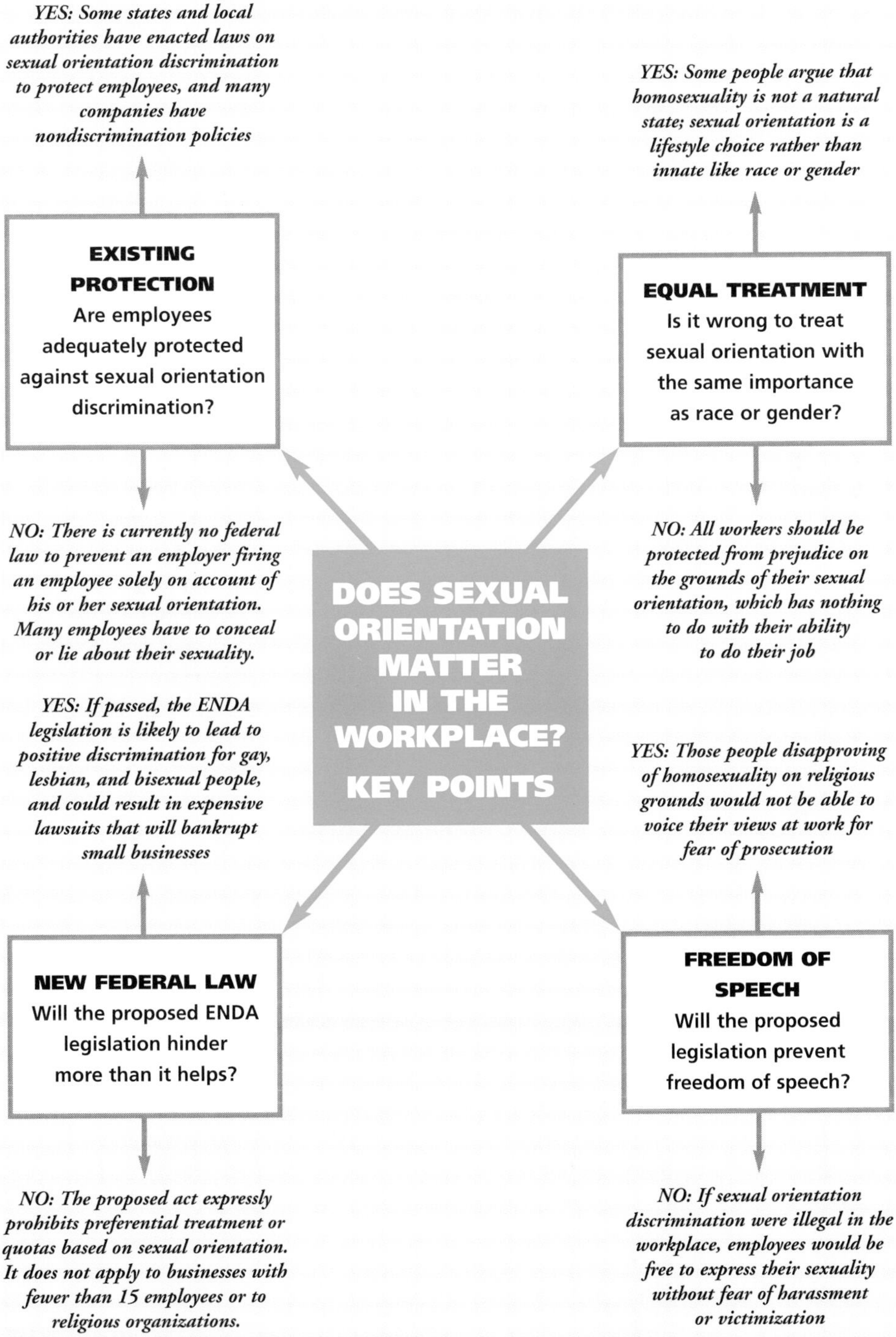

IMPROVING YOUR CONCENTRATION

"Concentration is the secret of strength in politics, in war, in trade, in short in all management of human affairs."

—RALPH WALDO EMERSON (1803–1882), ESSAYIST

Concentration is central to learning. If you find it difficult to concentrate—to focus your thoughts on a particular objective to the exclusion of everything else—you will find it hard to listen, retain and memorize information, study, or play sports, among other things. However, it is important to remember that most people suffer from the same problem. People who have good powers of concentration have most probably learned how to focus properly. The following article looks at a few key aspects to improving your concentration.

Barriers

The ability to concentrate depends on many factors. A positive, healthy attitude is central to good concentration, and this depends on feeling, eating, and sleeping well, and on factors such as time management and having a quiet study space and a good family and peer support structure. If you are overwhelmed by circumstances or feel that your goals are impossible to achieve, you will find it hard to concentrate, and your mind will wander. In certain circumstances—for example, if you are under pressure to learn something for an exam or an assignment—you will most probably feel panicked or stressed. Stress is a huge barrier to concentration, and there are various things you can do to manage stress levels (see Volume 21, *U.S. Judiciary, Stress management*, pages 124–125). But if you are have a positive attitude, feel well, and believe you can succeed, you have a far greater chance of being able to concentrate properly.

Time span

There is a limit to how much time anybody is able to concentrate. Try to time how long it takes before your concentration is broken. It can vary according to the task at hand. Once you have figured out your basic period of concentration, try to study again for that length of time before stopping. Take a break, and then study again, but this time try to increase the time by a minute or two. By doing this, you can gradually increase your concentration span. The longer you concentrate, the longer the break you should take—for example, if you concentrate for 30 minutes at a time, take a 5–10 minute break, especially if you are using a computer. If you can study for two or three sessions without your concentration going completely, you will have had an effective study time.

Carrots and sticks

Once you have established what your maximum concentration span is, you should set that as your target for each session. Setting targets and achieving them will help reduce the likelihood of last-minute panics or cramming sessions. Giving yourself rewards will also help you meet targets. However, concentration also depends on certain outside factors: Just because you were able to concentrate for an hour one day does not necessarily mean that you will be able to do the same the following day—you might be tired or upset, for example. Do not be demoralized if that happens. Work for as long as you can, and then take a break. Tomorrow is another day.

Concentrating on a topic that you dislike or find boring

This is one of the most common problems in concentration breakdown. If you find yourself in either situation, search for areas in the subject matter that might be useful to you or that could be turned into useful information. Use mind-maps or spider diagrams to record the search, and write test questions to summarize your learning after each study session. Use rewards to help you focus.

CONCENTRATION AND ENVIRONMENT

Helping you concentrate in the classroom:

Stop: When you notice your thoughts wandering, say or think "Stop!" It will help you refocus. You may have to do it many times, but you will find that the length of time between having to say it will gradually increase.

Focus: Classrooms are full of distractions. People talk, cough, and fidget. Focus on your teacher by keeping your eyes on him or her, and blocking out outside noise. The same technique can be used in a one-to-one conversation or debate.

Worry time: If you are anxious about something, especially if it is unrelated to school or work, try to set aside a specific time in which to deal with issues. This will allow you to focus on what you need to do at other times in the day. Research has shown that people who do this spend 35 percent less time worrying within four weeks.

At home:

1. **Study place:** Find a place where you can study without interruption. It should have a good-sized desk or table, a comfortable—but not too comfortable!—chair, adequate lighting, and not be too hot or cold. It should not have a TV or DVD player.
2. **Be realistic:** If a project is daunting, it will be easy to find things to distract you. Sit down, and divide your work into small, short-range goals that are achievable.
3. **Daydreaming:** If your mind begins to drift, take a break. Stand up and stretch. Try to refocus your mind on the task at hand.
4. **Time management:** Set a certain time each day at which to begin studying.
5. **Finish what you start:** Finish other tasks before you begin to study. If they are preying on your mind, it can be hard to concentrate.
6. **Notes:** Keep a pad and paper by your side. If you suddenly remember something that needs doing, write it down to do later.
7. **Don't panic:** Try to relax—if you are panicked, you will find it hard to concentrate.

PART 3
WORK IN THE UNITED STATES

INTRODUCTION

Most jobs in the United States are based on a 40-hour working week—that is, eight hours per day, five days per week (Monday through Friday). Paid vacations are usually two weeks, while other benefits usually include sick days and personal days. Most Americans retire around age 65, or before if their pension plans and savings allow it.

Ways of working

Since colonial times a number of different trends, cultural and social upheavals, and laws have helped shape the nature of work in the United States. Among them have been the Puritan work ethic of the early European immigrants, the arrival of mechanization, industrialist Henry Ford's invention of the assembly line, the economic and social influences of World Wars I and II, increased immigration, women's increasing participation in paid employment, and the sexual revolution of the 1960s. More recently the 1970s oil crisis and consequent inflation, widespread unemployment during the 1980s, downsizing, the expansion of world trade, and the increasing power and influence of transnational corporations have also all made for a more productive, flexible, dynamic, and innovative workforce. However, such factors have also caused many workers to complain of an excessive workload, hours far in excess of the standard 40-hour week, fewer vacation days than workers elsewhere in the industrialized world, boredom, lack of recognition at work, and anxiety about the future security of their job, income, and retirement. Downsizing, in particular, combined with an increased use by firms of short-term contracts and part-time workers, has resulted in charges of there being a "culture of overwork" in the United States. Topic 12 looks at this issue.

Labor laws in the United States

Present federal laws regulating labor-management relations are largely a product of the New Deal era of the 1930s. By far the most important labor legislation of that period was the National Labor Relations Act (NLRA) of 1935, popularly known as the Wagner Act, which guaranteed all employees who were covered by the act rights to join unions, bargain collectively, and strike. Nonetheless, laws enacted since, including the Taft–Hartley Act of 1947 and strike-breaking action by President Ronald Reagan in the 1980s, have restricted union activities. Since then many working Americans have come to believe the government and many U.S. firms are antilabor, and that the two sets of institutions work together to actively discourage labor organization. As a consequence, critics argue that poor and declining unionization are behind America's failure to uphold many labor rights and freedoms. Topic 13 discusses whether or not U.S. labor unions retain sufficient—or indeed too much power—when negotiating wages, terms, and conditions of employment for their members.

Equal opportunities

Most notable among American labor legislation designed to ensure equal employment opportunity (EEO) are the federal laws established by the Civil Rights Act of 1964. The numerous EEO guidelines are intended to provide equal opportunities regardless of race, religion, national origin, gender, age, or disability, while also establishing requirements for affirmative action. Of particular concern to many civil rights groups at the moment is whether or not such legislation should be expanded to ensure equal opportunity for people regardless of sexual orientation at the federal level.

Other of America's labor laws are designed to ensure the fair treatment of employees providing military service, health and safety in the workplace, and fair pay. For instance, although a number of employment sectors are excluded, there are federal minimum wage laws. Some states have set higher minimum wages than those mandated by the federal government. In addition to pay worker safety is an important consideration, and laws exist to protect employees by ensuring that certain requirements are met in the workplace, particularly in industries using hazardous materials. Whether these laws go far enough is discussed in Topic 14.

Globalization and domestic law

Globalization has come to be probably the most significant modern influence on ways of working in the United States today. While it provides the nation with increased opportunities for trade and exchange with the rest of the world, it also opens up domestic markets to foreign competition and allows firms to take action to cut costs by locating in parts of the world where operations can be more economical.

Labor unions and activists have taken issue, in particular, with the relocation by some companies of certain of their (often labor-intensive) activities overseas. Some people believe that U.S. law should actually prevent domestic companies from relocating jobs abroad, not only because of local unemployment, but on the basis that such moves act as a downward pressure on domestic wages or force local workers to accept sweatshop conditions rather than face layoffs. This issue is examined in Topic 15.

The final debate looks at the highly contentious question of whether U.S. executives are paid too much. This has received much attention in the media.

"Coming together is a beginning, staying together is progress, and working together is success."

—HENRY FORD (1863–1947), INDUSTRIALIST

Topic 12

IS THERE A CULTURE OF OVERWORK IN THE UNITED STATES?

YES

FROM "THE LOSS OF LEISURE IN A CULTURE OF OVERWORK"
WWW.OFSPIRIT.COM
LINDA MARKS

NO

"MORE YOUNG PEOPLE PURSUING SIMPLER LIFE"
MSNBC NEWS, JANUARY 26, 2004
CHRIS DEVITTO

INTRODUCTION

According to the Economic Policy Institute in Washington, D.C., in 2003 the average American worked 199 more hours a year than in 1973, when the average working week was 40 hours. Therefore, Americans today work the equivalent of an extra five weeks a year. Many people are concerned that Americans are working too hard, especially compared to workers in other countries. This has led some commentators to claim that there is a culture of overwork in America.

The number of people who work long hours each week has increased for a variety of historical reasons. Among them, some critics claim, is the weakening of the labor movement. Whereas in 1970, 27.8 percent of nonagricultural workers belonged to a union, by 2000 only 13.6 percent were members. Since 1973 wages, which had risen steadily in real terms since World War II (1939–1945), began to fall, partly as a result of the Middle East oil crisis, and partly because workers had lost much of their former power to negotiate pay rises. Another contributory factor to the erosion of wages in the late 20th century was the entry into the labor market of increasing numbers of women—they are generally paid less than men, whom they often replaced. The only way that many people could make up the shortfall in their income was by working longer hours.

The most significant recent development in working conditions in the 20th century, however, was the downsizing of businesses that took place in the 1980s. The widespread introduction of computers and new technology in the workplace has meant that many firms need fewer staff, but in practice these employees often end up working longer hours than before.

More firms have also begun to hire people on a temporary or "contingent" basis, employing extra staff whenever they need them. Since these people are most often self-employed and have no formal vacation entitlement, when they do not work they do not earn any income; this puts them under pressure to accept any work that is offered to them, no matter how tight the deadline may be. They are also aware that there are many other people in the same position as them, competing for the same job, and this also sometimes discourages them from asking for improved rates of pay. Many workers of this type have found that the only way to increase their earnings is by taking on extra work, and that the only way to create more leisure time is by finishing their jobs more quickly.

"Feeling overworked is a psychological state that has the potential to affect attitudes, behavior, social relationships, and health both on and off the job."

—FROM *FEELING OVERWORKED: WHEN WORK BECOMES TOO MUCH* (2001)

While full-time staff members are contractually entitled to take time out, many of them, too, are increasingly faced with the choice between working longer hours and earning less money. As a consequence of inflation, blue-collar workers and nonmanagers in service industries (who together comprise 80 percent of the private sector) earned in real terms less in an hour in June 2004 than they did in November 2001.

The increase in working hours has led to a corresponding reduction in leisure time. Some workers try to make a virtue of necessity, claiming that they enjoy long hours, boasting about their pay, and buying status symbols, such as bigger houses and cars to show off. However, studies show that they are the exception to the rule, and that most people working extremely long hours are stressed, unhappy, and suffer from illnesses such as depression.

Many Americans also resent the fact that they appear to work much longer hours than their European peers. Europeans work on average 350 fewer hours a year than their American counterparts, some observers claim. To draw attention to this discrepancy, in some parts of the United States activists now hold a "Take Back Your Time Day" annually on October 24, a date chosen on the basis that it would be the last day of the year for U.S. workers if they enjoyed the same conditions as their European counterparts. This is one of the initiatives of the Simplicity Forum, an organization that advocates a more simple and just way of living. They contend that around 50 million Americans are trying to slow down and work fewer hours, but the number of people who have actually achieved this is statistically very low.

The adoption of an "alternative" lifestyle is generally only an option for those people who reject materialism and consumerism, or those who have made enough money to last them a lifetime during short but hectic careers in highly paid areas such as banking or the law.

The following articles take a closer look at some aspects of this debate.

THE LOSS OF LEISURE IN A CULTURE OF OVERWORK
Linda Marks

Linda Marks is founder of the Institute for Emotional-Kinesthetic Psychotherapy in Newton, MA. She has taught and lectured both nationally and internationally, and is a leader in the emerging field of somatic psychology. This article was originally published in Spirit of Change *Magazine.*

YES

Having grown up in the 50's and 60's, I got the message from our culture that as we approached the 21st century, we could look forward to more leisure time and a better lifestyle as the miracle of technology made work easier and shorter.... Over the last several decades, it has become clear that this message is [both] a fantasy and a myth.... People seem to be working longer and harder. Their jobs are more and more demanding, and the pressure to do more and more seems to be increasing infinitely. At the end of the day people are spent from working hard, so the evening is about grabbing a bite to eat, vegging in front of the television, and going to sleep only to awake the next morning to do it all over again....

How did this way of life come to be?... In order to gain insight ... I spoke with historian Benjamin Hunnicutt, Professor of Leisure Studies at the University of Iowa, and community activist Barbara Brandt, founder of the Shorter Work-Time Group in Somerville, Massachusetts.

Benjamin Kline Hunnicutt and Barbara Brandt have both written several highly successful books on the culture of overwork in the United States. Look at the Further Information section on page 164 for more details.

The loss of leisure and the secularization of work

Over the past 100 years a series of political and economic factors have dramatically changed the way we live and work. We actually work more, not less, and no longer experience leisure as it existed 100 years ago....

Benjamin Hunnicutt notes that the evaluation of our modern concept of work [has] subordinated the former meaning and experience of leisure.

> *... Rather than a time to be with family and a time to do things important in and of themselves, like community, spiritual and artistic pursuits, leisure became a time to be fully passive. Now, people watch sporting events and consume. Leisure is seen as down time, a time to cease being human rather than a time to be fully human. Today, leisure is as foreign to us as is time outside of the marketplace.*

"Leisure" is the time available to relax, or free time away from work. If Americans are working as hard as this article suggests, is it inevitable that they will want to do as little as possible in their spare time?

Barbara Brandt cite[s] a series of political and economic factors that have contributed to the change in our quality of life and the way we live. "This change has not necessarily been for the better."

The decline of the labor movement in the 1960's and 1970's contributed to a decline in the value of wages. With a weakened labor movement and anti-labor legislation, no one was looking out for the best interests of the American worker. Also, the active participation of women in the workplace contributed to the decline in the value of wages. Women were paid less than men for their work.

Since the 1970's, families have been putting more hours into the paid workplace than in the 50's or 60's to compensate for the drop in the value of wages. Brandt [has] noted that 70% of families have both partners in the paid workplace. If two parents must work to assure the family survives, who has time for the children?

Finally, without protection for paid workers, the composition of the workforce has changed. The corporate trend of downsizing to increase profits has created two large categories of workers: More workers working longer hours and more contract or temporary workers (known as contingent workers). Contingent workers don't want to be trapped in corporate jobs. They escape this trap, but lack employee benefits and job security. Brandt [has] noted that 30% of the workforce is contingent and that a lot of people are working several part-time jobs adding up to more than 40 hours per week with no benefits. Those left behind after downsizing work more hours for the same pay to make up for the cuts.

As a result of all of the above, [Brandt says]:

> *... [P]eople are working terrible schedules and going crazy. Those hit hardest are families with both parents in the workplace, lower-class families (people of color and immigrants), and white-collar professionals (like computer people) who are expected to do more work for the same pay.*

Addicted to work

Brandt also acknowledges that it is hard for people to say "no" to work....

> *... We live in an addictive culture, so it is hard to say "no." ... There is a feeling that "I am an American, so I can do anything." Realistically, people don't know how*

Does this suggest that unions push up wages? See Topic 13 Do labor unions have too much power in the United States?

About a third of families in the United States are headed by one parent—more than 80 percent of them by a woman. Most have to work to maintain their families. Do you think that this has an adverse effect on children? See Volume 11, Family and Society, Topic 4 Is the two-parent family best?

Contingent workers are people who are part-time, temporary, or contract workers.

Do you think minority status—gender and race, for example—is a defining influence on people's earning power? See Volume 23, Poverty and Wealth, Topic 5 Is income inequality related to race? *and* Topic 6 Are women more likely to be poor? *respectively for more information.*

Quoting an expert can give your argument more weight and authority.

to set limits and boundaries. This is exacerbated by the New Age belief that you can create your own reality. We've been trained culturally to feel guilty if we say "no" to our paid work.

Go to http://www.familiesandwork.org/index.asp?PageAction=VIEWPROD&ProdID=8 to read a 2001 study on U.S. work culture and the reasons why Americans work so much. Does the study back up what Brandt is saying here?

Downsizing has created speed ups (a faster pace of work and life), longer hours or both. Because this country is economically addicted, we think anything that enables people to make money is good. Therefore, if an employer has to overwork you to make a profit, that is considered valid because we look at the money, not at people's quality of life. Brandt notes that this pattern is not limited only to the for-profit sector of the economy. "The pattern holds in a lot of government jobs and non-profits. Non-profits are some of the worst offenders. People trying to save the world have a hard time saying 'no.'"

Trading "luxuries" for leisure

... Hunnicutt traces the origins of how we have traded luxuries for leisure to three different sources:

Industrialist Henry Ford shortened the working day for his employees to eight hours; he also increased pay to $5 a day with the result that productivity increased and worker morale improved. Go to http://www.detnews.com/2003/specialreport/0306/09/f10-186947.htm to read an article on how Ford's $5 day altered America.

1. The emergence of commercialism in the 1920's. In his book *Work Without End* (Temple University Press), Hunnicutt links consumerism with "the threat of leisure." The beginning of consumerism and the practice of advertising designed to generate consumerism is linked directly to this "threat." Henry Ford asked "How can we compete with leisure?" People valued their leisure time and wanted to work only as much as was necessary to enjoy it.

2. Politics and how Roosevelt responded to the Great Depression. As a political maneuver to get out of the Great Depression, Roosevelt endorsed "the new gospel of consumption." He made it federal policy and came up with the strategy of "jobs, jobs, jobs."

Roosevelt defined the government's primary domestic responsibility as finding new work for people to do. Prior to this time, people would have said, "Go away business and government. We'd rather have our time to do the things we are working for."

3. A change in values and a change in our culture. Hunnicutt feels these changes have to do with the challenges we are facing as humanity in the 20th century. If you have got to the place where your needs are being met, then what? The changes ask us essentially religious questions, questions that in a secular society we would rather not think about.

Work as our cultural religion

Work in the 20th century comes close to answering the three basic questions that ... the world's religions [are based on]: Who am I? (a question of identity); Where am I going? (a question of destiny, meaning or purpose); How do I get out of the mess that I'm in, meaning the human condition? (a question of salvation).

> *"A lot of people profess not to have religions, but work fits the criteria for finding these answers in our culture," acknowledges Hunnicutt. "If there is a common morality in this culture, it is work. If you work hard, all your sins are forgiven. Work provides a high moral ground, allowing comments like, I work hard for my money. If people are starving, too bad for them.'"...*

Do you think this is a valid argument? Does work really provide a moral high ground?

Saying no to work

... Barbara Brandt founded the Shorter Work-Time Group in 1988 to encourage people to say no to overwork, to give people the courage to set boundaries and look at their quality of life.

> *People have a right to push for better quality of life and say no to work. If our values and political structures were different, we could have gone in a direction similar to Europe. There people work 30-35 hour weeks with 5-6 week vacations, and contemplate the idea of redoing work further because of unemployment. In the U.S., when we meet someone at a party we ask them, "What do you do?" meaning what is their paid work. In Europe this kind of exchange is considered discourteous. People talk about their hobbies.*

Go to http://uk.geocities.com/balihar_senghera/corpunhappy.html to read an article by journalist Polly Toynbee on the problem of overwork in Great Britain. How do you think it compares to the situation in the United States?

Can leisure be restored?

... Hunnicutt is concerned that work has such a hold on our culture that it would take a revolution for leisure to be reinstated. "The way we spend our days, the way art and music are practiced, entertainment—these and many other things would have to change in fundamental ways...."

While having a healthier cultural backdrop will certainly help tremendously.... [w]e do need to come together with others who share our values and empower one another to say no to excess consumerism, overwork, and treadmill existence. Maybe it's time for a revolution.

MORE YOUNG PEOPLE PURSUING SIMPLER LIFE
Chris Devitto

Journalist Chris Devitto published this article on MSNCB News on January 26, 2004.

Research shows that it is not just Americans who are doing this. In June 2004 the British newspaper The Guardian *reported around one million people in their 30s were using the equity gained from property to downshift to a less stressful life and were retraining or getting jobs in more meaningful professions. Go to http://www.guardian.co.uk/britain/article/0,2763,1247871,00.htm to read the article.*

NO

Sandi Garcia was living her dream—or so she thought. With a marketing degree from the University of Wyoming, she moved to Florida, started climbing the corporate ladder and was making good money.

There was only one problem: She was miserable. She was up at 6 A.M, and getting home from work just in time to watch the late-night news, and she often worked weekends, too.

"I got burnt out pretty quickly," says the 26-year-old, who longed for a life that was "calmer and simpler." She found it back in her native Cheyenne, Wyo., where she now has plenty of time to ski, volunteer at an animal shelter and enjoy her friends and family.

Experts say Garcia is one of a growing number of Americans—particularly people in their 20s and 30s—who are making a conscious decision to slow down and cut back on all that overwhelms them.

"It's true among people of all ages. But it's much stronger, much more notable among the younger generations," says Bruce Tulgan, a Connecticut-based consultant who tracks generational relationships and trends in the workplace.

They're simplifying at home: Pierce Mattie, a 28-year-old New Yorker, recently sold his car, moved into a smaller apartment and gave away much of his wardrobe.

"It feels great!" he says, noting that having "so much junk I don't use" was stressing him out.

Control over schedules

Gregg Steiner, a 29-year-old in Sherman Oaks, Calif., escaped the busy high-tech world to work at home, and sold his beach home near Malibu—he says he grew tired of never having time to spend there. He also couldn't stand commuting two hours a day.

"I hate traffic. I hate dressing in a suit. I hate sitting under fluorescent lighting," says Steiner, who now does customer service via the Web for Pinxav, his family's diaper rash ointment business.

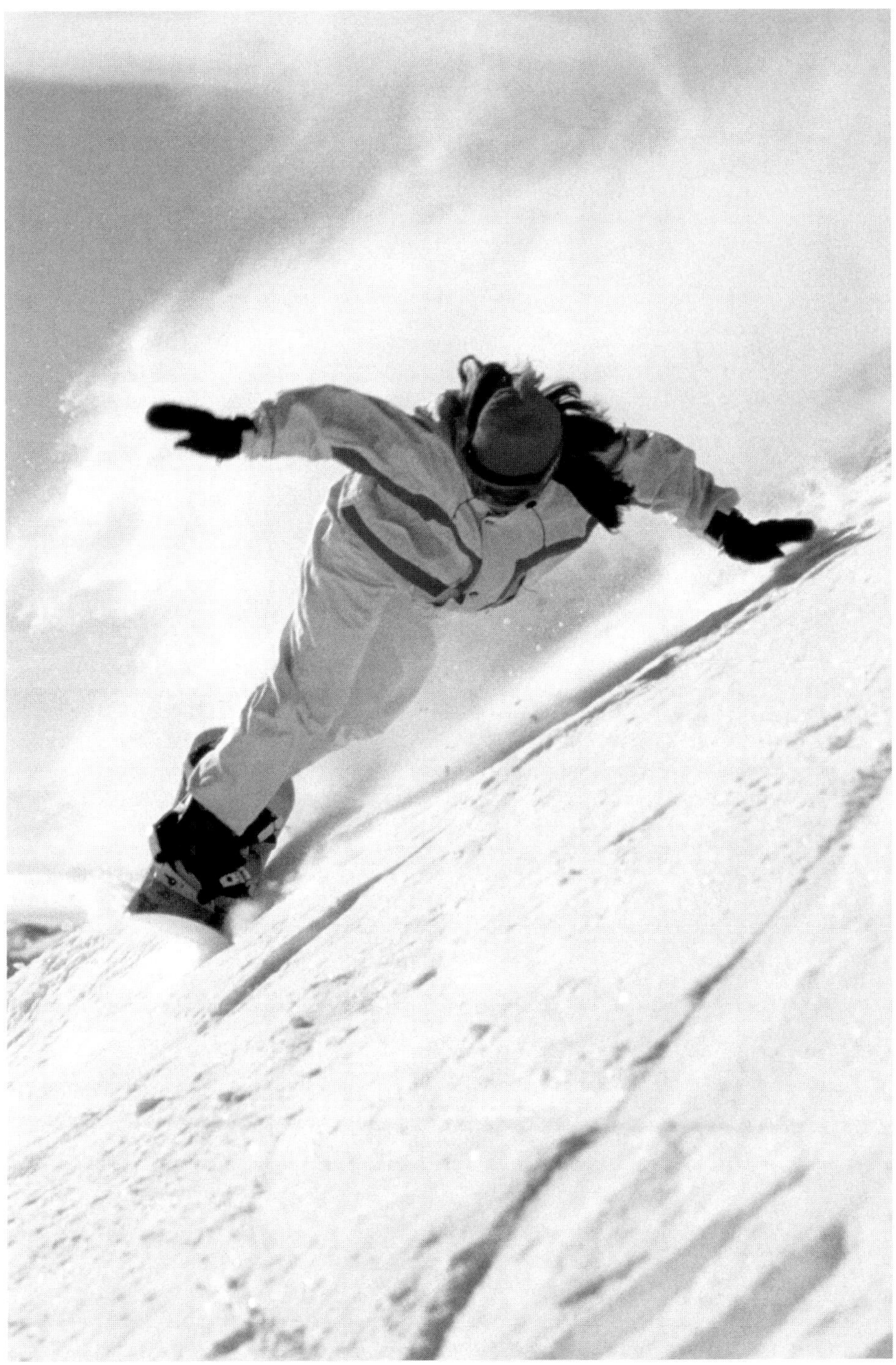

Increasing numbers of people are choosing to give up stressful jobs and move out of the rat race. Many take up activities such as snowboarding and skiing to help them relax.

Tulgan says all those gripes are common for young professionals.

"The idea of working in a particular building with certain hours seems ridiculous to them," he says.

Bruce Tulgan wrote Managing Generation X: How to Bring out the Best in Young Talent *(1996). "Generation X," or "GenX," is applied to people born in the post-baby boom period, between about 1963 and 1980.*

But he and other generational experts say that doesn't mean young people are lazy. They just want flexibility.

"It's much more likely they're going to tell you that they'd like more control over their schedule—and more time for the life part of life," says Tulgan, whose books include *Managing Generation X.*

An issue of trust

Michael Muetzel, another author who has studied twentysomethings, calls it a movement toward family and social activities.

"Why not put your trust and resources in things that you absolutely can trust?" he says.

Indeed, trust is an issue for many young Americans. While they're into volunteering at a local level, they have little faith in such institutions as Social Security or government in general. And many, given recent scandals, don't trust the political process or corporate America.

"A lot of us saw our parents or knew other people's parents who were laid off. There was loyalty to the company, and people were getting huge salaries, and all of the sudden it disappeared," says Garcia, who now works for the Wyoming Business Council.

Generation Y refers to the group of around 72 million people born in the baby boom period between around 1977 and 1997.

And so while their parents' generation may have focused on trying to "have it all," many in Gen X and Y are taking a step back to reassess and prioritize.

"I see my parents; they just worked so much, and I don't think they had much chance to enjoy stuff the way they would have liked to," Garcia says.

Do you think making this kind of decision is only possible if someone has a thriving career and is financially secure?

Katherine Josephs said she, too, had to do some soul-searching.The 29-year-old from Miami was a journalist for *Money* magazine in New York but quit her job after a road trip to the Pacific Northwest. She found a part-time job and moved in with her parents while figuring out what to do next.

Later this year, she'll head to a small town in Colorado to write and get a degree in ecopsychology, a field that explores the connection between the environment and personal well-being.

"I'll be spending most of my time outdoors and transporting myself on a bike and letting my spirit dictate my actions—not Madison Avenue execs," Josephs says.

Simpler vs. status

"The upshot is that people who value money and image and status are actually less happy," says Tim Kasser, a psychologist at Knox College in Galesburg, Ill., who has researched the phenomenon.

He says they often report being less satisfied with life and are more likely to experience depression, anxiety and such physical symptoms as back aches and headaches.

Those who weren't focused on possessions, fame and fortune were, overall, more content with life and felt better, too.

"We found this in people from age 10 to 80 all around the world," says Kasser, author of the book *The High Price of Materialism.*

Kasser heads the research committee for The Simplicity Forum, a group of authors, speakers and leaders interested in "voluntary simplicity," also the title of a 1981 book that some say is the movement's bible.

Garcia has never heard of the movement or the book. Like many others her age, she just listened to her gut and found the simpler life she craved in Wyoming, the state she once wanted to escape.

"Someone told me that you can never appreciate what you have until you've left," she says. "I never thought that was true—but now I really do."

Tim Kasser's book was published in 2002. It offers a scientific explanation of consumerism and materialism in society, and was critically received.

The mission statement of the Simplicity Forum says that it is committed to "achieving and honoring simple, just, and sustainable ways of life." Take Back Your Time Day, which challenges the culture of overwork is one of its initiatives. Go to http://www.simpleliving.net/simplicityforum/default.asp to learn more about its activities.

Summary

According to Linda Marks, in the first article, many people are working longer hours than a generation ago despite predictions in the two decades following World War II that technological advances would soon give people more leisure time than ever before. The author speaks to and quotes extensively from academic Benjamin Hunnicutt and social activist Barbara Brandt, both writers on the culture of overwork. The former suggests that work has filled the spiritual void created by the decline of religion; the latter contends that effective wage reductions and the increasing amount of work that people have had to take on in order to make up the shortfall are consequences of the erosion of labor union power. Both respondents share the view that the culture of overwork has also been fed by a growth of materialism and consumerism, and by the increasing credence given to the notion that earning money is a justifiable end in itself.

Journalist Chris Devitto, however, describes the experiences of many Generation Xers and Yers who have given up well-paid jobs and clearly mapped out career paths in the interests of more rewarding, although less well-paid, lifestyles. Those quoted compare their new lives favorably with their former responsibilities. One is pleased to have swapped long working days for recreation and voluntary work; another rejoices in no longer having to commute; a third quit her job because she suspected that her employers would keep her only for as long as she was useful. Devitto quotes psychologist Tim Kasser, who states that people who value money, status, and image are actually less happy than their peers.

FURTHER INFORMATION:

Books:

Brandt, Barbara, *Whole Life Economics.* Philadelphia, PA: New Society Publishers, 1995.

Galinsky, Ellen, *et al., Feeling Overworked: When Work Becomes Too Much.* New York: Families and Work Institute, 2001.

Hunnicutt, Benjamin Kline, *Kellogg's Six Hour Day.* Philadelphia, PA: Temple University Press, 1996.

Schor, Juliet, B. *The Overworked American: The Unexpected Decline of Leisure.* New York: Basic Books, 1992.

Useful websites:

http://abcnews.go.com/sections/us/DailyNews/work_howmuch_dayone.html
Article on Americans working harder than workers in other countries.

The following debates in the Pro/Con series may also be of interest:

In this volume:

Part 2: Work culture, pages 86–87

Topic 7 Is stress taken seriously enough as a health issue in the workplace?

Topic 13 Do labor unions have too much power in the United States?

IS THERE A CULTURE OF OVERWORK IN THE UNITED STATES?

ENOUGH OR TOO MUCH?
Do Americans work too much?

YES: Many Americans work 50 percent more hours a week than 30 years ago; Europeans, by comparison, work fewer hours and take more vacation

NO: Many members of GenX and GenY are choosing to work part time and spend more time enjoying life

ALL WORK AND NO PLAY
Have leisure activities taken a back seat to work?

YES: By the time they finish work, most Americans are too tired to do anything other than watch sports and eat. Obesity has become a national problem.

NO: Recreational pursuits have changed in the last 30 years as new technology has brought more leisure activities into the home

IS THERE A CULTURE OF OVERWORK IN THE UNITED STATES?
KEY POINTS

STRESS
Should employers be concerned about work-related stress?

YES: More workers are suffering from stress-related problems, such as depression. Man-hours lost to sick leave and the cost of employee health care worry many employers.

NO: Many employers are aware of the problems caused by overwork and are taking measures to help employees lead less stressful lives, including installing gyms in the workplace and having "family days"

CONSUMERISM
Are Americans driven to work hard because of consumerism?

YES: The media are constantly pushing people to buy bigger houses, better cars, designer clothes, and so on, and this takes money

NO: Increasing numbers of Americans are getting off the treadmill and adopting "alternative," less consumer-driven lifestyles

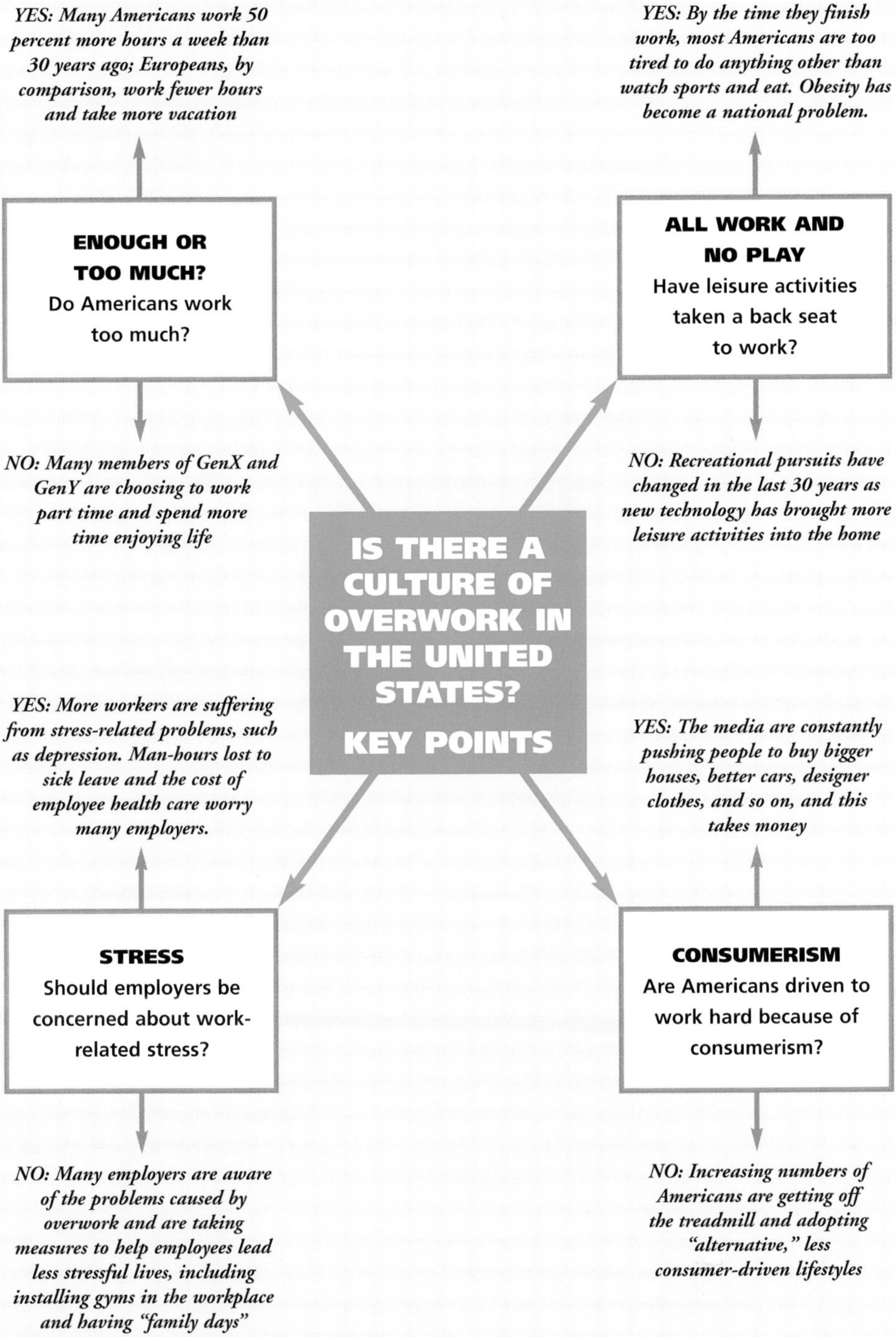

Topic 13

DO LABOR UNIONS HAVE TOO MUCH POWER IN THE UNITED STATES?

YES

"BUSH INVOKES TAFT–HARTLEY ACT TO OPEN WEST COAST PORTS"
THE NEW YORK TIMES, OCTOBER 9, 2002
DAVID E. SANGER WITH STEVEN GREENHOUSE

NO

"THERE IS POWER IN A UNION"
"IN THE PUBLIC INTEREST," SYNDICATED COLUMN, FEBRUARY 21, 2001
RALPH NADER

INTRODUCTION

Unions are made up of workers who group together to negotiate better working conditions and the protection of workers' rights through collective bargaining. Unions help protect their members against such things as unfair dismissal, discrimination, and exploitation, and they provide a range of services, including support for people claiming compensation for work-related injuries.

Supporters claim that U.S. labor unions act as a check against employer exploitation, but some observers counter that unions are far too powerful in America: They work against the interests of those people whom they are meant to protect.

The first organized labor groups were established in the United States in the 19th century. In 1881 at a meeting in Pittsburgh representatives of various workers' organizations joined together to form the Federation of Organized Trades and Labor Unions of the United States and Canada; five years later it reorganized to become the American Federation of Labor (AFL). From the beginning the AFL emphasized the grouping of skilled labor by craft. Samuel Gompers (1850–1924), its president, worked to win "bread and butter" gains, such as better hours. The more political Committee for Industrial Organizations (CIO), founded in 1935, represented both skilled and unskilled labor. Although initially antagonistic toward each other, the AFL and CIO merged in 1955; today the AFL–CIO is the main labor organization in the United States and has around 13 million members.

U.S. labor union membership grew in the first half of the 20th century: By 1954, 35 percent of the workforce was unionized. However, as the importance of manufacturing declined, membership began to fall, particularly from the 1970s onward. Some historians also cite such factors as difficulties in recruiting workers from new industries, such as information technology, in which collective bargaining is often seen as irrelevant, and the gradual erosion of legal rights and safeguards protecting unions in many countries as influencing membership levels. In 2002, when 65 unions were active in the United States, around 13 percent of the U.S. workforce were union members, a level that had remained steady for five years.

Union advocates argue that they are important: They protect workers, especially the low paid, and they give a much-needed political voice to those who might not have one otherwise. Without unions, some people say, business would be able to do whatever it wanted—it could lengthen working hours, drive down wages, and abuse workers' rights.

"Every advance in this half-century—social security, civil rights, Medicare ... came with the support and leadership of American labor."

—JIMMY CARTER, 39TH PRESIDENT (1977–1981)

Unions also claim that they are responsible for better worker conditions: Members enjoy higher wages, for example, and the benefits feed back into the economy, which is stimulated by increased worker spending power. According to the Bureau of Labor Statistics, union members in 1999 had median weekly earnings of $672 (equivalent to $34,944 per year) against a nonunion median of $516 ($26,832). Members also tend to have better health benefits and pensions.

By increasing the costs associated with their labor, some observers claim that unions are pricing their members out of a global market that is becoming increasingly competitive. Union opponents also argue that in industries with small profit margins, the extra costs imposed by unionization sometimes lead to them having to close down operations. In some cases companies relocate production abroad.

Advocates believe that far from having too much power, the strength of the movement has been systematically stripped away over the last few decades. For example, in 1947 Congress passed the Taft-Hartley Act, which gave the government the right to halt a strike if it would jeopardize "national health and safety." It also allowed states to enact laws restricting union shop contracts, prohibiting any that required union membership as a condition of employment (the "closed shop"). Opponents point out that many other countries have even more liberalized conditions: The United Kingdom, for instance, has abolished closed and union shops completely.

Union supporters also cite the billion-dollar corporate union-busting industry that has grown up in the United States—unique in the western world—as having had a major effect on union power. This industry employs some 7,000 consultants and lawyers to prevent new unions forming and to break up existing ones. Critics claim that tactics involve threats and bullying.

The following articles further examine the issue of U.S. union power.

BUSH INVOKES TAFT–HARTLEY ACT TO OPEN WEST COAST PORTS
David E. Sanger with Steven Greenhouse

This report by David E. Sanger with Steven Greenhouse is from The New York Times.

YES

President Bush intervened in the 11-day shutdown of 29 West Coast ports today [October 8, 2002], successfully seeking a court order today to halt the employers' lockout of 10,500 longshoremen, because the operation of the ports is "vital to our economy and to our military."

Judge William Alsup of Federal District Court in San Francisco issued a temporary injunction tonight that ordered the ports reopened immediately.

The Taft–Hartley Act—named after its sponsors, Senator Robert Taft and Representative Fred Hartley—was passed in 1947. It outlawed the closed shop and enabled presidents to order the end of a strike or lockout if it endangered the national health and safety. See http://hnn.us/articles/1036.html for an article putting the act in historical context.

In seeking to suspend the shutdown for 80 days, Mr. Bush became the first president to invoke the Taft-Hartley Act emergency provisions since President Richard M. Nixon sought to stop a longshoremen's strike in 1971.

Judge Alsup said he would hold a hearing in a week on whether to grant a full 80-day injunction. If he grants it, the dispute would be pushed past the Nov. 5 election, past the Christmas buying season and, perhaps, past the start of military action against Iraq.

Ports vital to war

Mr. Bush said he was worried about the movement of military supplies. The Pentagon often uses commercial shipping lines to send supplies and equipment overseas, and those lines would undoubtedly fill that role from the West Coast if fighting erupted in Iraq or elsewhere in the Middle East, because the route avoids the Panama Canal.

The president sought the court order after Labor Secretary Elaine L. Chao was unable to negotiate a 30-day contract extension to reopen the ports. The International Longshore and Warehouse Union agreed to a 30-day extension. But the employers' group acknowledged that it had rejected an extension, saying it feared that the longshoremen would engage in a work slowdown.

Mr. Bush's aides said he was reluctant to act, but feared that a continuation of the shutdown would undermine a sputtering economic recovery. Some economists estimate that it has already cost the economy more than $10 billion.

Some people believe this estimate is far too high. See http://www.andersoneconomicgroup.com/Publications/articles_pressreleases/aegreports/flash_estimate_port.pdf for a detailed breakdown of the losses.

"This dispute between management and labor cannot be allowed to further harm the economy and force thousands of working Americans from their jobs," Mr. Bush said in a hastily called announcement for reporters in the Rose Garden.

On Sept. 29, the Pacific Maritime Association, a group of port operators and shipping lines, shut the ports and locked out the longshoremen, accusing the workers of engaging in a slowdown. Union officials said the workers were merely observing safety precautions, because five longshoremen have died on the job this year. The union said the lockout was a management ploy intended to have the president intervene. Unions traditionally oppose back-to-work orders as government interference in contract disputes.

Between March 14 and September 5, 2002, five longshoremen died in accidents their union attributed to an increase in the work rate in order to meet an increase in cargo caused by importers stockpiling products in anticipation of a strike. In response the union imposed a return to the normal work rate. The PMA claimed workers were only in danger in the first place because in order to save jobs, unions insisted on doing some work by hand that in other ports was automated.

The major issue in this dispute is management's proposal to introduce new technologies to speed cargo handling.

The union has said it will not accept the new technology unless all new jobs resulting from it are in union jurisdiction.

Presidential miscalculation?

For the White House, the decision today was a difficult political calculation. With union leaders opposed to a cooling-off period, some of Mr. Bush's political advisers feared that the move might mobilize union members against Republican candidates [in the upcoming] midterm elections.

The November 2002 elections saw the Republicans take control of the Senate and increase their majority in the House of Representatives.

Several unions that Mr. Bush has courted say such injunctions undercut labor's power in contract disputes. "We're extremely disappointed," said Bret Caldwell, a spokesman for the International Brotherhood of Teamsters, the union that Mr. Bush has wooed most vigorously. "The whole strategy of locking out the workers and urging the president to invoke Taft-Hartley was clearly an employer strategy to get around negotiating a contract with these workers. It's a bad precedent. It gives management the upper hand."

The presidential emergency powers of the Taft–Hartley Act were invoked 33 times in the first 24 years after it was passed, but only once in the 31 years after that until 2002. Do you think that this means that the provision has become redundant and should be revoked?

Some White House officials argued that labor itself was divided on the issue.

"With every passing day, as the harm to economy increased, the president leaned more and more in this direction," a senior administration official said. "It buys some time. It gets us past Christmas."

Moreover, there is a chance that Mr. Bush may reap some benefit. Many business groups lobbied for him to seek an injunction, and they have sounded the alarm about the shutdown's potential to damage the economy.

Tracy Mullin, president of the National Retail Federation, said: "The President has shown political courage and leadership. He has put national security and the economy first."

Mr. Bush made his announcement one day after appointing a board of inquiry led by former Labor Secretary Bill Brock to report to him about the damage caused by the shutdown of ports that handle $300 billion in cargo each year. The board gave Mr. Bush a report this morning that said, "We have no confidence that the parties will resolve the West Coast ports dispute within a reasonable time."

Do you think there is a danger that presidents might use the Taft–Hartley provisions as a means to gain short-term political advantage rather than acting in the national interest?

A New York Times/CBS News poll published on Monday reported that voters were increasingly disenchanted with Mr. Bush's handling of the economy. Although the White House has argued that there is little that a president can do to control the business cycle, discussion in the administration grew over the weekend that inaction would only contribute to concerns that Mr. Bush was too remote from economic worries.

In his brief Rose Garden statement, Mr. Bush said: "The crisis in our Western ports is hurting the economy ... the security of our country, and the federal government must act. Americans are working hard every day to bring our economy back from recession. This nation simply cannot afford to have hundreds of billions of dollars a year in potential manufacturing and agricultural trade sitting idle."

Since it directly affects the physical flow of trade across borders, should longshore work be treated as an emergency service and subject to no-strike laws?

Not worth the damage

Many business leaders praised the president for seeking a cooling-off period, noting that the amount of money separating the two sides, $20 million by some estimates, was infinitesimal compared to the damage the dispute has done to the economy.

A spokesman for the National Association of Manufacturers, Darren McKinney, said: "While the NAM would have preferred the parties' coming together amicably and resolving the issue before governmental intervention became necessary, they failed in that and all the while the economy was being severely damaged. So we support the president's move."

Administration, management and union officials said the Labor Department solicitor, Eugene Scalia, contacted the heads of the union and the Pacific Maritime Association, the port operators' group, this morning to propose a 30-day contract extension. Several union leaders praised that approach, because it showed that the administration was seeking to heed union concerns and avoid invoking the Taft–Hartley Act.

According to the International Longshore and Warehouse Union (ILWU), Scalia had implied in his call to the union that the PMA had already agreed to the contract extension. This was not the case. See http://www.wsjwj.org/news/longshore_2002.asp for more details on this interpretation of the events.

An official in the talks said that the union agreed to a 30-day extension, but that the companies rejected it. Joseph Miniace, president of the operators' group, based in San Francisco, said in a telephone interview he could not accept such an extension when the longshoremen seemed quite likely to work at a slow pace when they were back on the job.

The union wanted to extend the existing contract because it would allow it to maintain a "safe" rate of work. The PMA rejected this idea; it preferred work to resume under the terms of a Taft–Hartley injunction, which allowed for the prosecution of the union if workers failed to meet the management's productivity targets.

"A 30-day extension, while we believe it would be a good short-term solution, clearly does not answer the questions of what happens in the long term," Mr. Miniace said. "We have been negotiating for five months without a solution."

But when the maritime association ruled out the extension, administration officials decided that they had no option but to seek an injunction.

Officials of the union accused the employers' group and the Bush administration of conspiring to order an injunction to weaken the workers' hand, an assertion that the administration and employers denied.

A phony crisis?

The AFL–CIO also denounced the president's move.

"We're absolutely furious," said Richard Trumka, secretary-treasurer of the AFL–CIO. "The PMA locked the workers out, contrived a phony crisis and then gets rescued by the administration. They're getting their way and have the weight of the government behind them."

He said it was especially infuriating that the companies had rejected the extension proposed by the administration and then still had the administration do what it wanted, seeking an 80-day cooling off period.

The Taft–Hartley Act, passed in 1947, allows presidents to seek injunctions against strikes and lockouts that "imperil the national health or safety."

The act calls for a 60-day cooling-off period while mediators continue working with the feuding parties. Then the National Labor Relations Board has 15 days to poll employees to see whether they will accept management's final proposal and an an additional five days to tally the votes. If the workers reject the proposal, they can strike.

The NLRB (see www.nlrb.gov) was created in 1935 by the Wagner Act. It administers unionization elections and investigates labor practices that infringe on both the Wagner Act and other later labor-related acts.

THERE IS POWER IN A UNION
Ralph Nader

Ralph Nader (1934–) is a well-known political activist, lawyer, and writer. He has defended consumer rights, the civil justice system, and has supported moves to make corporations more accountable, among other things. Go to his website—www.nader.org—to read more about his work and to find out more about him.

NO

There can be no vibrant American democracy without a vibrant labor union movement. Unions enable working people to band together to enliven our modest political democracy, and they are by far the most important institution working to infuse at least a modicum of the nation's democratic values into the economic sphere. Whatever their limitations and imperfections, there should be no dispute that our nation is far stronger than it would be in the absence of a labor movement.

That makes the latest figures on unionization rates a matter of serious concern, not just for union leaders or even all union members, but for all Americans. Despite an increased investment in union organizing in recent years, the number of unionized Americans declined last year [2000], not just as a percentage of the workforce, but in absolute numbers.

Unions weakened by harassment

See http://www.aflcio.org/aboutunions/joinunions/howjoin/upload/vatw_issuebrief.pdf for some examples of the kind of harassment that has been alleged.

Over the last two decades corporate America has waged a sustained campaign to weaken unions in the United States. Employing union-busting consultants and motivated by an anything-goes anti-union animus, employers regularly confront union-organizing campaigns with threats to close plants; harassment, intimidation, and firings of key union supporters; captive meetings; supervisor one-on-one meetings with fearful employees; threatening literature; use of surveillance technologies; and much more. Strikebreaking techniques, including the use of scab replacement workers and armed guards, is now so evolved that unions are fearful of using what at least once was their most powerful tactic: the strike.

Have the Republicans and the Democrats favored the interests of corporations over those of unions? Go to http://www.republicans.org/ and http://www.democrats.org respectively to find out more.

The two-party duopoly, featuring one party that too often takes labor unions for granted, and another that wants to take them out altogether, has aided and abetted corporate America. Lawmakers and the executive branch have let stand a legal regime that tremendously disempowers workers and they have worked hard for passage of key policies further undermining worker power.

Much of U.S. labor law, on the books and, even worse, in practice, is a disgrace.

Ralph Nader pictured during the 2000 presidential election campaign. Nader made his name as a consumer advocate before moving into issues of wider corporate accountability.

See http://library.lp.findlaw.com/articles/file/00565/003764/title/Subject/topic/Employment%20Law_Concerted%20Activities/filename/employmentlaw_2_2798 for an article about NLRB v. Mackay Radio & Telegraph, *the 1938 Supreme Court ruling establishing the distinction between "firing" and "permanenetly replacing" workers. Is the distinction made a convincing one?*

Although it is illegal for employers to fire striking workers, it is legal to "permanently replace" them—a distinction without difference to any worker or employer, but one the Supreme Court has embedded in the law and which Congress has not seen fit to remedy.

Although it is illegal for employers to fire workers for supporting a union, approximately 1 in 10 union supporters in union-organizing drives are, in fact, fired. The chilling effect from such practices is obvious and the insignificant penalties for illegal firings are little deterrent whatsoever to employers.

And then there is Taft-Hartley, the labor law deform that remains on the books 50 years after passage. Taft-Hartley's sweeping anti-union provisions deprive workers of many of their most important tactics—including calling boycotts of those who continue doing business with boycotted companies.

Rules made in the corporate interest

Corporate globalization, with rules fixed in the corporate-managed trade agreements that go by names like General Agreement on Tariffs and Trade (GATT)/World Trade Organization (WTO) and North American Free Trade Agreement (NAFTA), has tilted the labor-management playing field further in corporations' direction. New technologies and ways of organizing business did not inevitably lead to an international system of laws and regulations that leave workers ever more defenseless; that result has come from the business manipulation of the emerging norms and rules.

See http://www.ilo.org/public/english/dialogue/ifpdial/ll/observatory/profiles for a comparison of labor law between different countries. Does this back up Nader's statement?

The rules of the WTO are so skewed that they make it illegal for the United States to ban the import of goods made with brutalized child labor.

Most serious for U.S. workers, NAFTA and the WTO have ensured that U.S. employers can pull up stakes and move operations without restraint. The well-documented record of U.S. employers closing plants and moving to Mexico, China, and other low-wage havens casts a pall over most U.S. contract negotiations: American workers must always deal with the threat that, if they ask for too much, they will lose their jobs. Even worse, U.S. employees seeking to exercise their rights to unionize routinely find themselves facing threats that their employers will close their plant and move. Cornell University researcher Kate Bronfenbrenner has found in her groundbreaking research (her paper "Uneasy Terrain" is available as an 86-page pdf file requiring Acrobat reader)

See http://www.ustdrc.gov/research/bronfenbrenner.pdf to read "Uneasy Terrain" online.

that employers issue such threats in more than half of all union-organizing drives.

Under attack from Congress

As yet another blow, U.S. unions are now forced to devote resources to addressing extraordinarily aggressive investigations and congressional saber rattling. There can be no tolerance for corruption in the labor movement, of course. But one cannot but help question the motivation of tough-talking members of Congress who focus their rhetorical salvos and investigative authority at some of the most aggressive members of organized labor's leadership, while regularly ignoring massive defrauding of shareholders and consumers and a broad corporate crime epidemic—not to mention the massive corruption in their legislative-lobbying midst.

Organized labor—and all who understand the importance of labor unions to American democracy—needs Congress to stand up on behalf of working Americans and their representative unions.

Scandals such as the accounting frauds perpetrated by Enron (exposed in 2001; see the box on page 108 in Volume 18, Commerce and Trade*) and Worldcom (2002) have shaken public confidence in big business. Do you think the media holds unions more accountable than big corporations? Why might this be?*

Summary

Do labor unions have too much power in the United States? The first article, from *The New York Times,* cites the damaging effects of the 2002 industrial action brought by the International Longshore and Warehouse Union, when 29 West Coast ports were shutdown. The authors point out that the dispute between the union and the Pacific Maritime Association had been going on for over five months without a solution, and that the repercussions were far-reaching. Although the stoppage was brought about by an employer's lockout rather than the union's strike, the situation would not have arisen if the union had had less power, and thus less ability to affect negotiations. The damaging carryover effect of the stoppage on the economy at large might have led to thousands of Americans losing their jobs, as well as major financial losses.

Civil and political activist Ralph Nader, however, argues that it is corporate business that has too much power in the United States—and in many other countries too—not the unions. He states that unions are vital to the United States and that the nation would be far weaker without them. Nader points out that far from being too powerful, the unions have had much of their power and influence eroded by laws weighted in favor of big business. He continues by saying that corporate America has waged a war on unions in an effort to destroy their ability to function and has effectively been blackmailing workers into not unionizing by threatening to move their jobs abroad. In parallel with this Republican politicians have been repeatedly targeting often minor union corruption in congressional investigations, while ignoring much worse corruption among their corporate allies.

FURTHER INFORMATION:

Books:

Nicholson, Philip Yale, *Labor's Story in the United States*. Philadelphia, PA: Temple University Press, 2004.

Smith, Robert Michael, and Scott Molloy, *From Blackjacks to Briefcases: A History of Commercialized Strikebreaking and Unionbusting in the United States*. Athens, OH: Ohio University Press, 2003.

Yates, Michael, *Why Unions Matter*. New York: Monthly Review Press, 1998.

Useful websites:

www.laborresearch.org/union_busting_watch.php
Labor Research Association's Union-Busting Watch page.

http://www.nlpc.org/olap.asp
NLPC's Organized Labor Accountability Project page.

http://vi.uh.edu/pages/buzzmat/tafthartley.html
The text of the Taft–Hartley Act.

The following debates in the Pro/Con series may also be of interest:

In this volume:
Topic 15 Should companies be allowed to relocate jobs abroad?

In *Education*:
Topic 9 Do teachers' unions hinder educational performance?

In *Commerce and Trade*:
Topic 4 Do unions adversely affect economic growth?

DO LABOR UNIONS HAVE TOO MUCH POWER IN THE UNITED STATES?

DO LABOR UNIONS HAVE TOO MUCH POWER IN THE UNITED STATES?

KEY POINTS

JOB SECURITY
Do unions endanger job security?

YES: Unions and industrial action actually endanger jobs by making companies unprofitable and damaging the economy at large

NO: Labor unions protect jobs by seeking collective bargaining with employers and actively work to prevent layoffs

NEED FOR LEGISLATION
Should the government have the power to overrule unions?

YES: Union disputes must not be allowed to adversely affect national security or threaten the economy. Sometimes antiunion legislation is the only answer.

NO: Government should not have the power to overrule the right to strike. This is an infringement of civil liberties.

PEOPLE POWER
Are the views of workers distorted by unions?

YES: Unions work to increase their own power. Some workers, especially those from minority groups, feel that they are not properly represented by unions.

NO: Unions are duty bound to have the best interest of their members at heart. By showing a united front, unions can achieve more for their members.

PRODUCTIVITY
Are unions bad for business?

YES: Unions allow the workforce to stagnate by protecting lazy and inefficient workers. They drive up costs by demanding unrealistic pay and often make it difficult for small businesses to operate.

NO: Unions fight for better standards for their members. Well-paid staff with secure jobs and higher benefits will work harder, achieving higher productivity.

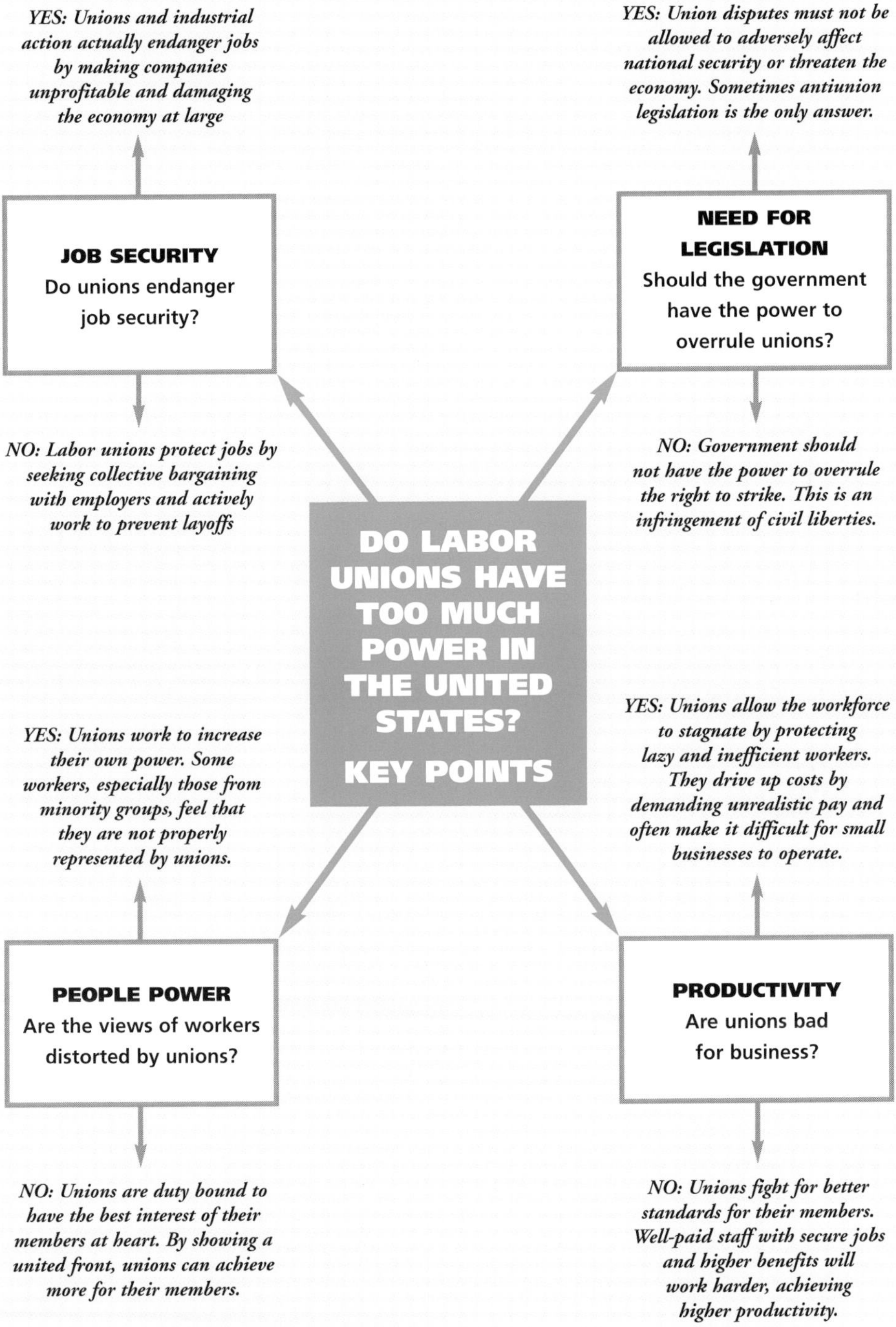

Topic 14

DO COMPANIES TAKE ENOUGH RESPONSIBILITY FOR WORK-RELATED INJURIES?

YES

"DUPONT'S CEO TAKES THE LEADERSHIP ROLE IN SAFETY"
OCCUPATIONAL HAZARDS, SEPTEMBER 12, 2003
MICHAEL A. VERESPEJ

NO

FROM "IT'S ABOUT TIME!—CAMPAIGN FOR WORKERS' HEALTH"
HTTP://WWW.NMASS.ORG/NMASS/WCOMP/WORKERSCOMP.HTML
NATIONAL MOBILIZATION AGAINST SWEATSHOPS

INTRODUCTION

In the United States employers are legally responsible for ensuring that the workplace is a safe and healthy environment. Even so, there were 5,534 work-related fatalities in the United States in 2002. Recent estimates from the International Labour Organization (ILO) suggest that globally about 2 million people are killed by their work every year. Another 270 million people are injured in work accidents.

Industrialized countries have seen a decrease in occupational injuries. Data from the U.S. Bureau of Labor Statistics, for instance, show that there were 11 injuries and illnesses for every 100 full-time workers in 1973; by 2002 this figure had decreased to 5.3. However, global figures for work-related injury have risen slightly. Some experts believe that this increase is due to more reporting of work-related cancers and other occupational diseases.

Critics counter that increased figures could be due to the negligence of many western-owned transnational corporations (TNCs), many of which do not have a good safety record. Incidents such as the 1984 mass gas poisoning at the U.S.-owned Union Carbide factory in Bhopal, India, have resulted in huge loss of life or serious injury to native labor. Some observers suggest that TNCs, which are not bound legally by any international regulations on human rights, are continuing the exploitative employment conditions that prevailed in the 1800s.

In the United States worker rights have come a long way since the slave and child labor of the 1700s and 1800s. Since the organization of skilled workers in the 1860s, leading to the formation of the labor movement and the American Federation of Labor in 1886, workers have been given a voice by labor unions and activist groups. During the 1800s social reformers such as John P. Altgeld (1847–1902), the governor of Illinois, supported by philanthropists, worked to legislate for reduced working hours for women and children. It was not until the Wagner Act of 1935 that labor regulations became law and the exploitation of women and children was regulated, however.

Some commentators consider union action and litigation to be a major force in improving employer responsibility for working environments. Others point to continuing exploitative conditions, particularly in the garment industry, and to the existence of child labor, with many countries failing to enforce their own labor laws—including parts of the rural United States and much of the Mexican farming community.

> *"OSHA's mission is to assure the safety and health of America's workers by setting and enforcing standards."*
> —OCCUPATIONAL SAFETY AND HEALTH ADMINISTRATION (2004)

All U.S. employers are legally accountable to the Occupational Safety and Health Administration (OSHA). This agency helps employers comply with the 1970 Occupational Safety and Health Act and also imposes penalties if they fail to do so. Commentators point out that since the act came into effect, there has been a significant reduction in workplace injuries and illnesses. They say legal penalties, along with higher safety standards, inspection, and safety training, are fundamental to improvement. Others argue that successful litigation by injured employees, which started in the 20th century, has caused major companies to take more responsibility for safety, if only to preserve their own interests.

In the past century rapid change in industry has brought new safety issues. The growth in technology, particularly in the computing industry and automated manufacturing, has led to the emergence of repetitive strain injury (RSI) and other illnesses caused by repetitive tasks. The pressured nature of the modern business world has also brought about a culture of overwork, leading to stress and fatigue.

Companies are increasingly aware of the dangers of pathogens such as nuclear waste or asbestos, and some people say that employers cannot be held responsible for diseases caused by pathogens that were not identified at the time people were exposed to them. Critics counter that employers have often left workers at risk long after the dangers have been known. Some point out that lack of enforcement can allow employers to avoid responsibility, while companies often deliberately slow down the compensation procedures that are available to most employees.

Many think responsibility lies with employees as well. A 2003 survey by the Missouri Employers Mutual Insurance found that most workers did not think injuries could happen to them, and critics assert that employers are often equally complacent for the same reason.

The two articles that follow examine this issue further.

DUPONT'S CEO TAKES THE LEADERSHIP ROLE IN SAFETY
Michael A. Verespej

Michael A. Verespej is a journalist who writes on human resources issues. This article first appeared in Occupational Hazards *in September 2003.*

DuPont is one of the world's largest chemical companies. In the 20th century it led the way in the development of polymer materials such as nylon, Teflon, and Kevlar.

The word "ergonomics" is derived from ergon, the Greek word for "work." It is the study of adapting work or working conditions to suit the worker.

YES

There's no question as to the importance of safety to the way that $25 billion life sciences giant DuPont operates. All employees need to do is look at who the company's chief safety, health and environmental officer is—CEO and chairman Charles O. Holliday Jr.

"The message [his title] sends is that safety is more than a priority—that it is a value. He is the chief environment officer. He's not just writing a memo," says Michael S. Deak, corporate director of safety and health at the Wilmington, Del., company that has 79,000 employees in 367 locations worldwide. "Priorities change. To really have a good strong safety culture, you have to have safety, health and environmental as a value, not a priority. We try to weave it into everything—performance evaluations, pay progression and career promotions."

A reduction in work-related injuries

That continued commitment to safety was reflected in DuPont's 2002 safety performance, which was its best since 1997. Acute and chronic work-related injuries were down almost 30 percent. Over 80 percent of its location sites completed 2002 with zero lost time injuries and 50 percent had zero total recordable injuries.

What's more, after an overall increase in recordable injuries between 1997 and 2000 because of DuPont's efforts to educate employees about ergonomic-related injuries, the number of recordable injuries/illnesses per 200,000 hours worked has declined by 33 percent to a level that is one-half the chemical industry average and one-fourth the manufacturing average.

"We have an internal ergonomic standards that is similar to the federal ergonomics safety standard that was repealed at the end of the Clinton presidency," says Deak. "We videotape employees to look for what's causing stress on knees, shoulders and wrists and have established zones of caution (similar to those used in the state of Washington) for repetitive motion and overhead movements.

In the movie The China Syndrome *(1979) actor Jane Fonda plays opportunistic journalist Kimberly Wells. While reporting on alternative energy sources, Wells witnesses an accident at a nuclear power plant. She tries to make it public, but there is a conspiracy to cover it up.*

But DuPont's safety efforts aren't just confined to the workplace. Since 1990, greenhouse gas emissions are down 68 percent and energy consumption is 6 percent lower, offsetting all growth over the past 12 years. Toxic waste generated is down 24 percent since 1999 and there have been just five significant environmental incidents in the last six years.

DuPont also credits its safety success to a philosophy that makes line management—not the 750 environmental, health

COMMENTARY: Repetitive strain injury (RSI)

Computers are essential to the modern workplace, from the workstations in offices to the automated machinery on assembly lines. Most people welcome the advances brought by technology, but it has also brought the emergence of a new occupational hazard—repetitive strain injury, or RSI.

What is RSI, and how is it caused?

RSI is a musculoskeletal disorder that can result from both physical and psychological stresses on the body. Other names for this disorder include repetitive motion injury (RMI) and occupational overuse syndrome (OOS). Most people associate RSI with computer use, but it can be caused by many tasks. Injury often starts with occasional numbness or muscular twinges but can gradually develop into a very disabling condition requiring strong painkillers and steroid treatment. People with severe carpal tunnel syndrome (CTS), the form of RSI most usually brought on by computer use, might be unable to use their hands for the simplest tasks.

The inflammation can be reversed with rest, but sometimes people are permanently affected. Current research is unclear on exactly how injuries arise, but most studies recommend prevention and early diagnosis. Devices such as wrist supports, screen shields, and software that has regular reminders to "take a break" are all helpful in reducing the occurrence of RSI. People whose jobs require heavy lifting benefit from training on how to lift and move weights efficiently.

In the United States OSHA counts cases of work-related RSI with other musculoskeletal disorders, making it difficult to tell just how many cases there are annually. A community health survey by Statistics Canada in 2000–2001, however, found a significant increase since 1996, with about 2.3 million Canadians reporting personal experience with RSI.

Reducing the risks in the workplace

Industrial workers in the mills and mines of the 19th century would probably recognize only too clearly the chronic pain from repeating tasks in uncomfortable conditions, but today medical advancement and legislation to protect workers means that the risks of RSI are increasingly addressed. Although some people still regard RSI as a "myth" or an excuse for laziness, medical evidence consistently supports the fact that it is a real occupational hazard in the modern working world.

In 1996 three women with RSI sued the Digital Equipment Company and were awarded almost $6 million, triggering many similar claims. Apple Computer, which in 1990 advised employees of the risks of RSI, faced action from thousands of consumers who had bought Apple keyboards without receiving a similar warning. Since then most employers promote ergonomic design in the workplace to reduce the likelihood of RSI occurring.

and safety professionals—personally accountable and responsible for safety, health and environmental.

"That is a cornerstone of our efforts," says Deak. Line managers are responsible for the incident investigation process, for making employees clear what is expected in terms of safety performance, for conducting safety training and for integrating safety, health and environmental expectations into the fabric of how work is carried out daily.

In addition, since 1990, DuPont has created competency networks (teams of individuals) to continuously look at safety performance in seven key areas: general safety, occupational health, ergonomics, fire safety, process safety, product stewardship and contractor safety.

"The networks have been the glue that has kept us together and kept us improving," says Deak. "They look at training, safety performance gaps and analyze incidents and equipment issues to drive improvement. It gives us solid core knowledge of safety issues and gives employees a group of mentors to learn from."

Go to http://www1.dupont.com/NASApp/dupontglobal/corp/index.jsp?page=/content/US/en_US/social/SHE/index.html to find out more about DuPont's health and safety record.

Eleuthère Irénée du Pont (1771–1834) was born in Paris, France, and moved to the United States in 1799. He founded the DuPont company to manufacture gunpowder, which was of poor quality in the United States at that time.

The French chemist Antoine Lavoisier (1743–1794) is considered to be the father of modern chemistry.

Safety from the start

Safety at DuPont began with the founding of the company. Eleuthère Irénée du Pont (E.I.) broke ground on July 19, 1802, for the company that bears his name.

He studied advanced explosives production techniques with the famous chemist Antoine Lavoisier. He used this knowledge and his intense interest in scientific exploration to continually enhance product quality and manufacturing sophistication and efficiency. He earned a reputation for high quality, fairness and concern for workers' safety.

E.I. du Pont paid Wilmington, Del., businessman Jacob Broom $6,740 for a site on the Brandywine River on which to build his first powder mill. The falling water on the lower Brandywine could drive the machinery of a large mill and ensure nearly year-round production. Willow trees on the riverbanks would make excellent charcoal, a key ingredient in black powder. The site also was close to wharves for shipping, yet far enough from the city for safety in case of explosion.

The DuPont family lived on the site, so they had a vested interest in running and maintaining a safe facility. Since its founding, DuPont established a global reputation for excellence in safety management. In 1805, DuPont was one of a few companies to hire a physician for employees. In 1935, it established one of the world's first industrial medicine facilities.

IT'S ABOUT TIME!—CAMPAIGN FOR WORKERS' HEALTH
National Mobilization against Sweatshops

National Mobilization against Sweatshops is a workers' membership organization founded in 1996. It campaigns on a number of work-related issues.

NO

"I didn't really think it was so bad until I got hurt," says William Ross when describing the long hours he had to put in working for the Postal Service. "We were forced to work overtime, especially when the volume of mail picked up like during the holidays or elections," he recalls. "You felt horrible. You didn't see your family." Ross injured his back in 1983 while lifting a bag of mail. The sound of his back "popping" was so loud that Ross' supervisor, standing 10 yards [9 metres] away, heard it. Hurt on the job at 27, Ross has been "put on ice for 15 years," and is in pain 24 hours a day, 7 days a week. Describing what the injury has done to his life, Ross says, "It destroys your life. You don't even care about money. You don't know if you'll be alive tomorrow, if you'll have a viable way of surviving. I don't know about marriage, family. I don't know if I could provide. But why should these things be taken away from me?"...

According to the Bureau of Labor Statistics, workers in the United States work more hours than workers in any other industrialized country.

Some injuries, like the one Ross suffered, are sudden and obvious—though they are more likely to happen when we are tired from long hours on the job. Other maladies develop over years of being overworked. Whether we are blue-collar or white-collar, low-wage or high-salaried workers, we suffer from a growing array of health problems. Repetitive-stress syndrome, back problems, asthma, vision problems, and nerve damage are just a few examples....

Long work hours are killing us

In the name of greater productivity, we are all being sweated. Businesses are downsizing and laying workers off, forcing the remaining workers to pick up the slack by working longer hours or doing more work in the same amount of time. Most of us in the U.S. do not have the right to say "no" to long hours. As Rekha Devi, one domestic worker put it, "I felt like I had to impress my boss—work harder and longer, or else she would fire me."...

In 1999, close to 6 million people reported work-related health problems in the U.S. More than 600,000 workers had serious injuries due to overexertion and repeated motions—almost one-third of all serious job-related injuries. Sixty thousand people in the U.S. died from work-related illnesses in 1998. The actual number of workers suffering from occupational diseases and injuries is much higher, as many of us do not report such health problems, telling ourselves that it is part of aging or "the nature of the job." Long hours also lead to chronic stress and anxiety, sleep deprivation, depression, high-blood pressure, cardiac problems, digestive problems and a general feeling of "burn out." We experience strains in our relationships. We lose track of our children; our kids are often asleep by the time we get home. Some of our children stop going to school. Some join gangs. Our ties to friends and community disintegrate. We are suffering in all aspects of our lives as a result of toiling long hours.

The Bureau of Labor Statistics reported that 6,055 people died from work-related injuries in the United States in 1998. The figure for 2002, the latest available, is 5,534—see http://www.bls.gov/iif/oshwc/cfoi/cftb0170.pdf for more information. It is important to use credible sources when fact-checking statistics.

New York State's workers' compensation: A dehumanizing "nightmare"

When workers get hurt on the job (except for certain categories of workers such as Federal employees) most turn to the Workers Compensation Board (WCB). Many describe their experience at the Board as a dehumanizing "nightmare" in a "system that doesn't work."

The WCB was created in 1914 to protect employers from getting sued by employees who get hurt on the job by providing quick medical treatment and weekly payments to cover living expenses while workers are unable to work. All employers are required to purchase Workers Compensation insurance. Workers whose employers do not purchase insurance qualify for benefits under the uninsured fund of the WCB.

Go to the Labor Department's website at http://www.dol.gov/esa/owcp_org.htm to find out more about workers' compensation programs in the United States.

In reality, insurance companies and employers, aided by the WCB, reap large profits at the expense of those of us who are injured. We are treated like criminals. Judges silence us, while allowing employers and insurance companies to say whatever they please to justify their denial of our benefits and medical treatments....

The writer is making some strong assertions here, claiming, for example, that injured employees are "treated like criminals." In a debate statements such as these should always be backed up by evidence.

During all this delay and denial, we are left without income or medical treatment. Many of us are forced to return to work to survive, and end up making our injuries worse. Those of us too disabled to work become dependent on our family or on public assistance. Sometimes we become homeless. By allowing delays of WCB cases and providing public assistance to those who are eligible, the State is, in effect, subsidizing insurance companies by paying money to workers when insurance companies should be paying benefits.

Insurance companies profit from pain

The insurance companies are permitted to appeal cases repeatedly for any reason to delay medical treatment and weekly living expenses. Huang Sheng Ku, who routinely worked overtime as a potato-chip packager at the Terra Chips factory, fell on a machine, injuring her back, legs and fingers in 1993. After 7 years and 18 hearings, during which her boss was allowed to falsely testify as a doctor, Ku still has not received the medical treatment or payments she is entitled to.

The source for these statistics is the National Association of Insurance Commissioners' "Report on Profitability by Line by State," 1998.

In 1994, private carriers in N.Y. State collected $2 billion in Workers' Compensation premiums and paid out only $1 billion in wage replacement and medical costs. This difference is among the highest in the nation. Commercial insurers in NYS are in the top 8% of the most profitable such companies in the U.S.

In addition, insurance companies sometimes deny payments to doctors, who in turn refuse to continue providing treatment to injured workers. For this reason, Arek Tomaszewski, a former asbestos remover, was unable to get any medical treatment for 7 years.

Using case studies to support an argument can be a very effective technique in a debate.

Many workers who have sustained injuries or developed occupational disease have claims dismissed, after being dragged out for years. Stanislawa Kocimska, a former home attendant for 8 years, injured her knee and back in 1994 when she ran to catch a patient who was falling out of bed. However, the WCB dismissed her case and denied her any benefits or medical treatment. Without benefits and unable to work, she is now homeless.

Denying our reality

A number of states allow employers to select a physician or require employees to select a physician from their employers' list.

Often, we are denied benefits because doctors paid by insurance companies tell us we are "fine" and able to work. Notably, New York is the only state that limits our choice to a list of physicians prepared by the WCB. Mussa Abdulkader, a former custodian, suffered a herniated disc on the job from lifting a trash bag, but has been given a clean bill of health by two of the carrier's consulting physicians. One doctor said, "At the age of 38 anyone could have this injury." His case was closed.

Furthermore, numerous illnesses and injuries are not even recognized as work related. For instance, those of us who are exposed to hazardous chemicals or develop repetitive stress syndrome have a particularly difficult time getting our injuries recognized. For 10 years Eva Herrera was exposed to chemicals at the T-shirt factory where she worked. The long hours of chemical exposure in a poorly ventilated factory, along with repetitive motions, led to nerve damage, chronic migraines, respiratory weakness, and muscle pains in her back, neck and shoulders. The WCB has questioned Ms. Herrera's claim that her health problems are job related.

Many injured workers who do receive weekly payments from the WCB, find that their payments are either very low to begin with or are arbitrarily slashed to as low as $40 per week. While New York State ranks lowest amongst all states in the maximum amount it allows for disability benefits—two-thirds of one's pay or $400 per week, whichever is lower—an even worse problem is its minimum rate. New York's minimum is absurdly low: $40 a week. This puts New York with the bottom 10 states in the nation for minimal protection of injured workers.

In 2003 the minimum rate in New York state remained at $40 per week; in some states, such as Florida, it was as low as $20. Go to http://www.dol.gov/esa/regs/statutes/owcp/stwclaw/tables-html/table-6.htm for more information on workers' compensation rates.

No longer silent and alone: Workers fight back

Many of us have silently watched our time, health and humanity stolen from us. Women, especially, know what this means. We toil long hours to make a living. We scramble endlessly for benefits, medical treatments, or a place to live. Many of us have been through the Workers' Compensation system, an experience that has caused countless numbers of us to lose our families, our dignity, and our self-respect. Our friends and relatives accuse us of not wanting to work, of being lazy. Those of us who are injured mothers can no longer enjoy simple pleasures with our children: prepare a bubble bath, jump rope, or ride a roller coaster. Instead, our children worry, take on jobs and more responsibilities at home, and accompany us to WCB hearings and doctors' visits.

We have tried it on our own—looking for a better lawyer, looking for a better doctor—but have come up against a system that frustrates, humiliates and discourages us at every turn....

It's About TIME! The Campaign for Workers' Health brings together injured workers and not-yet-injured workers to fight for what we value: our health, families and lives. We are exposing the greediness of employers and insurance companies whose profit-driven practices and policies put our time and health at a rock-bottom premium....

The National Mobilization against Sweatshops' website at http://www.nmass.org/nmass/index.html has more about the organization's campaigns.

We are fighting to win the wages and benefits that we can live on.... We are also building a new movement to take control of our time so that we can live our lives the way we choose, giving time to what we consider important....

Summary

Some commmentators say that the increased incidence of class action and personal injury claims by workers has forced companies to become more proactive toward and accountable for worker safety. The preceding articles look at some of the issues in the debate.

In the first article Michael A. Verespej describes how the DuPont chemical company implements health and safety procedures, and he also considers why the company is successful. The chairman is the chief health, safety, and environmental officer for the company, and the corporate director of safety and health argues that this signals "that safety is more than a priority—that it is a value." At DuPont managers are "personally accountable and responsible," and pay rises and promotions are tied to safety concerns. The company is proud that "over 80 percent of its location sites completed 2002 with zero lost time injuries." Verespej charts the company's philosophy from its beginnings as an explosives business in 1802, whose founder "earned a reputation for high quality, fairness and concern for workers' safety."

The second article, from the National Mobilization against Sweatshops site, takes the worker's point of view of work-related injury and illness. A postal worker describes how "We were forced to work overtime, especially when the volume of mail picked up," and a domestic worker feels she had to "work harder and longer, or else she [the boss] would fire me." The latter part of the article describes how methods to help injured employees are sometimes abused by employers and insurance companies that want to avoid payouts. When Workers' Compensation Board cases are disputed, delays can lead to loss of income, making some injured employees dependent on family or even homeless. Delays can also mean that medical bills are not paid, forcing injured workers to go without medical treatment for years.

FURTHER INFORMATION:

Books:

Green, Gareth M., *Work, Health, and Productivity*. New York: Oxford University Press, 1991.

Sullivan, Terrence, *Injury and the New World of Work*. Seattle, WA: University of Washington Press, 2000.

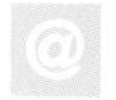

Useful websites:

http://www.bls.gov/iif/home.htm
Bureau of Labor Statistics data on work-related illness, injuries, and fatalities.

http://www.cdc.gov/niosh/homepage.html
National Institute for Occupational Safety and Health site.

www.osha.gov
Occupational Safety and Health Administration site.

The following debates in the Pro/Con series may also be of interest:

In this volume:

Topic 2 Should employees have the right to disobey company orders?

Topic 12 Is there a culture of overwork in the United States?

DO COMPANIES TAKE ENOUGH RESPONSIBILITY FOR WORK-RELATED INJURIES?

DO COMPANIES TAKE ENOUGH RESPONSIBILITY FOR WORK-RELATED INJURIES? KEY POINTS

WORKPLACE SAFETY
Do companies adequately implement health and safety policies?

YES: Many large corporations concentrate on worker education to prevent injury. OSHA statistics show that this approach is effective.

NO: Despite legally enforced penalties, lawsuits have drawn attention to continuing sweatshop conditions in U.S. territories such as the island of Saipan

ERGONOMICS
Do employers take workplace comfort and efficiency seriously?

YES: Companies are realizing that it is more cost-effective to take safety in the workplace seriously

NO: Changes to legislation that would have made ergonomic standards enforceable by OSHA were repealed by the U.S. government in 2001 under strong pressure from business lobbyists

PATHOGENS
Do employers have a responsibility to inform workers about toxic environments?

YES: The Occupational Safety and Health Act requires that employers communicate information on hazardous substances and conditions to their employees

NO: Globally, the International Labour Organization (ILO) estimates that cancer caused by exposure to asbestos and other cancer-causing substances is responsible for 32 percent of work-related deaths

COMPENSATION
Do injured workers receive adequate support?

YES: Companies contribute to funds to help employees who are injured at work through the Workers' Compensation Board

NO: Research shows that insurance companies obstruct justice. Injured workers can be subjected to even more distress, and temporary or foreign workers often do not qualify for support in the first place.

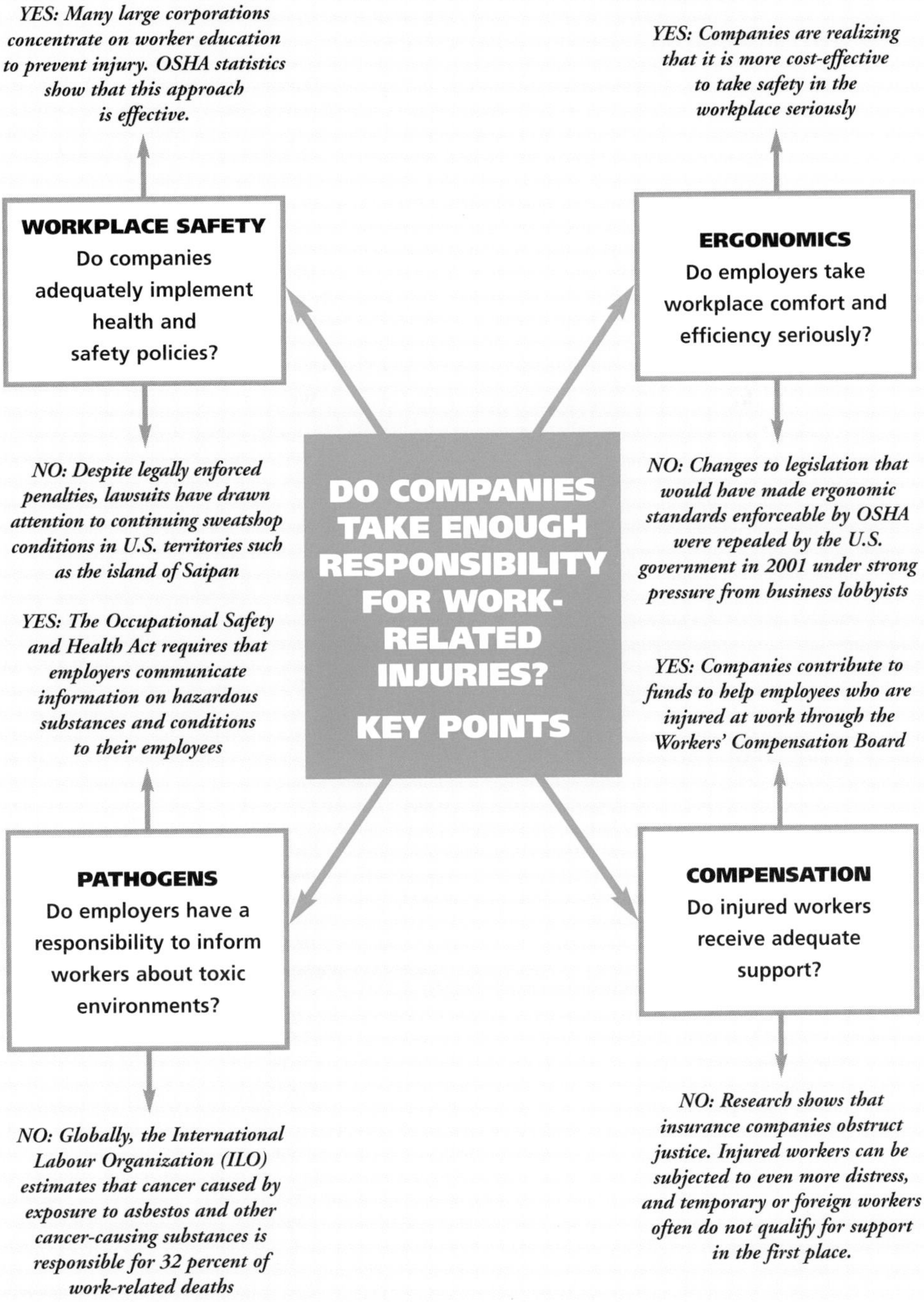

Topic 15
SHOULD COMPANIES BE ALLOWED TO RELOCATE JOBS ABROAD?

YES

FROM "OUT OF INDIA"
WWW.CBSNEWS.COM, JANUARY 11, 2004
MORLEY SAFER

NO

"MONEY FOR NOTHING AND CALLS FOR FREE"
CORPWATCH, FEBRUARY 17, 2004
NIDHI KUMAR AND NIDHI VERGHESE

INTRODUCTION

Outsourcing overseas—the practice of moving jobs to low-wage countries—has become the topic of much debate in recent years. Call centers, financial services firms, and many IT companies have been outsourced abroad. Relocating jobs overseas, also referred to as "offshoring," is a very tempting prospect for U.S. companies that are eager to reap the financial benefits and competitive edge that they argue comes with a huge reduction in wage bills. Estimates suggest that as many as 400,000 jobs may have moved from America since the outsourcing trend began in the 1990s. Research has shown that 3.3 million jobs may have gone overseas by 2015, with the potential loss of $136 billion in wages.

Advocates of outsourcing argue that it has been going on for centuries, and that certain industries, such as textiles, fashion, and electronics, have always looked to place jobs overseas to make the most of cheap labor or to be close to valuable resources. They point out that relocating jobs overseas is in line with the continuing positive globalization of the world economy, in which rich countries invest and create jobs in poorer developing nations.

Many people cite high domestic wages, labor laws, and unionization as the reasons why companies are forced to relocate jobs overseas in lean economic times. They argue that many developing countries, such as Mexico, China, and India in particular, have benefited from the outsourcing boom. NASSCOM (National Association of Software and Service Companies), for example, states that the Indian outsourcing industry accumulated $712 billion in 2000 and is heading for $1.2 trillion worth of business market by 2006. More and more companies from Europe and the United States are looking at outsourcing IT and call center operations to India, attracted by cost savings and access to a large number of highly educated staff. In recent years around 250,000 call center jobs have gone abroad. The savings are massive, experts say; the average call center salaries in the United States are about $22,000 a year, compared with $2,100 in India, for example.

> *"Outsourcing is just a new way of doing international trade."*
> —GREGORY MANKIW, CHAIRMAN, COUNCIL OF ECONOMIC ADVISERS (2004)

Opponents, however, insist that it is bad business sense to relocate jobs overseas. Developing nations, they say, often have far less stable business environments than western countries. They also tend to be politically more unstable, more bureaucratic and corrupt, and possess poor infrastructure in comparison to western nations. Critics also point out that there are massive security risks in sending private data, such as tax return information, abroad. They argue that it is far harder to protect consumer privacy once data leaves the country.

In the case of call centers observers also cite poor cultural affinity between foreign workers and U.S. customers as a main reason for loss of business. Although call center staff receive training, including watching U.S.TV and movies, critics argue that workers have no real experience of living in places like America.

Critics also accuse companies relocating jobs abroad of betraying U.S. workers: They argue that U.S. citizens are losing jobs because companies are relocating their business operations to countries that have less than adequate worker rights legislation, where they can pay much lower wages, make their employees work far longer hours, and can treat them generally as and how they want. U.S. unions also claim that outsourcing is just another example of corporate greed at the expense of the U.S. worker.

Many critics now believe that legislation is needed to curb the practice. They have welcomed the passing of the 2004 Appropriations Bill by the Senate, which contains provisions limiting agencies receiving federal funding from outsourcing subcontracts to foreign countries.

Advocates of outsourcing, however, believe that such legislation is wrong. They argue that companies should have the right to export jobs to countries like India if it is economically more viable. They claim that it could actually result in a win-win situation for all concerned. U.S. consumers could benefit from cheaper products produced by foreign labor, companies could use the profits to fund other U.S.-based operations, and employment in developing nations could help lessen the rich-poor divide.

Some economists suggest that outsourcing is an easy and obvious target for politicians who want to shift blame for an underperforming domestic economy. They argue that these people are using the issue to deflect attention from the real problems facing the U.S. economy.

The following articles further examine relocating jobs abroad.

OUT OF INDIA
Morley Safer

Morley Safer is a correspondent for CBS News and has been coeditor of the program 60 Minutes since 1970.

YES

"We're doing customer servicing there," says Raman Roy, chairman of Wipro Spectramind, a leading outsourcing company. He helped start the Indian call center boom in the '90s when he came up with a business plan for American companies to direct their calls to India.

Wipro had to build their own generators and their own satellite phone systems. The call centers are cool, self-sufficient islands in an uncertain sea of chaotic Indian street life. Inside, round-the-clock, they keep America on the line.

Do you think that getting people to work through the night is a form of exploitation?

"We service the globe. We service all parts of the world irrespective of what time it is here or there," says Roy.

New Delhi is nearly 11 hours ahead of New York, so manning the phones is largely night work. By day, the agents—as they're called—are dutiful Indian sons and daughters. By night, they take on phone names such as Sean, Nancy, Ricardo and Celine so they can sound like the girl or boy next door.

"The real name is Tashar. And [the] name I use is Terrance," says one representative.

Most western nations are multicultural societies. Is it really necessary for workers with foreign-sounding names to adopt more western ones?

"My real name is Sangita. And my pseudo name is Julia," says another representative. "Julia Roberts happened to be my favorite actress, so I just picked out Julia."

Training agents

American movies are part of an agent's training in how to sound all-American.

Lavanya Prabhu is a call center trainer who guides young Indians through the labyrinth of American English. And she says she is able to pick up some of typical American accents while instructing her students.

"Well, you have Brooklyn. 'You walk the walk and you talk the talk.' And you have the southerner's thing. 'Oh hello, there. What can I do for you today,'" says Prabhu, who spends most of her time trying to de-Indianize her countrymen.

But it's difficult to get in. In fact, Prabhu says they accept approximately five applicants out of 100 applications.

Do you believe that American jobs should be lost so that Indians can find a job?

On any given day in New Delhi and Bombay and Bangalore, the call goes out for new call center recruits as more and more American companies come calling. The call center

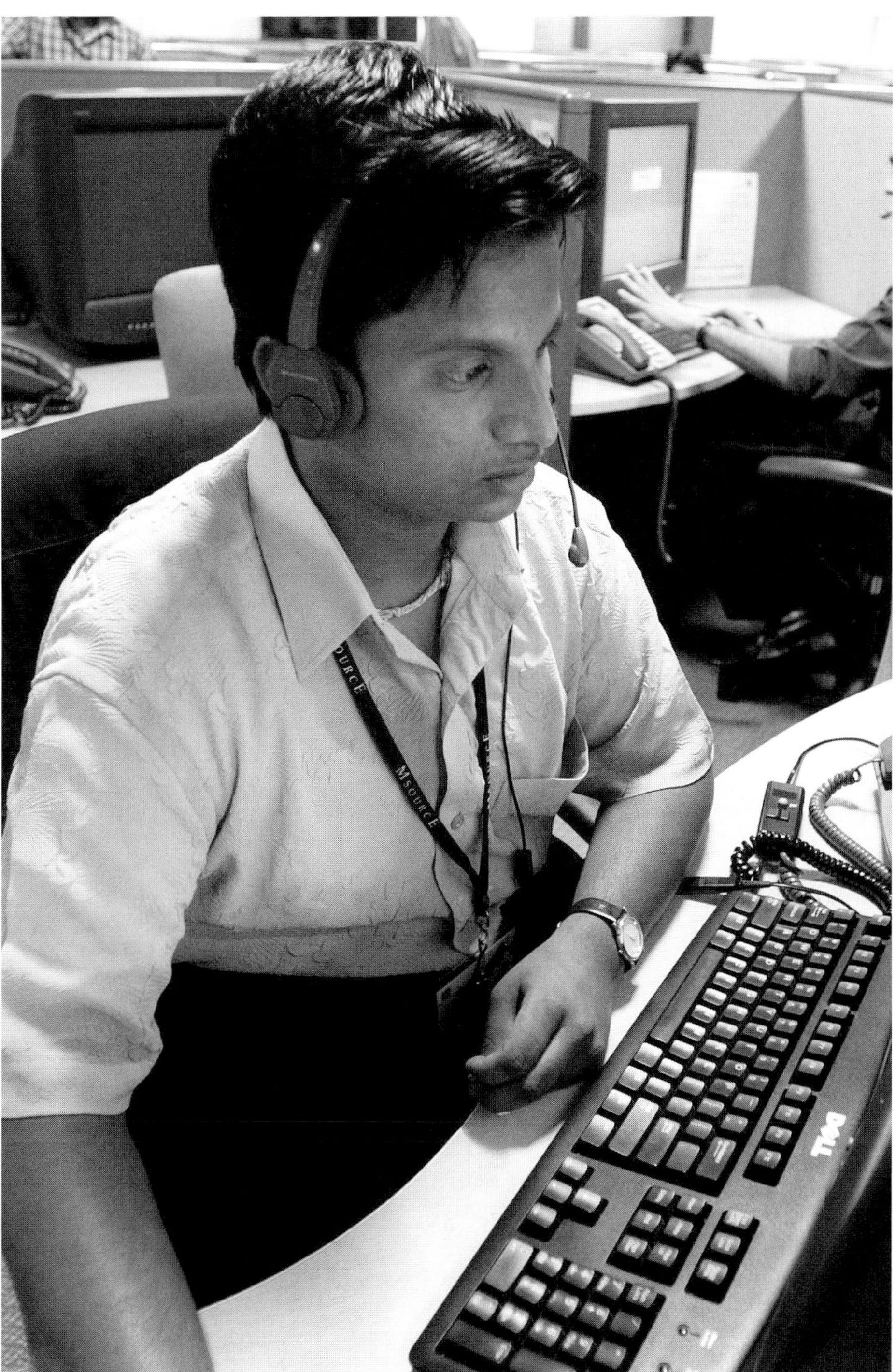

An Indian employee of an international call center in Bangalore, India, deals with customers. Many U.S. businesses now use overseas call centers.

employees earn $3,000 to $5,000 a year, in a nation where the per capita income is less than $500. The perks include free private transport to and from work plus the sheer heaven of an air-conditioned workplace.

There are few aspects of your telephonic life that do not sooner or later end up in India....

Debt collection

Debt collection is, as it has always been, a growth industry.

Arjun Raina, a Shakespearean actor, helps debt collectors and others trying to wheedle money out of you play the part.

"There's also a hierarchy of bill collectors. There's the sweet gentle one who's first calling in and saying, 'Just reminding you,' right? And then the toughies come in, you see? And the toughies have it quite good because the, for example, a lot of men have no problem being aggressive, right? Accent doesn't matter," says Raina. "You know, once I'm being aggressive with you, I don't have to be polite and neat. I can be tough with you, right?"

Do you think that globalization is unavoidable? For more on this debate go to Volume 3, Economics, Topic 9 Is globalization inevitable?

Partha Iyengar, an analyst in India..., says this is probably the best example of globalization.

"Absolutely. We've had globalization in the manufacturing sector with the auto industry, and Japan really emerging as a major auto power. We've had globalization in the low end manufacturing industry with China emerging as a global power," says Iyengar. "But this is the first time in the knowledge industry we have globalization impacting two countries at such a large scale—India and the U.S."

According to The Economist *magazine, this accounts for a tiny proportion of the jobs being created and destroyed in the U.S. economy. Over two million people change jobs every month in America.*

The U.S. government does not keep track of how many American jobs have gone overseas, but there are estimates that in just the last three years, as many as 400,000 jobs have gone to places like China, Russia, and India.

"The reason the companies are coming here is to really be more competitive and that cannot be bad for the U.S. economy," says Iyengar, who believes the effect of outsourcing on the Indian economy has been quite dramatic.

"There are some estimates that say that the whole outsourcing revolution, if we can call it that, will really be one of the key factors in moving India towards developed economy status."

Is the loss of U.S. jobs a fair price to pay for cheaper goods in America?

At which time, India would probably outsource to China, for the same four reasons the U.S. outsources to India—money, money, money and money.

What would be the savings to a multi-national company?

"You save anywhere between 30 to 50 percent," says Wipro chairman Roy....

Indians also answer some of the Amazon.com's e-mail. And AOL and Dell send technical calls to India. Plus, if your doctor prescribes an MRI at Massachusetts General Hospital in Boston, it may be processed by a radiologist in India.

Can you think of any disadvantages of getting Indian workers to do these jobs?

Tax returns

So what's left? Well, there's taxes. Last year, only a thousand U.S. tax returns were prepared in India. This year, there were 25,000.

"And next year, people are estimating that about 200,000 returns will be prepared in India," says Dave Wyle, a 31-year-old American entrepreneur who expects to make a fortune on outsourcing for U.S. accounting firms through his company, Sureprep, based in Bombay.

What makes India such a good candidate for outsourcing taxes specifically?

"The cost of the labor—it's a fraction of the cost," says Wyle. "You might be paying somebody $300 to $400 a month there that might make $3,000 to $4,000 a month or more in the United States."

Sureprep currently does work for more than 150 U.S. accounting firms, and its client list grows larger each month.

"These accounting firms range from small local firms to right now, it's about 20 of the top 100 firms including one of the national firms," says Wyle....

But most people regard their tax returns as among the most private things they have. Is there any risk of that security being broken with tax returns flying through the ozone?

"The type of security you see in this facility is generally much more so than you would see in any U.S. accounting firm. Everything is paperless," says Wyle. "You'll notice in the facility there's no pens or papers on the desk. There's no printers in the work room. Everything's done on screen."

Does a paperless office necessarily mean that it is more secure?

Young successful businessmen like Wyle and Roy no longer view the world as a place with boundaries.

"This is a global economy," says Wyle.

"Geography is history. Distances don't matter anymore," adds Roy.

Is Roy being overly optimistic? Some people believe that foreign companies choose to use Indian educated labor because it is cheaper and easier to exploit. What do you think?

But beyond the success and the money that's being made in this business, there's a terrific sense of national pride that India is making its mark in this very sophisticated way.

"There is a huge amount of nationalistic pride," says Roy. "Because we want to show that as a work force, as a labor pool, we are equivalent to, if not better than, anybody else. Anywhere in the world."

MONEY FOR NOTHING AND THE CALLS FOR FREE
Nidhi Kumar and Nidhi Verghese

Nidhi Kumar and Nidhi Verghese write for Unequal Sphere, a project of the Social Communications Media Department at Sophia Polytechnic in Mumbai (Bombay), India.

NO

The teacher lights a candle. The student whispers a thank you, gently blowing out the candle. The candle is relit. Once again the student says thank you the flame flickers and then glows steadily. The teacher smiles. Another day, another lesson learnt. This is one of the exercises in an accent neutralization class in India. Many such training institutes have sprung up which prepare youngsters for working in call centers. Call centers are mushrooming around the country and youngsters are queuing up to join the "may I help you" brigade. The Customer Service Executives (CSEs), or agents, keep in touch with foreign clients, sell products to prospective customers, offer after-sales services, handle queries, attend to complaints, etc. The CSEs assume different names and identities. They are trained to understand and speak with a neutral accent. Growth industry call centers provide employment on a large scale in India; currently, about 200,000 young men and women are working in call centers. They are mostly restricted to metropolitan cities and recruit youngsters from the upper middle class bracket.

Do you think it is reasonable to expect well-educated Indian workers to have to pretend to be someone else and change the way they speak? Do you think such treatment of workers in America would be tolerated?

According to a research done by callcentre.net, an Australian research and consulting firm, the Indian call center industry is expected to grow by 68 percent in the next twelve months, overtaking Australia to become the largest call center country across Asia by 2004. If one starts out as an agent in a call center, one can become the manager in just a few years. An entry-level worker earns about 100,000 rupees ($2,211) a year. According to call center representatives, the pace at which wages are raised is exceptionally fast. An official from a call center recruitment and training center in Mumbai says, "There is room for both horizontal and vertical development. In five years one can go from a CSE to an Operations Manager, earning 50,000 rupees ($1,105) a month."

The rupee is the primary unit of Indian currency. In August 2004 one rupee was worth about U.S. $0.021.

Elsy Thomas, Head of Economics Department, Sophia College, has a different point of view. She says, "Growth may be fast but what does one do after five years? There is stagnation and there is no new learning. However, Call centers have proved beneficial to India." According to US State Legislation, all products that cost more than one dollar require customer service operations that are often relocated to developing countries like India. There is much hype about how India could become the global hub for outsourced businesses. But the reality is that the current boom is based on a single premise—cheap labor. But is cheap labor a virtue? Is it something to be proud of? The call center industry could move overnight to another country where the cost of labor would be lower. In the US, a CSE is paid eight dollars per hour whereas in India they are paid 72 cents for the same work.

The authors use a series of questions to explain their point. Do you think this is an effective way of putting across an argument?

Physical costs

The job comes with all sorts of problems. The working hours at call centers are odd, due to the time difference in various countries. Centers offer pick-up and drop-back facilities but only at night. Sameer used to work at Wipro Spectramind at Powai, Mumbai during the graveyard shift from 2:30 am to 10:00 am. "Traveling by locals, at rush hour, after a sleepless night's work was extremely tiring", he says. Besides the odd working hours, repeating the same task over and over again can be very monotonous.

Mayur, who recently quit his job at Epicenter in Malad, Mumbai, says, "This is a kind of assembly line job that assures you a salary, but nothing more. There's not much skill or training required and people come in and go like they're working at McDonald's." Dhaval works for an inbound call center where customers call in. He says that one cannot take a break even to go to the toilet in between calls. Cris works for an outbound call center E-serve in Malad, Mumbai, where an automatic dialer dials numbers. His work starts at 10:30 pm but there is no fixed ending time. He has to log out each time he takes a break. He has to complete six hours of log-in time, no matter how long it takes and is paid only for the log-in hours.

Is this an abuse of human rights? Would workers be justified in disobeying such orders? *See* Topic 2 Should employees have the right to disobey company orders?

Many callers hang up or use foul language over the telephone. CSEs are trained to hit the mute button in order to be unheard and listen patiently without interruption. Girls sometimes get asked out over the telephone. Also the US has strict telemarketing laws and one can be sued for calling unlisted numbers for sales. Mayur, who works for Epicentre in Malad, Mumbai, states that he misses Indian holidays and that he, has to work even on Diwali and New Year's Eve. "One has no social life and one loses touch with friends", adds Darion, a CSE at Prudential (PPMS). Sameer and Nikita, both having

Do all jobs require a certain amount of personal sacrifice to achieve promotion and success?

COMMENTARY: Indian call centers

In the 1990s the trend to outsourcing, or "offshoring" as it is sometimes called, took off. India quickly became one of the most popular locations for outsourcing. Many top American companies, including American Express and General Electric, have moved some of their operations to India. India is ideally positioned to benefit from this practice. It is the world's second most highly populated country, and English is the common language. In fact, more than 1 million English-speaking students graduate from over 200 Indian universities every year. However, is there a price to pay for this new working environment for the graduates themselves?

Training

Most of the outsourcing jobs in India go to call centers. These centers answer queries from customers who telephone from America and Europe. They are also used to sell goods and services for western companies, such as insurance. In order for the Indian employees at the centers to sound as American as possible, they are put through a training program that is designed to teach them to sound like native Americans and know something about U.S. culture. Trainees are made to watch popular movies such as *Titanic* and TV programs such as *Ally McBeal*; they are also taught U.S. history and geography. They have to adopt a western name at work, so that Amit and Heena become Jeff and Julia, for example, and they are told to tell their customers that they are calling from a U.S. city. All of this is designed to put their customers at ease. Since there is a time difference between the United States and India, employees often have to work through the night—their computers tell them what the local U.S. time is and what the weather is like. Other techniques to "Americanize" staff include feeding workers cola and pizzas, and displaying U.S. flags at work.

Cultural erosion

Although these workers receive salaries that are high by Indian standards, there are concerns among critics that the call centers are starting to erode traditional Indian culture. The Indian writer Arundhati Roy has said that the adoption of foreign accents for jobs in call centers shows "how easily an ancient civilization can be made to abase itself completely." Indian employees, many of whom have conservative values, are exposed to a western culture that can be shocking for them, while the effect of splitting personalities—an American one for work and an Indian one for home—can be bad for family life. Inconvenient and long working hours mean that there is a high burnout rate. Call centers have opened up new employment opportunities for Indian graduates, but in the long term Indian companies might find it increasingly difficult to retain workers and end up facing high staff turnover—the same problem that has emerged in the West.

worked the night shift from 2:30 to 10:00 am, complained about health problems due to lack of sleep. Sameer could not adjust his sleep cycle to sleep during the day. As a result he was always stressed. His nightmare was when he had 159 calls on hold to attend to. Nikita developed liver and eye infections.

How important are health and safety in the work environment? Should they always be considered before productivity?

Most of the youth working in call centers are aware that it is an interim two-year stint—wage labor rather than a career option. Reasons for joining a call center are varied. The biggest attraction is the money. Although call center employees in India are paid only 10–15 percent of the salary of their American counterparts, it is considered adequate by Indian standards.

Outsourcing elsewhere

With the increase in opposition against outsourcing several states in the US are planning regulations to ban government operations from being shifted abroad. Thus, this great Indian dream could soon come to an end. Cadjetai Fernandes, economics teacher at Xavier's College says, "The employment benefits of Call centers are only for a short term and will not last for a long time. In such a scenario, thousands of graduates will be left in the lurch." Already countries like China and Philippines are gearing up to take India head-on. According to the *Outlook Magazine*, China has made English compulsory at all levels of education. Research reveals that Americans find it easier to understand Filipino English speakers than Indians.

Go to http://www.outsourcing-asia.com/china.html to see a list of possible reasons why China could become the next big outsourcing center.

Whether the call center industry moves elsewhere or not, the real beneficiary will always be the developed countries. While US based companies work during the day, their back offices in India and other developing countries continue their work even while they sleep. While developed countries reap the benefits, the fringe "benefits" are shared among the underdogs. The larger piece of the pie will go to the one who bids the lowest.

Summary

Morley Safer and Nidhi Kumar and Nidhi Verghese agree that the outsourcing boom to India has brought increased employment but disagree about the other relative benefits. Safer argues that outsourcing is good for America and good for India. American companies benefit, he says, because they are able to become more competitive due to the huge amounts of money they can save by paying relatively cheap wages. He points out that they can also take advantage of a highly educated workforce that is prepared to work hours that suit the needs of the business, and that in India wages for outsourced work are much higher than the national average, so the industry can choose from the best applicants. He also dismisses concerns over security as unfounded. Safer says that outsourcing from the United States to India is a positive example of globalization, pointing out that this new industry is propelling India into becoming a more developed economy and has engendered a sense of national pride there.

Kumar and Verghese argue against outsourcing. They say that although jobs in the call center industry are highly sought after in India, many workers do not view them as a long-term career move because they will reach a wage and learning ceiling after five years. While they admit that wages are relatively high compared to the national average, they argue that workers are paid far less than those doing a similar job in America. They also fear that workers are being exploited by working long, inconvenient hours and being forced to miss traditional holidays. They are skeptical that the boom will be of long-term benefit to India and believe that the companies will eventually relocate to countries that offer even cheaper labor rates. They conclude that the real beneficiaries of outsourcing will always be the developed countries.

FURTHER INFORMATION:

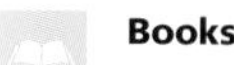

Books:

Davies, Paul, *What's This India Business? Offshoring, Outsourcing, and the Global Services Revolution*. Yarmouth, ME: Nicholas Brealey, 2004.

Heywood, J. Brian, *The Outsourcing Dilemma*. New York: Financial Times Prentice Hall, 2001.

Kobayashi-Hillary, Mark, *Outsourcing to India: The Offshore Advantage*. New York: Springer, 2004.

Useful websites:

www.outsourcing.com
Outsourcing Institute site.

http://yaleglobal.yale.edu/display.article?id=3422
Debate about outsourcing on site for Yale Center for the Study of Globalization.

The following debates in the Pro/Con series may also be of interest:

In this volume:

Topic 7 Is stress taken seriously enough as a health issue in the workplace?

Topic 13 Do labor unions have too much power in the United States?

SHOULD COMPANIES BE ALLOWED TO RELOCATE JOBS ABROAD?

SHOULD COMPANIES BE ALLOWED TO RELOCATE JOBS ABROAD? KEY POINTS

A BETRAYAL?
Should American companies be allowed to outsource jobs to foreign countries?

YES: They can become more competitive by saving on labor costs, make larger profits, and pass on the benefits to U.S. consumers via cheaper goods

NO: Outsourcing means that American jobs will be lost, and it devalues the worth of American workers

ETHICS
Is it morally right for businesses to pay foreign workers only a fraction of what their American counterparts would earn?

YES: Wages are still much higher than the national average in developing countries, and the cost of living is relative

NO: By paying foreign workers a fraction of what American employees would earn for the same work, businesses are exploiting them

BUSINESS SENSE
Does outsourcing abroad make good business sense?

YES: Companies can save money and tap into a pool of highly qualified workers

NO: Cultural differences and misunderstandings can cause problems with communication, resulting in consumers taking their business elsewhere

BENEFITS
Is the relocation of jobs overseas of equal benefit to America and developing nations?

YES: It helps accelerate nations such as India toward developed economy status and makes America more competitive

NO: The real beneficiaries of outsourcing will always be the developed countries, which have no commitment to any particular nation and go wherever labor is cheapest

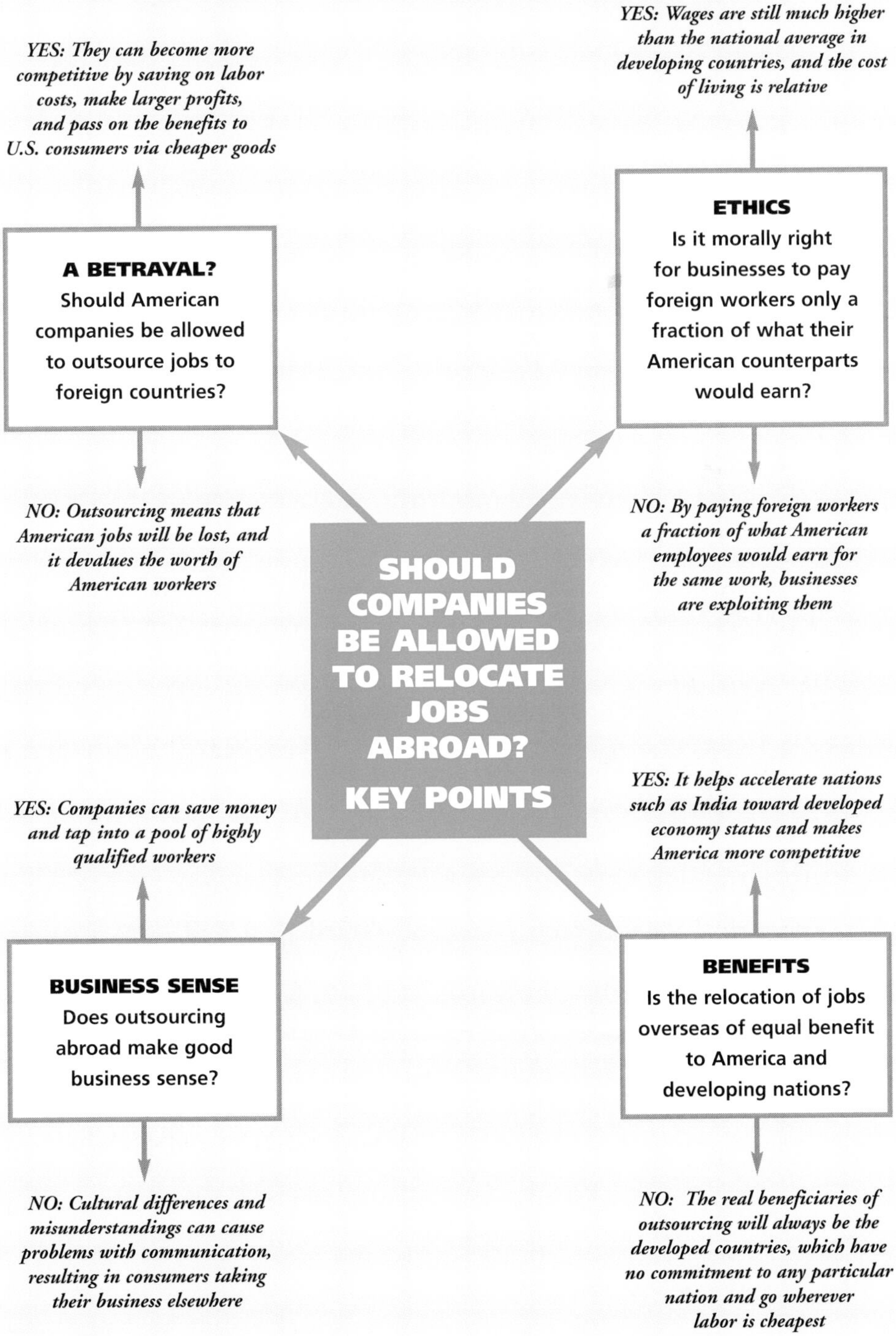

Topic 16
ARE U.S. EXECUTIVES PAID TOO MUCH ?

YES
"WHERE'S THE STICK?"
THE ECONOMIST ONLINE, OCTOBER 9, 2003
THE ECONOMIST

NO
"WHY ARE CEOS PAID SO MUCH?"
CAPITALISM MAGAZINE, APRIL 12, 2004
ELAN JOURNO

INTRODUCTION

In 1999-2000 Charles Wang, chief executive (CEO) and chairman of the software company Computer Associates, earned over $650 million—a world record for executive pay. Though his case is extraordinary, an executive at a major U.S. company can receive over $10 million in compensation, and some get much more.

Some people maintain that such enormous pay deals are fair because an executive is in a position of great responsibility that demands an understanding of the complex legal and financial issues affecting a company. Others, however, cite plain greed as the main reason for inflated payments. They point out that such huge payouts contribute to the growing income gap between rich and poor.

Income inequality is greater in the United States than in any other western country. A survey by professional services company Towers Perrin in 2002 revealed that on average, U.S. CEOs took home paychecks that were 475 times more than their workers, while European executives took home between 11 and 24 times as much. *BusinessWeek* magazine reported that executives at 365 major U.S. companies earned on average $8.1 million in 2003, up 9 percent from 2002. That works out to $22,000 a day. The average production worker made $31,928 in 2003, while the average salary increase was 3.4 percent. Critics assert that this huge difference in incomes is immoral, particularly in light of the fact that 12 percent of Americans live in poverty.

Supporters counter that it is unrealistic to compare executives and regular employees. People in executive positions need to have vision, strong leadership qualities, and to be highly competitive. Often they are required to turn around the fortunes of a failing company and will need to make big changes, perhaps laying off thousands of people or making enormously risky financial decisions. An executive is responsible for the success or failure of a company, they say, and may be realizing profits that amount to millions or billions of dollars. Executive pay of several million dollars is fully justified, advocates claim, given the vast wealth that executives can generate for company shareholders.

Opponents of this view argue that no individual can make that much difference to a large company. They contend that richly rewarded CEOs are often arrogant and have a complete disregard for shareholders, whose money indirectly finances their pay. Furthermore, they argue that arrogance and disregard can go hand in hand with corrupt business practices at the highest level, as has been seen in corporate scandals involving companies such as Enron and WorldCom.

"I think greed is healthy. You can be greedy and still feel good about yourself."

—IVAN BOESKY, FINANCIER (1986)

In addition to a basic salary executive pay packages usually include other forms of financial compensation such as stock, stock options, and performance-related pay. Options—the right to buy shares of company stock at a set price over a certain period—can provide an incentive for an executive to make the company succeed, thus increasing the value of the company's shares; but they can also mean that falling stock values significantly decrease executive pay.

A performance-related bonus is intended to reward an executive for leading a company to greater profitability. However, critics claim that the connection between bonus payments and long-term performance is unproven. They argue that there should be greater emphasis on accountability when it comes to negotiating pay deals. Executive earnings have spiraled out of control, they say, because company directors are too willing to offer overly generous packages in order to attract prestige candidates. In 2003 the Securities and Exchange Commission (SEC), the government agency that regulates financial markets, proposed rules making it easier for shareholders to nominate candidates to a company's board of directors. Advocates claim this will make boards more independent and therefore more rigorous in regulating compensation for executives.

Some people believe, however, that government intervention is required to curb pay excesses. More stringent reporting requirements on executive pay to the SEC have been in place since the early 1990s, but critics say this is not enough. For example, the AFL–CIO, which represents most labor unions in the United States, has called for legislation to curb executive-only pensions. Observers point out, however, that governments are usually reluctant to interfere in such matters. In the United Kingdom there has been a parliamentary inquiry into the large severance payments frequently given to departing CEOs when a company is taken over. Although the British government criticized such "rewards for failure," it stopped short of imposing new laws.

The following two articles examine issues in this debate in greater detail.

WHERE'S THE STICK?
The Economist

The Economist *is a British weekly business and current affairs magazine. This article first appeared in October 2003.*

YES

Running a large public company is a stressful and important job. Thousands of employees and business partners and millions of customers and shareholders rely on the good judgment of corporate chief executives, who have to make decisions in a climate of constant uncertainty. Only the savviest and most determined need apply. Lately, though, these adjectives hardly spring to mind when company bosses are mentioned. For many, top bosses are not the toughest or most talented people in business, just the greediest.

See the box on page 108 in Volume 18, Commerce and Trade, *for an explanation of the Enron scandal. By mid-2004 charges had been brought against a total of 30 people involved in Enron's collapse, including the former CEO and the chairman.*

Corporate scandals

A string of corporate scandals in recent years, from Enron to WorldCom to Tyco, have revealed senior executives apparently plundering their companies with little regard to the interests of shareholders or other employees. And even when no wrongdoing is alleged, huge pay awards are provoking growing outrage. Just ask Richard Grasso, the former chairman of the New York Stock Exchange, who went from folk hero to a symbol of excess almost overnight when it was revealed that he was due to receive $188m in accumulated benefits.

A "golden parachute" is a clause in an executive's contract specifying the severance pay that he or she will receive if the company is taken over, and the executive's employment is terminated.

"Golden parachutes" rile many

What is now causing the most indignation, in Europe as well as in America, are "golden parachutes" and other payments which reward bosses even when they fail. Not only does it seem that bosses are being fed ever bigger carrots, but also that if the stick is finally applied to their backside, they walk away with yet another sackful of carrots to cushion the blow. Bugs Bunny couldn't ask for more.

The highest-profile cases of excessive pay, unfortunately, are not isolated exceptions. Bosses' pay has moved inexorably upwards, especially in America. In 1980, the average pay for the CEOs of America's biggest companies was about 40 times that of the average production worker. In 1990, it was about 85 times. Now this ratio is thought to be about 400. Profits of big firms fell last year and shares are still well down on their record high, but the average remuneration of the heads of America's companies rose by over 6%.

In 2003 the average salary increase for workers in the United States was 3.4 percent, the lowest rate for 30 years.

Richard Grasso, chairman of the New York Stock Exchange, resigned after outcry at what many people viewed as his exhorbitant compensation.

A survey in 2003 found that over the previous year the average pay rise for senior executives in the United Kingdom increased 23 percent, while average earnings rose by just over 3 percent. Despite this rise, senior UK executives earn on average less than half what their U.S. counterparts earn.

This one-way trend in top executives' pay has rightly raised eyebrows, on both sides of the Atlantic. The supply of good bosses may be short, but can it be that short, even during an economic slowdown and stockmarket slump? A recent poll in Britain found that 80% of people believe that top directors are overpaid. This summer customers boycotted a Dutch retailer, Ahold, to express disapproval of the pay awarded to that company's new chief executive.

Unions in America and Britain want governments to be more directly involved in regulating bosses' pay. But that cure threatens to be even worse than the disease itself. It would be much wiser to play to capitalism's strength—its flexibility—and to encourage shareholders themselves, the ostensible owners of companies, to sort the problem out. For too long the missing element in the setting of top executives' pay has been the active interest of shareholders. Only once that comes into play can the bargaining between boards and bosses become a more equitable affair.

Do only the top executives make a difference to a company's value? Do you think regular employees should also benefit from, for example, profit-sharing plans?

Lavish pay-outs are not only costly in themselves but can also damage the long-term health of a company. Too many bosses have manipulated corporate results to fill their own pockets. Moreover, pay packages thought excessive or unfair can destroy morale among the rest of a company's workforce.

In 2004 a third of shareholders in the British supermarket chain Sainsbury's voted against the company's pay policy, objecting to its decision to give a $4.4 million bonus to the ousted chairman.

So what should shareholders do? For a start, big institutional investors can often make better use of the powers that they already possess. In Britain this year shareholders received the right to vote on top executives' remuneration. And yet at only one company (GlaxoSmithKline) did big investing institutions vote against an existing package—not an impressive performance if they are genuinely aggrieved.

Beyond Lake Wobegon

The pay-setting process is characterised by what has come to be known as the Lake Wobegon effect, after the novel *Lake Wobegon Days* by Garrison Keillor. All Lake Wobegon's children are said to be "above average". Most boards appointing a new chief executive will seek the advice of a pay consultant, who will tell them the going rate. The trouble is, no board wants to pay the average for the job. The above-average candidate which directors have just selected as CEO, they invariably reason, deserves more. And so bosses' pay spirals upwards.

If shareholders want to break this mould they need to be far more diligent. Greater transparency about executives' pay will undoubtedly help, and moves in that direction in both

America and Europe are to be welcomed. And yet shareholders must also exercise more say in choosing genuinely independent directors to select and monitor the CEO. Few public companies today in either America or Europe have a majority of independent directors. This week, America's Securities and Exchange Commission took steps in the right direction by proposing an increase in the power of shareholders to nominate and appoint directors. Once they have these powers, shareholders should make use of them.

The main aim of the U.S. Securities and Exchange Commission (SEC) is to protect investors and maintain the integrity of the securities markets. Go to www.sec.gov for more information.

How much should top bosses be paid?

That leaves the vexed question of how, and how much, to pay top bosses. There can never be any simple, single formula for this. Much will depend on the situation of each company. The boss of a firm in a stable or declining industry should probably not be paid in the same way as one in a fast-growing high-tech market. Some corporate boards ought to at least consider a return to what was once the norm in both America and Europe (and still is in Japan) and largely ditch pay-for-performance and instead pay largely through a straight salary (most lower-level employees are paid this way). Yet most boards will probably stick with pay-for-performance of some kind. Whether in the form of options, the outright grant of shares, bonuses tied to criteria such as earnings or revenue growth, or some other means, pay should be explicitly aligned with the long-term interests of the owners, not short-term blips in share prices or profits. Whatever formula is chosen, some bosses are bound to try to manipulate it. This is why, in future, capitalism's pillars, the shareholders who own the company, will have to become more actively involved in choosing the directors who represent them and in policing what they do. Shareholders, after all, supply the carrots.

Stock options give employees the right to buy company shares at a fixed price over a specified period of time. In the past some senior executives have overstated a company's profits or committed accounting fraud to push up the value of options.

In 2004 shareholders voted to separate the positions of CEO and chairman of the board of directors of the Disney Corporation. Michael Eisner kept his job as chief executive but had to hand the chairmanship to George Mitchell. In 2001 Forbes *magazine estimated that in the previous five years—a period when Disney's profits fell—Eisner earned $737 million.*

WHY ARE CEOS PAID SO MUCH?
Elan Journo

Elan Journo is a writer for the Ayn Rand Institute in Irvine, California. The institute promotes the philosophy of Ayn Rand (1905–1982), author of Atlas Shrugged *(1957) and* The Fountainhead *(1943).*

NO

Are America's CEOs paid more than they deserve? Many people's answer is a vehement: Yes. That view is reinforced anew every spring, when companies file their financial statements and we learn how much CEOs were paid last year.

In 2003 the average pay for CEOs at 200 of the largest U.S. companies was $11.3 million—but there are a good number whose compensation packages approach the $100 million mark. Faced with these figures, Americans from all walks of life—who revile CEOs as greedy fat cats—are overcome with bewilderment and indignation. Astonished to learn that what an average worker earns in a year, some CEOs earn in less than a week—people ask themselves: "How can the work of a corporate paper-pusher be worth so many millions of dollars?"

According to the Census Bureau, the average worker's pay was $42,400 in 2002.

The answer is that successful CEOs are indispensable to their companies. They earn their rewards.

CEOs can turn a company around

How big an influence can one man have on the fortunes of the entire corporation? Consider the impact of Jack Welch on General Electric. Before his tenure as CEO, the company was a bloated giant, floundering under its own weight. Splintered into dozens of distinct and inefficient business units, GE was scarcely making a profit. Welch turned it around. He streamlined and reorganized the company's operations and implemented a sound business strategy yielding more than $400 billion worth of shareholder wealth.

Jack Welch was chairman and CEO of General Electric from 1981 to 2001. His generous post-retirement package attracted a lot of criticism, and eventually he asked the board to take back some of the perks. Go to http://www.businessweek.com/bwdaily/dnflash/sep2002/nf20020918_7629.htm to read a BusinessWeek *article about the controversy.*

In business, success requires long-range thinking. But CEOs must project a strategic game plan in terms not merely of a month or two, but of years and decades. A biotechnology company, for example, may spend 15 years and billions of dollars developing a new cancer-fighting medicine. Success is impossible without the business acumen of its CEO. For years before a marketable product exists, he must raise sufficient capital to sustain the research. What long-term business model will attract venture capital? Should the company accept short-term partial sponsorship from a large drug manufacturer in exchange for a modest royalty on the drug

Many people believe that U.S. executives receive too much compensation in salaries, bonuses, stock options, and payoffs.

COMMENTARY: Steve Jobs and Apple

Steve Jobs is the CEO and cofounder of Apple, a leader in personal computers, and Pixar, the Academy-Award-winning animation studios that made *Toy Story* (1995) and *Finding Nemo* (2003). By the time Jobs was 25, he was worth $165 million. Regarded as a visionary in the industry, today Jobs is a billionaire with a pay package worth about $75 million per year.

Jobs was born in Green Bay, Wisconsin, in 1955. He was adopted soon after his birth; he moved with his adopted family to Santa Clara, California. After graduating from high school, he went to college in Portland, Oregon, but dropped out after one semester. His interest in computers was already evident, however, and it was through the Home Brew Computer Club that he met Steve Wozniak. In 1976, at the age of 21, Jobs set up the Apple Computer Corporation with Wozniak, an outfit that the pair ran from the Jobs's family garage. Their mission was to produce affordable personal computers, and they scored an instant success with the Apple I and Apple II.

Apple: A study in how to succeed

The company went from strength to strength, but Jobs was ousted in a reshuffle in 1985. Twelve years later he was asked to return to the then-ailing company and proceeded to turn its fortunes around. Thanks to the marketing genius of Jobs, and the groundbreaking design of British designer Jonathan Ive, Apple's hardware and software products became widely regarded as the most innovative and user-friendly in the industry.

Sales of Apple computers had started to drop off by about 2002, however, and Apple's shares plunged more than 80 percent during its 2002 fiscal year. Yet in 2003 Apple directors agreed to trade in Jobs's stock options—which would have been valuable only if Apple's stock price rose significantly—for restricted shares worth almost $75 million. Supporters say his unique vision and ability to turn the company around make him worth every cent. Critics point out, however, that the chairman of Apple's compensation committee is William Campbell, who is a former colleague of Jobs at Apple and lives on the same street as he does.

According to Jobs, the money is not important. During a 1996 TV documentary entitled *Triumph of the Nerds* he said, "I was worth over $1 million when I was 23, and over $10 million when I was 24, and over $100 million when I was 25, and it wasn't that important, because I never did it for the money."

Apple's latest move has been into the digital music industry. It launched the highly successful digital music player the iPod in 2001. Two years later it opened the iTunes Music Store in the United States. Following its success, Apple opened one in Europe in 2004. In the same year Apple reported that U.S. iPod sales had more than tripled company profits—a success story that many believe will be reflected in Jobs's next pay package.

in the future—or risk going it alone and possibly running out of funds? It is on such decisions that a company's success is made—and lives of cancer patients may depend.

Does the author strengthen his argument by using the example of cancer patients, or detract from it?

In order to be successful in the long range, the CEO's strategy must encompass countless factors. He must devise a plan to grow the business in the face of competitors, not only from within the United States but from any and every region of today's global economy. The CEO calls the plays for a team of tens (and sometimes hundreds) of thousands of workers. All of the actions of every employee and every aspect of the business must be coordinated and integrated to produce the cars, computers or CAT scanners that yield profits to the company. It is the CEO who is responsible for that integration.

Exceptional thought and judgment

To successfully steer a corporation across the span of years by integrating its strengths toward the goal of creating wealth, requires from the CEO exceptional thought and judgment. Excellent CEOs are as rare as MLB-caliber pitchers or NFL-caliber quarterbacks. And in the business world, every day is the Super Bowl. There is no off-season or respite from the need to perform at one's peak.

If excellent CEOs should receive excellent rewards, do you think inefficiency in CEOs should be reflected in their paychecks? Some CEOs continue to reap huge compensation while running the company into bankruptcy, and others get enormous payoffs when they are no longer required by the company.

Given the effect a CEO can have on a company's success, we can understand why their compensation packages can be so high. One way employers reward excellence is through bonuses. For many CEOs, bonuses amount to a large portion of their earnings. Some CEOs are paid a token salary, but are rewarded with large parcels of company stock; last year, for instance, the CEO of Apple Computer, Steve Jobs [see box on opposite page], earned $1 in salary and received stock valued at $75 million. As is the case with athletes and other individuals whose talents are rare and much prized, the CEO's pay package is calculated with an eye on the competition. Companies pay millions of dollars to a valuable CEO, one who they judge will produce wealth for the shareholders, in part so he will not be hired away by a competitor.

Some companies, such as Microsoft and Apple, are replacing stock options for employees with restricted shares. There is less chance of making huge sums, but workers will not lose out altogether if the share price falls.

On the gridiron, the baseball diamond and the basketball court, we see and admire the physical prowess of a superlative athlete—one who earns the title of MVP—and we understand that it is morally proper to reward him accordingly. Though the efforts of CEOs are not televised on *Monday Night Football*, their achievements are real and have a profound benefit to all our lives. It is time that we learned to appreciate the work of successful CEOs and recognize that they deserve every penny of their salaries.

Baseball players earn, on average, more than 50 times the average U.S. worker's salary. Do you agree that it is "morally proper" to reward athletes with vast sums of money?

Summary

Senior executives, particularly in the United States, receive large pay packages, which usually consist of a basic salary plus stock options or shares. Popular opinion regards such compensation as undeserved, particularly when CEOs continue to receive huge payouts regardless of a company's performance.

In the first article the magazine *The Economist* notes that recent well-publicized corporate scandals have only confirmed that public opinion is justified. "Golden parachutes"—large payments to departing executives—also provoke understandable indignation, the magazine reports. Although the article accepts that good bosses are valuable, it urges shareholders to exercise control over the board of directors to ensure that bosses' pay is realistic. While reasoning that it is unfeasible to return to paying fixed salaries, *The Economist* suggests a compromise: Rather than tie performance to short-term profitability, it should be aligned to longer-term goals that have lasting benefit to the company and to shareholders.

In the second article Elan Journo agrees that pay awards can be considerable but argues that public disapproval is unjustified, since good executives have enormous individual influence on a company's success. Journo cites the example of Jack Welch, who turned around the fortunes of General Electric during his term as CEO and chairman. Journo argues that CEOs must use strategic planning, raise capital, and make difficult business decisions—and integrate all these skills. Comparing CEOs to other individuals with rare ability, such as athletes, he says that high pay packages reflect talent and ability, as well as the competition to keep such people. Rather than take money from the shareholders' investment, Journo believes that highly paid CEOs ultimately produce wealth for the company. Just like top-class athletes, he says, top-level executives deserve to be rewarded well.

FURTHER INFORMATION:

Books:

Bok, Derek, *The Cost of Talent: How Executives and Professionals Are Paid and How It Affects America.* New York: The Free Press, 2002.

Nofsinger, John, and Kenneth Kim, *Infectious Greed: Restoring Confidence in America's Companies.* Upper Saddle River, NJ: Financial Times Prentice Hall, 2003.

Useful websites:

http://www.aflcio.org/corporateamerica/paywatch/
Executive Paywatch from the American Federation of Labor–Congress of Industrial Organizations.

http://www.inequality.org/execsummay04.html
Article on U.S. corporate pay and inequality.

http://www.usatoday.com/money/companies/management/2003-03-31-ceopay2_x.htm
Article on CEO salaries from *USA Today*, March 31, 2003.

The following debates in the Pro/Con series may also be of interest:

In this volume:

Topic 13 Do labor unions have too much power in the United States?

ARE U.S. EXECUTIVES PAID TOO MUCH?

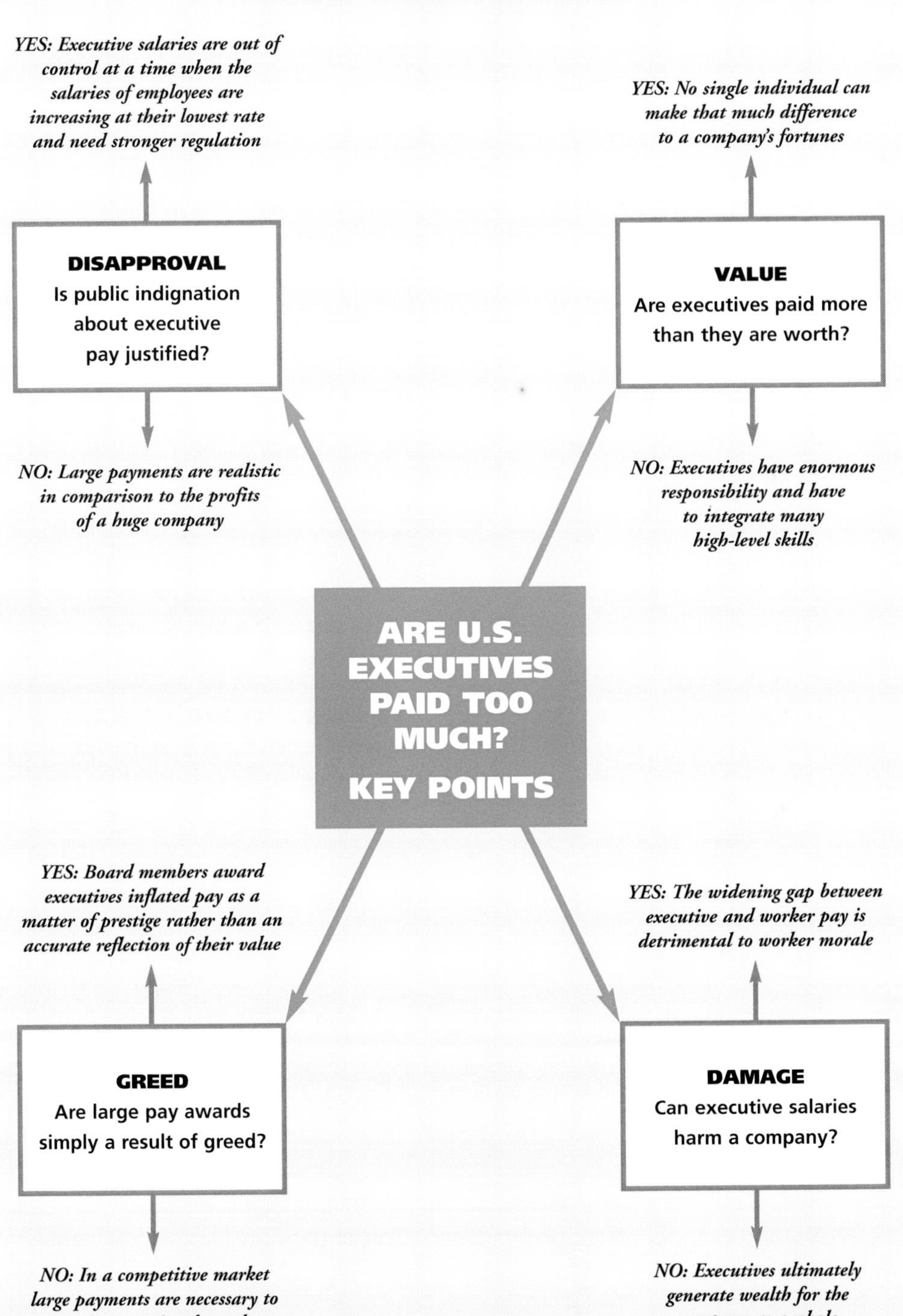
YES: Executive salaries are out of control at a time when the salaries of employees are increasing at their lowest rate and need stronger regulation
DISAPPROVAL
Is public indignation about executive pay justified?
NO: Large payments are realistic in comparison to the profits of a huge company
YES: No single individual can make that much difference to a company's fortunes
VALUE
Are executives paid more than they are worth?
NO: Executives have enormous responsibility and have to integrate many high-level skills
ARE U.S. EXECUTIVES PAID TOO MUCH?
KEY POINTS
YES: Board members award executives inflated pay as a matter of prestige rather than an accurate reflection of their value
GREED
Are large pay awards simply a result of greed?
NO: In a competitive market large payments are necessary to retain exceptional people
YES: The widening gap between executive and worker pay is detrimental to worker morale
DAMAGE
Can executive salaries harm a company?
NO: Executives ultimately generate wealth for the company as a whole

GLOSSARY

absenteeism a habitual absence from work.

affirmative action a set of policies and initiatives designed to redress past discrimination based on race, color, gender, or religion. Also known as "positive discrimination."

Bill of Rights the first ten amendments to the Constitution, passed by Congress in 1791, that grant citizens certain rights.

bullying using aggressive behavior to intimidate or frighten someone, usually weaker or less powerful.

carcinogen a cancer-causing agent. Carcinogens in the environment include viruses, tobacco, and forms of sunlight.

CEO stands for "chief executive officer," the managing director of an organization.

chain of command the system in which the tasks of people on each level of management are set and monitored by specific people on the level above.

civil rights rights guaranteed to the individual as a citizen, such as the right to vote. *See also* Bill of Rights.

civil rights movement a popular mass movement that emerged in the United States during the late 1950s that fought for equal rights for African Americans.

compensation money awarded as reparation for an injury, discriminatory behavior, or loss of job.

constitution a written codification of the basic principles and laws under which a government operates.

contingent workers part-time, temporary, or contract workers.

culture of overwork a phrase used to describe the fact that in many developed societies, including America and Japan peer and employer pressure results in people working longer hours. *See also karoshi.*

depression a mental state characterized by feelings of inadequacy and anguish.

discrimination the unfair treatment of an individual or group of individuals on the basis of their race, color, gender, sexuality, nationality, religion, education, or economic status.

ethics the system or code of morals of a particular person, group, or organization, or the study of those standards or codes.

Equal Pay Act a law that came into force in June 1963. It states that men and women performing substantially equal work in an establishment must be paid at the same rate. *See also* discrimination.

feminism the movement to attain equal rights and opportunities for women.

Framers in U.S. history the leaders who wrote and adopted the Constitution, including George Washington, Thomas Jefferson, Alexander Hamilton, and James Madison.

Fourth Amendment an addition to the Constitution that, among other things, protects persons, homes, and papers from unreasonable searches.

freedom of speech the right to express one's views and opinions, protected by the First Amendment. *See also* hate speech.

gender the physical, economic, social, and cultural attributes that are associated with being either male or female.

Generation X or GenX the group of people born in the post-baby boom period, between about 1965 and 1980.

Generation Y the group of people born in the period between around 1980 and 2000. *See also* Generation X.

glass ceiling informal barriers based on attitudinal or organizational bias that tend to prevent minority groups and women from advancing to the levels of senior management.

globalization the expansion worldwide of private corporations and of the cultures of the countries they come from.

hate speech in law public statements that "willfully promote hatred against any identifiable group." *See also* discrimination, freedom of speech.

homophobia a fear of, discrimination against, or hatred of homosexuals.

inequality disparity in distribution of a specific resource or item, such as income, education, employment, or health care. *See also* discrimination.

Internet the global network of computers by which users can communicate using protocols such as e-mail, file transfer protocol (ftp), or the World Wide Web.

karoshi the Japanese term for "death from overwork." See also culture of overwork.

meritocracy a system in which the most talented people are chosen and promoted on the basis of their achievement.

minimum wage the lowest wage that can be paid, as set by law. The U.S. federal minimum wage provisions are contained in the Fair Labor Standards Act. If a state has its own minimum wage, the recipient is entitled to the higher of the two.

MP3 a computer format that compresses audio signals—for example, music tracks—so that they can be more quickly copied from computer to computer via the Internet.

nepotism favoritism shown toward relatives in the allocation of a job.

not-for-cause testing a test carried out on a random or universal basis rather than because there is evidence that a particular individual might be, for example, alcohol or drug impaired.

pornography writings, pictures, films, or theater intended to stimulate sexual desire by a description or portrayal of sex. *See also* freedom of speech.

prejudice an opinion formed about a person or group that is not based on individual knowledge but on untested assumptions, particularly when leading to hatred, intolerance, or suspicion.

presenteeism a situation in which employees are afraid to call in sick so show up at work but are too stressed to be productive.

productivity the value each worker creates for each hour worked.

racism a belief that some races are inherently and naturally superior to others, which often leads to discrimination against or harassment of certain races.

rat race being part of an exhausting routine that leaves no time for relaxation.

RSI repetitive strain injury caused by overuse of certain muscles. People who use computers a lot are prone to getting this.

sexual harassment any form of unwanted sexual attention.

sexual orientation whether a person is homosexual, heterosexual, or bisexual.

stress a condition caused by physical or mental pressure, often caused by overwork. Symptoms can include sleeplessness, irritability, and depression.

taxation the method by which national, regional, or local government collects money from individuals and businesses to fund society's collective costs, such as education, defense, and public health.

transnational corporation (TNC) an enterprise that operates in several countries and has production facilities outside its home country. *See also* globalization.

unions organizations of workers whose purpose is to protect their common interests and improve working conditions.

welfare assistance in the form of money or necessities for people in need.

whistleblowing when an employee decides to publicize a company's malpractices or health-and-safety abuses.

World Trade Organization (WTO) an international organization founded in 1995 as a result of the final round of the General Agreement on Tariffs and Trade (GATT) negotiations. The WTO handles trade disputes between members and aims to reduce tariffs.

Acknowledgments

1. Should Workers Have a Right to Privacy in the Workplace?
Yes: "Where to Draw the Line" by Liz Hall, *Personnel Today*, June 1, 2004. Copyright © *Personnel Today*. Used by permission.
No: "Workplace Surveillance Reduces Liability, Raises Ethical Concerns" by Jennifer LeClaire, www.va-interactive.com/inbusiness.

2. Should Employees Have the Right to Disobey Company Orders?
Yes: "Facing Anthrax Threat, Employees Have Limited Right Not to Work" by Brian Friel, Govexec.com, October 30, 2001. Reprinted with permission by National Journal Group, Inc.
No: "Caught on the Net" by Helen Hague, *The Guardian*, Friday December 3, 1999. Used by permission.

3. Is Mandatory Drug Testing in the Workplace Wrong?
Yes: "Privacy in America: Workplace Drug Testing" by American Civil Liberties Union (www.aclu.org). Used by permission.
No: From "Drug Testing" Employer Tip Sheet No. 9, U.S. Health and Human Services Department and SAMHSA's National Clearing House for Alchohol and Drug Information (www.health.org). Public domain.

4. Is Workplace Sexual Harrassment Legislation Adequate?
Yes: "America's Overprotective Sexual Harassment Law" by Joan Kennedy Taylor, The Cato Institute, April 10, 2000. Used by permission.
No: "Same-Sex Sexual Harassment Cases Typically Held to Different Standards" by Beatrice Dohrn, Lamda Legal, *Legal Director's Update*: Fall 1997. Used by permission.

5. Do Parents Have Enough Rights in the Workplace?
Yes: "Courts Bolster Rights of Working Mothers" by David Crary, *The Philadelphia Inquirer*, July 24, 2004. Reprinted with permission of The Associated Press.
No: "Breastfeeding Mothers Need Workplace Support" by Tamara W. Wilson, www.momsvoice.com. Used by permission.

6. Should There Be a Mandatory Retirement Age?
Yes: "CBI Warns against Scrapping Retirement Age" www.management-issues.com, November 3, 2003. Used by permission.
No: "Should Retirement Be Mandatory?" by Reginald Stackhouse, *The Globe and Mail*, December 23, 2003. Used by permission.

7. Is Stress Taken Seriously Enough as a Health Issue in the Workplace?
Yes: "Employers Seek to Relieve Stress, Depression" by Jenna Colley, *Austin Business Journal*, May 15, 2000. Used by permission.
No: "Job Stress, Burnout on the Rise" by Jane Weaver, MSNBC News, September 1, 2003. Used by permission.

8. Is Nepotism in the Workplace Wrong?
Yes: "Good Timing" by Jenn Carbin, Philadelphia Citypaper.net, January 10–17, 2002. Used by permission.
No: From "In Praise of Nepotism: An Interview with Author Adam Bellow," *Family Business*, www.family-business-experts.com. Used by permission.

9. Do Women Make Better Managers than Men?
Yes: "Why Women Make Better Managers" by Joanna L. Krotz, www.bcentral.com. Used by permission.
No: "My Boss, the Bitch" by Michelle Hamer, *The Age*, February 26, 2004. Used by permission.

10. Should Sexual Relationships in the Workplace Be Allowed?
Yes: "Stretching the Meaning of Sexual Harassment" by Robyn E. Blumner, *St. Petersburg Times*, March 8, 1998. Copyright © Tribune Media Services, Inc. All Rights Reserved. Reprinted with permission.
No: "Dangerous Liaisons" by Ellyn Spragins, *FORTUNE Small Business*, February 14, 2004. Copyright © Time Inc. All rights reserved.

11. Does Sexual Orientation Matter in the Workplace?

Yes: "Don't Violate the Freedom of Speech and Religion of Nonhomosexuals on the Job" by Louis P. Sheldon, *Insight on the News*, April 1, 2002. Reprinted with permission of Insight. Copyright © 2004 News World Communications, Inc. All rights reserved.
No: "Ending Job Discrimination against Gay and Lesbians Is Good for Business" by Winnie Stachelberg, *Insight on the News*, April, 1, 2002. Reprinted with permission of Insight. Copyright © 2004 News World Communications, Inc. All rights reserved.

12. Is There a Culture of Overwork in the United States?

Yes: "The Loss of Leisure in a Culture of Overwork" by Linda Marks, www.ofspirit.com. Used by permission.
No: "More Young People Pursuing Simpler Life" by Chris Devitto, MSNBC News, January 26, 2004. Copyright © The Associated Press. Reprinted with permission of The Associated Press.

13. Do Labor Unions Have Too Much Power in the United States?

Yes: "Bush Invokes Taft-Hartley Act to Open West Coast Ports" by David E. Sanger with Steven Greenhouse, *The New York Times*, October 9, 2002. Copyright 2002 The New York Times Co. Reprinted with permission.
No: "There Is Power in a Union" by Ralph Nader, "In the Public Interest," February 21, 2001. Used by permission.

14. Do Companies Take Enough Responsibility for Work-Related Injuries?

Yes: "DuPont's CEO Takes the Leadership Role in Safety" by Michael A. Verespej, *Occupational Hazards*, Penton Media Inc., September 12, 2003. Used by permission.
No: "It's About TIME!—Campaign for Workers' Health" by National Mobilization against Sweatshops (www.nmass.org). Used by permission.

15. Should Companies Be Allowed to Relocate Jobs Overseas?

Yes: "Out Of India." Reported by Morley Safer on CBS News' *60 Minutes*, Sunday January 11, 2004. Used by permission.
No: "Money for Nothing and Calls for Free" by Nidhi Kumar and Nidhi Verghese, CorpWatch, February 17, 2004 (www.corpwatch.org). Used by permisison.

16. Are U.S. Executives Paid Too Much?

Yes: "Where's the Stick?" by *The Economist* Online, October 9, 2003. Copyright © 2003 The Economist Newspaper Ltd. All rights reserved. Reprinted with permission. Further reproduction prohibited. www.economist.com.
No: "Why Are CEOs Paid So Much?" by Elan Journo, *Capitalism Magazine*, April 16, 2004. Copyright © 2004 Ayn Rand Institute. Reproduced with permission.

The Brown Reference Group plc has made every effort to contact and acknowledge the creators and copyright holders of all extracts reproduced in this volume. We apologize for any omissions. Any person who wishes to be credited in further volumes should contact The Brown Reference Group plc in writing: The Brown Reference Group plc, 8 Chapel Place, Rivington Street, London EC2A 3DQ, U.K.

Picture credits

Cover: Corbis: Bob Rowan; Progressive Image.
Hulton/Archive. Corbis: 174/175; James L Amos 25; Bettmann 6/7, 188/189; Francoise De Mulder 88; Dallas & John Heaton 64; Francis G Mayer 91; **Hulton/Archive:** 116; **Popperfoto:** 54, 58/59; **Rex Features Ltd:** Fotos International 132; Sipa Press/Lena Kara 194; Richard Jenkins**,** 108/109; **Ronald Grant Archive:** 42, 166; **U.S. Customs Service:** James R Tourtelloti 17

SET INDEX

Page numbers in **bold** refer to volume numbers; those in *italics* refer to picture captions.

C

E

H

J

K

L

S

T